P9-EDV-036

JEAN SIBELIUS

Jean Sibelius

by Harold E. Johnson

GREENWOOD PRESS, PUBLISHERS
WESTPORT, CONNECTICUT

Library of Congress Cataloging in Publication Data

Johnson, Harold Edgar, 1915–
    Jean Sibelius.

    Reprints of the ed. published by Knopf, New York.
    "Complete list of compositions and arrangements by
Jean Sibelius": p.
    Bibliography: p.
    Includes index.
    1. Sibelius, Jean, 1865–1957. 2. Composers—
Finland—Biography.
 ₍ML410.S54J6 1978₎   780'.92'4 ₍B₎   78–5506
    ISBN 0-313-20470-5

36, 929

© Harold E. Johnson, 1959

All rights reserved. No part of this book may be reproduced
in any form without permission in writing from the publisher,
except by a reviewer who may quote brief passages and repro-
duce not more than three illustrations in a review to be printed
in a magazine or newspaper. Manufactured in the United States
of America.

Reprinted with the permission of Alfred A. Knopf, Inc.

Reprinted in 1978 by Greenwood Press, Inc., 51 Riverside Avenue,
Westport, CT. 06880

Printed in the United States of America

10 9 8 7 6 5 4 3 2 1

For Alice

CAMROSE LUTHERAN COLLEGE
LIBRARY

Preface

Normally when a well-known artist dies, tribute is paid him in an official biography written by his widow, his heirs, or an intimate friend. Whether the title is My Life with X *or* X as I Knew Him, *the net result is the same. It is a work of piety lightly interlarded with carefully chosen excerpts from the artist's memoirs and personal correspondence. If, after a decade or two, his reputation continues to endure, the inevitable* Secret and Intimate Life of X *appears. Generally this is one of those "now it can be told" books in which the muckraking reveals that its author was impelled to write it because of some personal grievance or jealousy, or merely by the desire to ride on the coattails of a great name. Finally the biographers move in and the arduous process of separating the man from the legend begins. By this time, however, myth has become fact, and many of the secrets lie buried with the artist. Thus, the promises implied in such titles as* X: The Man and the Legend *are fulfilled only in part.*

Jean Sibelius is an exception to this rule, and for reasons as unusual as the man and his music. From a musical point of view, it may be said that he died in 1926 after composing Tapiola. *During the final thirty years of his life—the "silence from Järvenpää"—he enjoyed reading the many pious books about his life and music, and even helped in their preparation. Actually this process was well under way by 1916, when Erik Furuhjelm's* Jean Sibelius: Hans tondiktning och drag ur hans liv *appeared. The most famous of these books was completed in 1935 by Karl Ekman, Jr., and published in English translation as* Jean Sibelius: His Life and Personality. *For more than twenty years, Ekman's vol-*

ume has constituted the "authorized" biography, the indispensable source book for all later writers such as Ringbom and Levas.

The sameness that characterizes most of this writing may be attributed to Sibelius himself, who in his final years saw his career through rose-colored glasses, and to his Finnish biographers, who considered it their moral and patriotic duty to respect his slightest wish. It must be clearly understood that in Finland, at least, Sibelius is far more than a great national composer. He is a national hero, a symbol of what a small nation can achieve, and thus it was inevitable that he should become a legend long before his death.

This is the consequence whenever a nation elects to deify one of her citizens. Before World War I, the English writer Mrs. Rosa Newmarch became aware of this deification while shopping in Helsinki. A merchant refused to accept payment for a purchase with the protest: "Impossible! Are you not the friend of our great Sibelius?" This concept of "our great Sibelius" denotes not only a pride in common ownership—and because of the composer's lifelong and generous state pension, that ownership is very real—but also the realization that Finland found her place in the sun thanks to Sibelius. And a very considerable place it is, too.

It is not at all surprising that the Finnish writers have been obliged to discuss their great composer with reverence. The sheer greatness of the man precluded any reference to the common human frailties, for Sibelius linked Finland's present with her past, and stood above and apart from her political and military figures. On the occasion of his eighty-fifth birthday, Finns considered it fitting and proper

*that the President of the Republic should motor to Järven-
pää in order to pay the official respect of the entire nation.*
In this study I have not attempted to write a Secret
and Intimate Life of Jean Sibelius—*he is hardly a suitable
subject for such an approach—nor do I claim that it is in any
way an "authorized" biography. Before leaving for Finland,
I had decided that no useful purpose would be served by ask-
ing the living legend to describe at ninety what he actually
thought and did at the age of twenty-eight. A few questions
submitted through an intermediary confirmed my belief that
the composer either did not remember the information I was
seeking or else refused to admit to anything that might run
contrary to the many myths that he and his biographers believed to be true. Furthermore, Sibelius—and frequently
with good cause—distrusted what he called "journalists." The
mere sight of pencil and pad in the hands of a guest was
enough to cause him to end all conversation.*

*My task was one familiar to those who have had to
produce dissertations—months of research in libraries and ar-
chives with microfilms of newspapers, programs, manuscript
letters, journals, etc. During the early stages of my research, I
came to the conclusion that much of the factual material concerning Sibelius's music was in error. In checking all of the
published music against old programs and critiques, I discovered that many pieces were lost. The results of these labors are to be found in the list of compositions at the end of
this volume. It is, I venture to say, the most complete and
accurate list of its kind which has appeared to date.*

*At times, it seemed highly amusing that my subject
was living but a short distance from Helsinki, that he and I*

were both listening to radio concerts of his own music, and that he was as near as my telephone—"Sibelius Jean, Prof., Ainola 28 73 22." Fortunately my office-like routine was interrupted by numerous visits to the excellent Sibelius Museum in Turku and meetings with older men who were willing and able to remember. During these meetings, I was frequently told: "But, remember, this is not for publication."

Often these "not for publication" stories were subjected to considerable variation, depending upon the imagination of the teller. Sibelius apparently had been seen riding a carousel in Brussels at midnight dressed in a top hat and frock coat—all this in 1900! Others assured me that his father had been a rather indifferent suitor of Miss Maria Charlotta Borg in Hämeenlinna. One story dealing with Sibelius's purchase of a kilo of butter in Helsinki I regarded as top-secret until I discovered it in a published interview with the composer's brother-in-law, Armas Järnefelt. And then—horror of horrors!—there were even a few stories of youthful indiscretions when he was a student in Berlin and Vienna.

The many stories dealing with Sibelius's visits to a popular restaurant known as Kämp were especially entertaining as an indication of how great the legend had become. What appears to be the original version of one dating from the first decade of this century tells how Sibelius participated in a drinking party lasting several hours. The conductor Kajanus left in order to conduct a symphony concert, and when he returned, Sibelius greeted him with: "Kajus, you certainly spent a long time in the washroom!" Later versions had Kajanus make a round trip to St. Petersburg. Another writer substituted Bruno Walter for Kajanus and the wash-

room became Stockholm. After the composer's death, a New York gossip columnist, displaying the special talents for which his profession is known, re-told the story as "The Longest Party on Record," in which Kajanus was replaced by a Hollywood movie star who made the round trip to London —by air!

And then there was the business of the famous "Eighth Symphony." Although I was convinced that the much-discussed and long-awaited Eighth no longer existed, I was told by people who knew people, etc., that such was not the case. Now it was in three movements, now in four. One conductor assured me that while Sibelius was visiting his dentist in Helsinki, one irreverent relative rummaged through his desk and discovered that it was "something between a symphony and a cantata." Even after the composer's death, when his eldest daughter solemnly announced to the press that there was no Eighth Symphony, Finnish musicians continued to insist that it existed. One assured me that it could be found in the city of Lahti.

Happily, many of these interviews produced the sort of information I was seeking. After waiting for more than six months, I was permitted to examine the original score for The Lizard, *which presumably had been lost for almost fifty years. One person offered to sell me the manuscript of an unpublished and unlisted composition for string orchestra which disappeared under mysterious circumstances one hour after I had identified it and photographed the first page. Many people generously brought to my attention manuscripts of minor, unknown compositions, letters, and old photographs.*

As I reread my manuscript, I cannot help feeling a genuine concern for these good and generous people who were so eager to help me write yet another book about their "great Sibelius." Some will undoubtedly feel that I have betrayed their trust in my attempt to reduce him to mortal stature. On innumerable occasions, when asked what I planned to write about him, I could only plead that as a detached foreigner I admired much of his music and wanted to discuss it as objectively as possible. I am not altogether certain that this was a satisfactory answer, but Sibelius as I have found him appears in the pages that follow.

In general, my approach has been that of the historian. Even here I have been forced to be highly selective in the choice of what I considered to be pertinent material. Only in rare instances do I venture opinions concerning the "correct" analysis of individual compositions. Those who are interested in such musical vivisection are advised to consult the special studies by Gray, Abraham, Wood, Ringbom, Parmet, and others listed in my bibliography. They are all most interesting, and clearly establish that, as far as Sibelius is concerned, analysis is like criticism: you can prove almost anything, once you have taken your stand.

The people to whom I owe, directly or indirectly, my inspiration for this study are too numerous to be listed. A few deserve special mention. It is with great pleasure that I take this opportunity to thank the following persons for the unstinted aid they rendered during my stay in Finland. To Professor Otto Andersson, Director of the Sibelius Museum, I owe much for his wise counsel and sympathetic understanding. Both he and his assistant, Mrs. Alphild Forslin, did everything possible to facilitate my research in their institution. Dr. Jorma Vallinkoski, Librarian, and the staff of the University of Helsinki Library showed me many courtesies for which I am deeply grateful. As a former music librarian, I cannot find words to express my profound debt to Mr. Sune Orell, the music specialist.

Dr. Nils-Eric Ringbom, Artistic Director of the Sibelius Festival and a well-known scholar, has been both a personal friend and a voluntary sounding-board for what many may regard as my unorthodox views. Our many differences of opinion have not interfered with cordial, lively discussions and the exchange of much valuable information. Professor Ilmari Krohn, Finland's most distinguished musicologist, honored me with many stimulating meetings during which we were able to turn back the clock more than sixty years. Professor Erik Furuhjelm helped me in dating and correctly identifying the A minor Overture.

Mrs. Nelma Sibelius generously permitted me to examine the letters from Sibelius to his brother, Christian, and Mrs. Lilly Kajanus-Blenner showed me many of the composer's letters to her distinguished father. To Mrs. Eva Paloheimo, Sibelius's eldest daughter, I am indebted for the hitherto unknown information concerning In Memoriam, *and his son-in-law Mr. Jussi Jalas made available several early and unpublished manuscripts.*

Messrs. Kai Maasalo, Director of Music for the Finnish State Radio, and Nils-Eric Fougstedt, Chief Conductor of the Finnish Radio Symphony Orchestra, have shown me many courtesies and on two occasions arranged public performances of compositions that it was my good fortune to un-

cover. My thanks are also due to Messrs. Veikko Helasvuo and Sven Enqvist, librarians, respectively, of the Helsinki City Orchestra and the Finnish Radio Symphony Orchestra, for permitting me to study many published scores and manuscripts.

To Messrs. Einari Marvia and Kai Kavanto of Fazer & Co. and to Mr. Lauri Solanterä of Westerlund & Co. I must express my thanks for help in locating many early editions of Sibelius's published music. The Danish publishing house of Wilhelm Hansen permitted me to examine the original manuscripts of the music for The Tempest *and their extensive correspondence with the composer. Professor Martti Turunen of the Y.L. Choral Society has given me much valuable information concerning contemporary Finnish music. Thanks to Mr. Birger Lagerman, I was able to examine the three manuscripts of* Sandels *and the other music that Sibelius wrote for the M.M. Choral Society.*

The composer's pencil drawing dating from around 1887 is reproduced in this volume through the courtesy of Mrs. Mary Gahmberg. Mr. Tauno Pylkkänen, a well-known contemporary composer and music critic, kindly provided me with a collection of foreign newspaper clippings dealing with Finnish music.

I would be remiss if I failed to mention Professor Heikki Reenpää and his son, Mr. Erkki Reenpää, of The Otava Publishing Co. for their early interest in my work and their willingness to publish it in Finnish translation. Nor may I overlook the assistance given to me by Mr. Martti Vuorenjuuri, the Music Editor of Helsingin Sanomat, for bringing to my attention a score of Sibelius's letters and

Preface

also for printing a number of my articles in his newspaper. I wish to thank E. P. Dutton & Co. for permission to quote from the Everyman's Library edition of Kalevala *(Kalevala: Land of Heroes, translated by W. F. Kirby, Everyman's Library Nos. 259 and 260) .*

This study was made possible thanks to a Fulbright Research Grant. I wish to thank the Board of Directors and the Staff of the United States Educational Foundation in Finland for their many courtesies. Finally, to Miss Hilkka Kokko of the United States Information Service in Helsinki I owe a debt of undying gratitude for her patience and tenacity in arranging interviews. There is no need to say that the views expressed in this study are, unless otherwise acknowledged, solely my own and that none of the above-mentioned persons is to be held responsible for them in any manner.

Helsinki, Finland   *H. E. J.*

Contents

xvii

Illustrations

JEAN SIBELIUS

Chapter I   *1865–1885*

*"I am told to my surprise that there are
people who have never seen a goblin. One
cannot help feeling sorry for such people. I
am sure there must be something wrong with
their eyes."*   *Axel Munthe*

●

Few composers have been so
fortunate as Sibelius in being born when and where everything he needed was in animation around him. He was born
in 1865 in Finland. Had he been born twenty years earlier,
twenty years later, or in another country, he might never
have become the world figure he is today.

The century of his birth witnessed profound changes
in the history of Finland. After more than five hundred years
of Swedish rule, Finland became an autonomous grand
duchy of the Russian Empire in 1809. The Finns, with their
traditional hatred for the Slavs, had resisted Russian conquest to the bitter end, and many were astonished that Tsar
Alexander I imposed so generous a peace. However, Alexander displayed a shrewdness lacking in many of his successors,
for he understood that any attempt to subjugate this proud
and stubborn people would be more trouble than it was
worth. Although the Finns were permitted to keep their own
Lutheran faith and the ruling classes to control the schools

and local agencies of government, the lot of the people remained unchanged.

Alexander was under the impression that he had conquered a Swedish province, and consequently he left the administration of the country in the hands of the Swedish-speaking aristocracy. If the Finnish-speaking majority had jumped out of the frying-pan, it was only to land in another. The Swedish minority built up a tight bureaucracy and maintained its language as the exclusive means of communication in government and education. The Finnish majority was still treated as a group of uneducated peasants who spoke a "barbaric tongue." Among the Finns arose a slogan that reflected their discontent. It ran: "We are not Swedes, we can never be Russians, so let us be Finns."

As the historian Jackson has observed, it was not clear at first just what to "be Finns" meant. By the end of the century, however, everyone knew what it meant. In 1899, under Nicholas II, the so-called February Manifesto virtually nullified all Finnish constitutional rights. When certain newspapers dared to voice protests, they were promptly muzzled. In November, the people of Helsinki countered by holding what were called "Press Celebrations." The grand climax was a series of historical tableaux depicting Finland's troubled history, and for these a rising young musician named Jean Sibelius was commissioned to compose and conduct some orchestral preludes and background music.

Among the many figures represented on the stage in the sixth and final tableau—*Finland Awakes*—were three men who had been the prime movers in this awakening.

They had come from widely divergent backgrounds, and during the second quarter of the century they had met regularly as the nucleus of a group that became known as the Saturday Society. The first was a teacher of the classics named Johan Ludvig Runeberg who wrote poetry in Swedish during his spare time. For Runeberg to "be Finns" meant a Romantic revival in which Finnish patriotism and courage in battle were extolled. His historical reputation rests upon a collection of poems entitled *The Tales of Ensign Stål*, recalling the exploits of Finnish heroes, generals as well as foot soldiers, who had fought against the Russians. The dedicatory poem, "Our Land" (*"Vårt Land"* in Swedish, *"Maamme"* in Finnish), was set to music by the German-born composer Fredrik Pacius, and became the national anthem. Oddly enough, Finland's greatest poet never mastered Finnish well enough to write in it.

The second figure in the tableau was a humble little district medical officer named Elias Lönnrot. He spent much of his time wandering through the eastern regions of Finland known as Karelia, where he recorded a vast amount of folk poems, or *runos*. These he published in 1835 as an epic poem to which he gave the title *Kalevala* (*Land of the Heroes*). After a dozen years or so, it was evident to many that Lönnrot had converted a great oral tradition into a written one, and in so doing had given his countrymen the greatest single source upon which Finnish art of the future would be based. The way was now paved for spoken Finnish to be fashioned into a literary language; Lönnrot devoted the final years of his life to the preparation of a dictionary.

The third figure in *Finland Awakes* was the national reformer, Johan Vilhelm Snellman. It has been said that Snellman turned Romantic nationalism into a movement for education. He argued that it was fundamentally wrong for Swedish to remain the exclusive language of government and education in a country in which the uneducated majority spoke only Finnish. There could be no genuine spirit of national unity, no communication between the rulers and the ruled, until Finnish was placed on a basis of equality with Swedish and taught in the schools. No impractical visionary, Snellman fought relentlessly for his ideas, and the battle of the languages soon became a bitterly contested political struggle. The Swede-Finns ultimately lost the battle of the languages, but they were fortunate in being able to safeguard their minority rights.

The consequences of the Romantic revival and the movement for popular education were inevitable—a desire for political and economic independence. By 1899, Finland was very much "awake," and the Russian overlords knew it. If they did not, the rest of the world soon hailed the music for this tableau as the symbol of Finnish national aspirations: *Finlandia.*

That Jean Sibelius composed the music for this tableau was singularly appropriate. He had already been acclaimed as Finland's greatest composer, and his life and work reflected the deep influence of these three honored national figures. As a Swede-Finn, he had been raised on the lyric poetry of Runeberg, which inspired many of his art songs. As a Swede-Finn, he had received his general education during the very years when the battle of the languages was most intense. Fortunately, he had attended one of the first Finnish-language secondary schools, and thus as a Finn he was able to find in Lönnrot's *Kalevala* the inspiration for much of his music.

The audience attending the "Press Celebrations" had known this young man for over a decade under the artistic name of Jean Sibelius, but that many ever addressed him familiarly as Jean is to be doubted. To his relatives and intimate friends he was known as Janne; some of his fellow musicians called him Sibbe; in the eyes of the law—in this case the records of his church parish—he had been baptized Johan Julius Christian Sibelius.[1]

He was born in Hämeenlinna,[2] located in the south-central interior of Finland, on December 8, 1865. His parents were Dr. Christian Gustaf Sibelius, a physician and surgeon, and Maria Charlotta Sibelius, *née* Borg. His paternal grandfather, Johan Sibelius, a merchant and town councilor in Loviisa, had married the daughter of a doctor who had emigrated from Sweden. His great-grandfather, a farmer named Johan Martinpoika, had moved from Artjärvi, in the interior, south to Lapinjärvi, where he married Maria Mattsdotter. Maria's father, in accordance with rural traditions, adopted as his surname that of the land he farmed—Sibbe.

[1] *It should be noted that in Finland he has never been known as "Jan" Sibelius.*

[2] *For the sake of uniformity I have employed Finnish regional names throughout this study. Thus: Hämeenlinna = Tavastehus (Swedish), Helsinki = Helsingfors, Loviisa = Lovisa, Porvoo = Borgå, Tammisaari = Ekenäs, Turku = Åbo, Vaasa = Vasa, Viipuri = Viborg.*

In settling here, Johan Martinpoika thus became known as Johan Sibbe and in time the name was given the fashionable Latin ending and became Sibelius. There is not complete agreement as to whether Johan's family name was Martinpoika (Finnish) or its Swedish equivalent, Mårtensson. The most recent genealogical research on the Sibelius family favors the former.

On his mother's side, the composer was descended from a long line of clergymen, government officials, soldiers, and landowners, all apparently Swedish in customs and language, and of mixed Swedish, Finnish, and German ancestry. In the eighteenth century, we encounter in the family tree such names as Anders, Prockman, Chydenius, Hornaeus, Welenius, Haartman, Macrolander, Floor, Justander, Utter, Florin, Amnorin, and Palenius. On the basis of a genealogical study made in 1925, the English writer Cecil Gray finds that out of thirty-two direct ancestors of Sibelius living around 1700, eighteen were Swede-Finns, nine pure Swedes, four pure Finns, and one a German. "So far as blood and race go," Gray concludes, "Sibelius is predominantly, even overwhelmingly Swedish, not Finnish."

Names, however, are not always reliable indicators of what constitutes "blood and race," and this is especially true in Finland. During the long period of Swedish domination, many Finns quite understandably adopted the names and customs of their rulers. Centuries later, as Finnish culture became the dominant one, this process was carried out in reverse. Thus, in many cases "Swedes" who assumed Finnish names were actually regaining those of their ancestors.

But as far as language and home environment are

concerned, it can be said that Sibelius was born a Swede-Finn. This means exactly what it says, and should not be construed as an attempt to deprive the composer of his nationality. He is as Finnish as Runeberg, Lönnrot, and Snellman. Many outsiders, bewildered by what appear to be contradictions in both the music and the personality of Sibelius, have attempted to resolve matters in terms of his Swedish and Finnish origins. His lighter, small instrumental compositions and his elegant manners are attributed to the sanguine, adaptable, and extroverted "Swede." On the other hand, the creator of the symphonies and the *Kalevala*-inspired tone poems, as well as his self-imposed isolation—largely a myth—are associated with the phlegmatic, obstinate, and introverted "Finn." Like many attractive theories, this one is easier to advance than to prove. Anyone who has had the opportunity to live in intimate contact with the Finnish people would find it rather difficult to assign these so-called racial characteristics to his acquaintances. Perhaps a sanguine friend, Mr. Olofsson, is descended from an introvert named Pekkala, whereas a phlegmatic Mr. Virkkunen might be the grandson of an extrovert named Snellman.

In spite of repeated denials, the legend still persists that Sibelius was descended primarily from uneducated Finnish peasant stock. Undoubtedly this assumption grew out of the "primitive" qualities that many profess to find in his music; it has been abetted by photographs of a stern, granite-like face frozen in what appears to be a perpetual scowl. On the contrary, Sibelius belonged to what is generally called the middle class.

Chapter I

Throughout his life, the composer made repeated references to aristocrats and things aristocratic. If we are to believe one of his intimate friends, Adolf Paul, he strove to become a super-aristocrat by means of his art. In Finland, at least, he more than succeeded in this ambition. Behind this aristocratic façade, however, there is another Sibelius—highly imaginative, nervous, and emotionally insecure—totally different from the *grand seigneur* who in his later years charmed visitors from near and far with his lofty mien, refined tastes, and continental *esprit*. This is the Sibelius who expressed his feelings in music that made him great.

One English writer has observed that it is very difficult to throw any interest into a chapter on childhood. There is the same uniformity in almost all children until they grow up. Janne was the second of three children. His sister, Linda, was three years his senior, and Dr. Sibelius died before the third child, Christian, was born. In as much as the widow possessed no independent income, she lived with the children's maternal grandmother, Katarina Juliana Borg, in Hämeenlinna. Summers were spent with Grandmother Katarina Fredrika Sibelius in Loviisa, on the southern coast of Finland. The children also made frequent visits to their bachelor uncle, Pehr Sibelius, in Turku.

Janne appeared to be no different from most Finnish lads raised in rural communities. He delighted in collecting plants, chasing butterflies, hunting, and exploring all of the mysteries of nature. Many years later, a boyhood friend, Walter von Konow, drew attention to Janne's highly developed imagination—he would insist that the surrounding dusky forest was inhabited by nymphs, witches, goblins, and other supernatural creatures. But most children enjoy the priceless privilege of being able to live in a fairy-tale world of their own creation. The extraordinary thing about Janne was that his childish visions remained with him when he became an adult.

Had there been any child psychologists in Hämeenlinna during those years, they might have expressed some mild concern over a few of Janne's "patterns of behavior." He was rather reluctant to engage in such group activities as sports, and, though not a backward child in matters of learning, he was extremely nervous when asked to recite in class. He disliked all forms of academic discipline, and preferred at an early age to follow his own "way." Some of his teachers called him a dreamer. Endowed with an excellent constitution, Janne employed the art of drawing attention to himself by feigning illness.

He was happiest, and apparently felt most secure, when in the company of an intimate friend or a small group of his own choosing. Then his shyness yielded to garrulity and he invented all sorts of games and pranks. If the group formed an "orchestra" out of one or two legitimate instruments and a variety of homemade noisemakers, Janne was always the self-appointed leader. If a play was improvised, Janne became the author, director, and king. Konow describes his playmate's creative process:

"In the beginning Janne thought out the main lines of the play the same evening it was to be given. As the plot evolved, new things were added, so that not even the actors knew how it was going to end. Unexpected ideas could give a completely new turn to the play. In every play there was always a king, a princess, a troll, and a robber. Janne was always the king, but sometimes he suddenly changed into a troll and caused the most preposterous scenes."

With a few minor changes, such scenes could be converted into any one of many descriptions of the mature Sibelian style, which we shall have occasion to examine. For example, Edward Robinson has written: "Sibelius's music is full of fine thoughts, fine moods, and fine emotions that are only too often hesitatingly stated and imperfectly developed. His most convincing work is still pervaded by an underlying sense of incompleteness and insecurity."

At the age of eight, Janne was placed in a Swedish-language elementary school. Because there was no Swedish secondary school in Hämeenlinna and the family was too poor to send him to Helsinki, he was moved to another private institution so that he could learn enough Finnish to be admitted to Hämeenlinna's pioneering Suomalainen Normaalilyseo (Finnish Normal School). Even for a child, the transition to the completely different Finnish language with its fifteen case endings and complicated syntax was not an easy one.

Janne soon became fluent in Finnish, but for the remainder of his life he lapsed into minor grammatical errors that revealed that he had not been born to the language. For him his first language—the language he instinctively counted in—was Swedish. But the gap had been bridged, and he no longer ran the risk of being labeled a "Swede" by the majority of his countrymen.

On the occasion of his fiftieth birthday, Sibelius was especially eager to have it known that musicians could be found on his family tree. Actually there were no professional musicians among his ancestors, though it is said that several of them were quite competent amateurs. Consequently, the three children were encouraged to develop similar interests. Linda elected the piano and Christian the cello, upon which he later became so proficient that he was asked to perform in public. Janne commenced with the piano, but soon favored the violin. The Finnish writer Furuhjelm has reproduced in his study of Sibelius a few measures from a piece entitled *Water Drops (Vatten Droppar)* which Janne composed at the age of ten. What it establishes more than anything else is the fact that the boy was eager to create his own music.

By the time he was fifteen, Janne's interest in the violin was serious enough to merit professional instruction from the leader of Hämeenlinna's military band, Gustaf Levander. These lessons, which also included some instruction in theory, continued for the next five years, until he left for Helsinki to begin his university studies. Apparently Levander accompanied sound instruction with strict discipline. Janne practiced the odious scales and exercises with such diligence that later he was able to begin advanced study with relative ease.

After his retirement, Sibelius confessed that during these early years in Hämeenlinna he undertook to instruct himself in the science of music with the aid of a copy of Marx's *Die Lehre von der musikalischen Composition,* which he studied assiduously. These studies resulted in a series of chamber-music compositions that were used to supplement the family's regular repertory of works by the classical and romantic masters. It has been estimated that Sibelius must have written seven or eight trios and several other compositions during these years. Although it would be difficult to prove that there are any marks of a boy genius in these works, they do indicate that he had musical interests and abilities far exceeding those one would expect from a student with so limited a musical background. In 1902, Sibelius employed a theme from one of these early string trios in his *Impromptu* for women's chorus and orchestra, opus 19.

On the occasion of his fiftieth birthday, the composer told his biographer Furuhjelm: "I knew just about everything—that is to say, everything concerning form—when I began my studies in Helsinki." Coming from anyone other than Sibelius, this would be considered the preposterous remark of a braggart who would soon be whittled down to size by his teachers and fellow students. Perhaps there is more than a grain of truth to this statement, especially if we interpret it as meaning that he *believed* this to be the case.

As we shall see, it is the formal structure of his symphonies upon which his critics have pounced with the greatest glee. Indeed, some of the critics have gone so far as to insist upon an almost complete disregard for form in these same works, saying that they constitute a series of unrelated and undeveloped musical ideas joined together by the crudest of means. On the other hand, the composer's warmest admirers have attempted to show through analysis that the symphonies contain radical formal innovations that entitle Sibelius to be ranked with Beethoven.

Are the symphonies of Sibelius different from those of his contemporaries or predecessors primarily because he was unwilling or unable—as some have intimated—to pre-

Mitrofan Wasiljeff and his violin students. Sibelius is
the third from the left.

Pencil drawing by Sibelius (about 1887) to accompany
a quartet for violin, cello, piano, and harmonium

sent his musical ideas in forms that would give them logic and continuity? Are the forms so highly personalized and intellectualized as to constitute a veritable revolution in music? Any attempt to answer these questions or to resolve the implied differences depends ultimately upon the individual listener.

At the age of twenty, Janne Sibelius, in spite of a fertile imagination, did not entertain any notions about becoming a famous symphonist. He had just earned the coveted white cap, a sign to all that he had the right to employ the honorable title of "student" and enter the Imperial Alexander University in Helsinki. The family counted on the youth to seek fame and glory in the field of law. But Janne had different ideas. The boy who had played at being a king was now a young man who dreamed of becoming a violin virtuoso.

Chapter II   1885–1889

O age of gold, O life that gleams
With purest joy and pleasure,
When one is young, and student dreams
Fill every rift with leisure,
And one's worst worry is the fear
That one's moustache will not appear!

from Runeberg's *Ensign Stål*

●

Young Sibelius made a feeble pretense at beginning his pre-law studies during his first year in Helsinki, but his heart was not in such work. In truth, one could not imagine a profession for which he was more temperamentally unfit than the law. He immediately enrolled in the Music Institute as a special student, and after one year even Grandmother Sibelius reluctantly concluded that Janne was bent on becoming the first professional musician in the family.

His progress with his new violin teachers—in the beginning with the Russian Mitrofan Wasiljeff, later with the Hungarian Hermann Csillag—was both rapid and promising. Near the end of his first semester, Sibelius performed in a trio for violins by the Austrian pedagogue Jakob Dont, and during the second semester he played the first movement of a David concerto. Perhaps the most gratifying recognition of his talent came during the second year, when he was appointed second violin in the Institute's faculty quartet.

Sibelius stayed with the quartet during his undergraduate years, and rejoined it when he was appointed to the faculty. This, however, did not prevent him from appearing in public as a soloist in such virtuoso compositions as concertos by Mendelssohn, Kreutzer, Rode, and Spohr. In 1888, at a special chamber-music soirée given in the popular Kämp restaurant, no less a musical figure than Richard Faltin served as his accompanist.

The German-born and trained Faltin (1835–1918) was one of those complete musicians able to serve in almost any capacity—composer, church organist, pianist, choir director, orchestra conductor, teacher, and music critic. In 1870, he had been given the position of music teacher at the Imperial Alexander University in Helsinki. His predecessor had been another German, Fredrik Pacius, the composer of the Finnish national anthem and *King Charles's Hunt,* the first Finnish opera. Thus, by virtue of his position Faltin could be considered one of the high priests in Finland's musical life and a man worth cultivating. As we shall see, his interest in the career of the young Sibelius, who addressed him as "Uncle," was so great that he proposed the younger man as his successor at the University.

Helsinki's Music Institute was founded in 1882 by Martin Wegelius (1846–1906), who served as its director and principal teacher in theory and composition. Wegelius enjoyed an exceptionally fine background for this dual role. At the age of twenty-three, he earned his Master of Arts degree at the University under Faltin and then proceeded to Vienna and Leipzig for further graduate studies. Among his famous teachers were Carl Reinecke, for many years conductor of the Gewandhaus Concerts; Salomon Jadassohn, a former pupil of Liszt; and the great Wagnerian conductor Hans Richter. Before founding his school, Wegelius had presented a concert of his own compositions in Helsinki at the age of twenty-seven, had served as a pianist and conductor on numerous occasions, and for a brief spell had held a post as music critic.

Because Sibelius in his later years insisted that he was self-taught and uninfluenced, it is difficult to properly assess the importance of the role played by Wegelius—or anyone else, for that matter—during these formative years. Sibelius described his teacher as being "a father to me" and ". . . if anyone, the right man in the right place." It is to be doubted whether the young student relished the heavy assignments in thorough bass, harmony, form, and strict and free counterpoint which were based on Bussler's *Practical School of Composition*. Sibelius evidently submitted to these musical disciplines reluctantly, and though he earned superior grades, he was crestfallen later when his post-graduate teacher in Berlin, Albert Becker, insisted that he return to them.

If we are to believe Sibelius and his biographer Ekman, the Director of the Music Institute was a "neo-romantic" who tried to "infect" his pupil with an admiration for Wagner's music. There is no doubt, however, that Wegelius was genuinely interested in acquainting his protégé with the prevailing musical styles and in introducing him to the great works in classical literature which were not available in Swedish translation. Sibelius soon became the favored pupil, and as the years progressed, he was permitted greater freedom in composing as his fancy dictated.

One mark of the teacher's esteem was an invitation to Sibelius to collaborate with him in the composition of incidental music to Gunnar Wennerberg's fairy-tale drama, *The Watersprite (Näcken)*, which was presented by the Institute during the spring of 1888. Around this time, Sibelius also wrote background music for piano trio to accompany the reading of verses by Runeberg, *Nights of Jealousy (Svartsjukans nätter)*.

Sibelius must have experienced a feeling of exhilaration in 1888 over the appearance of his first published composition, a song entitled "Serenade" to verses by Runeberg. Elsewhere in this collection of songs, *Singing Finland (Det Sjungande Finland)*, he was identified as "Jean Sibelius, music student." The composer has said that the idea for adopting Jean as his artistic name came when he inherited some calling-cards belonging to his seafaring uncle Johan Sibelius, who preferred the French form of his Christian name when traveling abroad.

About midway in his career as a music student, Sibelius had the good fortune to meet the highly respected music critic for the Swedish-language newspaper *Nya Pressen,* Karl Teodor Flodin (1858–1925). Flodin had also earned his Master of Arts degree with Faltin and had then continued his studies at the Leipzig Conservatory. As a critic possessing a broad musical background and owing no allegiance to anyone other than himself, Flodin kept a sharp lookout for new music that was distinctively "Finnish." In the young Sibelius he found what he had been seeking. He became the composer's friend and mentor during his formative years— one might even call him Sibelius's artistic conscience.

Shortly before his death in 1925, Flodin wrote a short article entitled "The First Meeting" in honor of the composer's sixtieth birthday. It provides us with a rare picture of Sibelius's personality as it appeared to the critic during the 1880's. Flodin recalls an afternoon when his friend Paul Leontjeff telephoned a request for him to come immediately to Forsströms Café. He said that he was with a young music student named Jean Sibelius, and he was unable to decide whether he was a genius or *"ein bischen meschugge."*

Flodin was introduced to an extremely talkative youth with a heavy shock of untidy blond hair that fell over his forehead. He was impressed by the young man's large, well-formed ears and his blue eyes, which were alternately misty or brilliant, depending upon his mood. "His speech overflowed with paradoxes and metaphors," Flodin recalled, "without allowing one to decide what was serious and what only played on the surface like bubbles born of the odd caprices in his nimble brain. . . . Little did we suspect then that a creative force was already breathing in this youth, that the canvas for a new world-picture was already being raised out of these fantasies, however confused they seemed to us, however little firm foundation and connection they seemed to possess." The similarities between this first impression and Konow's portrait of the child Janne are unmistakable.

Flodin followed with great interest the student's progress as a composer of chamber music. In May 1888, Sibelius's Theme and Variations in C sharp minor for string quartet was presented by the Institute. The critic pronounced it an "interesting number" that bore witness to the composer's newly acquired skills in theory and at the same time revealed a power of imagination worth cultivating. The following year, Flodin found a Suite in A minor for string trio less to his liking. "Such melody as there was," he noted, "was rather far-fetched and fragmentary." The violin teacher Csillag immediately wrote a strongly worded letter of protest, but the critic remained unshaken. Several years later, when the Piano Quintet in G minor was presented, he repeated the same charge: "I thought that I could again detect some of the melodic sterility that had already been evident in Sibelius's earlier works."

In May 1889, however, Flodin was delighted with the String Quartet in A minor, and wrote: "With this composition Mr. Sibelius has given such excellent proof of an original musical talent that we can expect the greatest things from him. There was a richness of ideas, an independence combined with a mastery of technical problems, which must be regarded as unique qualities in so young a composer. . . . Let us express our sincere joy at the fact that this work has been created and that Mr. Sibelius has placed himself foremost among those who have been entrusted to create Finnish music."

Some of these student manuscripts have survived, and fragments from most of them have been preserved by Furuhjelm in his excellent study of Sibelius published in 1916. Collectively they may be regarded as first exercises in free expression and as having little in common with the later works for orchestra, which were to mark the Sibelian style as unique in world music. In his later years, Sibelius refused many entreaties to publish them; he is represented in chamber-music literature only by the String Quartet in D minor (*Voces intimae*), opus 56, which appeared in 1909.[1] "I am myself a man of the orchestra," he told Törne. "You must judge me by my orchestral works."

Seated in the audience that heard the Quartet in A minor was Finland's most important musical figure, the man destined to help Sibelius along his "way" more than all others: Robert Kajanus (1856–1933). Also a protégé of Faltin, Kajanus had studied later at the Leipzig Conservatory with Reinecke and Richter, as well as in Paris with the Norwegian composer Johan Svendsen.

After returning to Finland, Kajanus founded the Helsinki Orchestra Association in 1882, claimed to be the oldest permanent symphony orchestra performing on a professional basis in northern Europe.[2] After procuring the necessary financial aid from private sources, Kajanus formed his small orchestra of thirty-six around a solid core of imported German musicians. The first public concert took place on October 3, 1882, with performances of Beethoven's Fifth Symphony and several shorter works.

In the hope of attracting greater public support for his venture, Kajanus presented programs in which standard classical symphonies were interspersed with lighter pieces, and engaged such famous soloists as Leopold Auer and Vladi-

[1] *Although the manuscript of a String Quartet in B flat major, composed in 1889, is listed as opus 4, Sibelius made this designation rather late in his career.*

[2] *In 1895 it became known as the Philharmonic Society, and in 1914 as the Helsinki City Orchestra.*

mir de Pachmann. As professional musicians were not available in large supply in Finland, he organized and was the principal teacher in the Orchestra School. This automatically placed him in competition with Wegelius's Music Institute.

In addition to his activities as conductor and teacher, Kajanus, until the advent of Sibelius, was considered one of Finland's leading composers. Between 1880 and 1885, he wrote *Kullervo's Death,* the so-called *Aino Symphony,* his first *Finnish Rhapsody*—all for orchestra—and numerous minor works. Much in this music betrays his deep admiration for such composers as Liszt and Wagner. But Kajanus stands revealed as an accomplished master of orchestration. In addition, he was among the first to draw upon the *Kalevala* for inspiration, thus pointing the way to such younger composers as Sibelius.

The "friendly" rivalry between Kajanus and Wegelius was so strong as to prevent any open fraternization between the members of their respective institutions. Because of this, Sibelius was very much the loser. Much against his teacher's wishes, he did manage to attend some of the orchestra concerts, but he was unable to benefit from Kajanus's experience and friendship until many years later. Had there been close co-operation between the two schools, Sibelius would have been able to acquire at an earlier date an adequate knowledge of orchestration. The limited facilities of the Music Institute did not include courses in orchestration; nor was there a student orchestra.

Veikko Helasvuo has written: "The mission of Kajanus in the creative music of Finland was ultimately . . . that of a John the Baptist, who prophesies the coming of the

Messiah: Sibelius's hour was about to dawn!" This Biblical analogy does not do Kajanus justice. As we shall see, he was Sibelius's close friend and promoter during the latter's creative life. Even more important, during those early years when the "Messiah" was woefully lacking in the techniques of scoring for orchestra, Kajanus was his unofficial but acknowledged teacher.

Kajanus was not the only one who had to import foreign musicians. Wegelius was faced with the same problem in recruiting a staff for his Music Institute. Among the most talented teachers he lured to Finland was Ferruccio Busoni (1866–1924). Although one year Sibelius's junior, Busoni was already considered the complete *Musiker*. At the age of nine, he had appeared as a pianist in Vienna and had excited the admiration of the famous critic, Eduard Hanslick. At fifteen, he had made a triumphal tour of Italy which merited him membership in the Philharmonic Academy of Bologna, the youngest member to receive this honor since Mozart.

As a piano teacher in Helsinki, Busoni had no direct influence on Sibelius's training, but the two bachelors soon became fast friends. Busoni was attracted by Sibelius's eccentric ways and vivid imagination. Together—generally at Busoni's expense—they spent many lively hours in Helsinki's popular restaurants and cafés. Later Busoni proved his friendship by championing the new Finnish music in Germany. When he composed his *Geharnischte Suite,* he dedicated the first movement to Sibelius, the second to Adolf Paul, and the remaining two to the brothers Armas and Eero Järnefelt.

Almost fifty years later, Adolf Paul (1863–1943) wrote for a Berlin newspaper:

"Sibelius, that remarkable man, first stepped into my life in 1886 when I enrolled as a student in the Music Institute of Helsinki in order to study piano. A handsome, slender youth of medium height with bright eyes, a blond mustache, and an impressive head of dark blond hair falling over an imposing forehead—so he appeared to me during my first day at the Institute. . . . We immediately became fast friends. We were both crazy about E. T. A. Hoffmann."

Paul was a Swede by birth who had gone to Finland at the age of nine. His father had had hopes that the boy would follow in his footsteps and become an agricultural specialist, but Adolf had his heart set on becoming a concert pianist. After working with Busoni in Helsinki, he continued his studies in Germany, where he soon convinced himself that his chances for success were far greater in literature than in music.

A tragic figure, this Paul. As his friend Janne's popularity grew, his own diminished. His efforts as a dramatist, journalist, and writer of scenarios for motion pictures may charitably be described as mediocre. He died in poverty before witnessing the final defeat of his idol, the only person other than Sibelius who, he felt, deserved the love of his people: Adolf Hitler.

Right from the beginning, Paul stamped his new friend as a rather odd but lovable character. He was merciless in taunting Janne for his many poses and especially for his tendency toward hypochondria. Once he visited the "deathly

Chapter II

sick" Janne, bringing him some roses. The following day, Sibelius dispatched his brother, Christian, with his own thank-you present to Paul. It was a suite for piano in four movements entitled *Florestan,* dated April 22, 1889. Over each of the movements Sibelius had written his own program:

1. Florestan goes out into the forest. He is melancholy and unhappy. There is an odor of moss and damp bark in the air.

2. Florestan comes to a rapid stream, and as he watches the ripples, they are changed into water nymphs. There is an odor of water lilies in the air.

3. One of the nymphs has black eyes and golden hair. Florestan falls in love with her.

4. Florestan beckons her to approach, but she vanishes. Depressed and unhappy, he returns through the forest.

Janne, who had seen those same nymphs during his school days in Hämeenlinna, would continue to see them at least until 1926, when he completed his last great composition, *Tapiola.* But in 1933, when Paul requested permission to publish *Florestan* in facsimile—he needed money desperately—Sibelius refused, perhaps because by that time he had thoroughly revised his notions concerning program music, and also because he wanted to forget what he considered to be his youthful indiscretions.

Another of Sibelius's close student friends was Armas Järnefelt (1869–1958), who later became a well-known conductor in Sweden, and whose modest international reputation as a composer rests upon two charming miniatures for orchestra, *Praeludium* and *Berceuse.* The Järnefelt family ranked high among the Finnish aristocrats. Lieutenant General August Alexander Järnefelt was distinguished both as a military figure and as an administrative official. His wife was born Baroness Elisabeth Clodt von Jürgensburg. In addition to Armas, the family included two other brothers, a writer named Arvid and a painter named Eero, as well as several daughters, one of whom, Aino, later married Sibelius.

When Armas introduced Janne to his family, Mrs. Järnefelt, his mother, was delighted with the young musician's violin-playing and found him "very pleasant, intelligent, and sensitive." As for Aino, it was love at first sight. Intimate contact with this family broadened Sibelius's intellectual horizons. They were all in the vanguard of the Finnish nationalist movement, and their infectious enthusiasm undoubtedly helped to convince him that his future as an artist had to follow similar directions.

By the spring of 1889, Sibelius had completed his course of instruction at the Music Institute. His grades, except in piano, were superior. With Wegelius's blessing, he was now ready to seek the stimulation, inspiration, and prestige associated with foreign study.

We have already seen that he possessed a highly developed imagination. Consequently it is likely that he was able to visualize his being invited to return to the Music Institute as a teacher within a few years. But it is to be doubted that even during his wildest flights of fancy he dreamed that fifty years later that same institution would be renamed the Sibelius Academy.

*"People don't have to know everything. If
they did, that Leporello index of yours would
constitute not one forbidden book, but a
whole library."   Adolf Paul to Jean Sibelius
(Berlin, 1919)*

•

In the spring of 1889, the name
of student J. C. J. Sibelius figured on the list of successful
candidates awarded state grants for the continuation of art
studies abroad. Painter Gallén-Kallela and sculptor Vikström
each received three thousand marks, and musicians Sibelius
and Ilmari Krohn, later to become Finland's most famous
musicologist, two thousand marks each. Actually, Sibelius
enjoyed a more generous sum than the others, for the Nyland
Student Corporation, of which he was a member, provided
him with an additional fifteen hundred marks. Thus began a
two-year sojourn on the continent which was to be of para-
mount importance in shaping the young artist's future.

When he arrived in Berlin in the fall, Sibelius immediately made contact with the teachers in violin, theory,
and composition recommended by Wegelius. His new in-
structor in composition, Albert Becker, was a strict task-
master of the old school who had very definite notions concerning what his students should and should not do. Young

Sibelius found to his dismay that he had to return to the monotonous diet of vocal and instrumental counterpoint, which he found most distasteful. With characteristic youthful impetuosity, he felt that he had already been subjected to enough of that sort of thing in Finland, and he yearned to compose as his fancy dictated. But Becker's will prevailed, and during this year his student managed to complete only one work in his spare time: the Piano Quintet in G minor.

Berlin was a far cry from relatively provincial Helsinki. Sibelius thoroughly enjoyed the greater social freedom and richer cultural environment. He and his fellow countryman Adolf Paul soon joined a coterie of foreign students, many of whom came from Scandinavia. Their quasi-Bohemian life has been admirably described by Paul in his autobiographical novel, *A Book About a Man,* to which we shall return presently.

For Sibelius, accustomed to Helsinki's chamber-music soirées and a few poorly performed symphony concerts, Berlin's musical life with its superabundant offerings of all kinds was dazzling. The lavish opera productions, and especially Wagner's works, opened his eyes to greater possibilities for self-expression than he had dared to imagine. These deep and lasting influences were the most important facts of the Berlin year.

Sibelius has frequently been described as one of the most "uninfluenced" composers in the entire history of music. The general impression appears to be that his art was born in extreme isolation and directly inspired by prolonged and intimate contact with the phenomena of nature. In his later years, the composer contributed to the spreading of this myth by frequent references to what he called "my way." But the expression "my way" connotes movement and even struggle in the search for self-expression, and any attempt to ignore or minimize those early influences is patently absurd. The composer's systematic attempt to deny any Wagnerian influence is a good case in point.

Sibelius's intemperate criticisms of the Master of Bayreuth were so frequent as to constitute a phobia. It should be noted, however, that most of his remarks were made after 1926, which year marked the beginning of the "silence from Järvenpää." In 1899, the young Finnish student was deeply impressed by this *Zukunftmusik* with its exciting harmonies, strong rhythms, and, above all, its lush and varied instrumental coloring. Early during his stay in Berlin, he heard performances of *Tannhäuser* and *Die Meistersinger,* and he wrote Wegelius: "There was such a mixture of surprise, disappointment, joy within me." Ekman's explanation that this was written merely to spare the feelings of a fanatic Wagnerian at any price is little more than undisguised sophistry. The young Sibelius considered Wagner "a great and incomparable human being." Even if we were to admit that he refused to drink at the Wagnerian fountain for his inspiration, his early compositions establish far better than words that he was unable to escape its spray.

As we have seen, the rivalry between Helsinki's Music Institute and Kajanus's Orchestra School was such as to preclude any warm friendship between the conductor and Sibelius as long as the latter remained under the watchful eye of Wegelius. The beginnings of their friendship date from

the composer's Berlin days, when Kajanus conducted his own
Aino Symphony—actually a tone poem for chorus and orchestra—with the Berlin Philharmonic. "Acquaintance with
this work was of thrilling importance to me," Sibelius later
recalled to Ekman. "It opened my eyes to the wonderful op-
portunities the *Kalevala* offered for musical expression. Earlier attempts to interpret our national epos had not encouraged imitation. And the environment in which I had
grown up was as far removed from the *Kalevala* as possible."

Many years after the death of Kajanus in 1933, Sibelius categorically denied the influence of the *Aino Symphony*
on his own work. "That was something that matured in me
quite by itself," he told Ringbom, "[something] that was in
the air." We shall have several occasions to see how the aging
composer denied the influence of Kajanus on his own music.
For the present, however, it should be noted that within one
year after hearing the *Aino Symphony* Sibelius made the
first sketches for his *Kullervo,* which, if more original and
ambitious in both scope and content, bears many similarities
to the earlier work.

It was also in Berlin that Sibelius had the opportunity to hear Richard Strauss's *Don Juan* for the first time.
Strauss was Sibelius's senior by one year, and was approaching
the height of his career. Hans von Bülow had fittingly nick-
named him "Richard the Second." Little did Sibelius know
at that time that twelve years later the Finnish critics would
hail him as Strauss's rival and even his superior. There can
be no doubt that upon hearing *Don Juan* the imaginative
young Sibelius was attracted to the programmatic tone poem

of heroic proportions. A few years later, he started work on a group of tone poems based on a similar subject—the amorous escapades of the legendary Finnish hero, Lemminkäinen.

In the spring of 1890, Sibelius returned to Finland, where he became engaged to Aino Järnefelt. Then he proceeded to Vienna for a second year of study. Once there, he made repeated efforts to see Brahms, to whom he bore a letter of introduction written by his friend Busoni. "True to his northern origin," Busoni wrote, "he has developed later than we. . . ." Ekman's explanation that this "half-jesting" letter may have been responsible for the lack of cordiality on the part of Brahms is improbable. Unlike Sibelius, both Brahms and Busoni had been child prodigies. Furthermore, Brahms did not have the reputation for being kindly disposed to rising young artists, and at this stage in his career Sibelius could hardly claim to be a rising young artist. By Viennese standards, he could at best produce a few specimens of what might pass for competently written *Schulmusik*, and consequently he must have struck Brahms as a complete nonentity.

Thanks to a letter from Hans Richter, Sibelius was accepted as a student by Robert Fuchs; another letter from Wegelius induced Carl Goldmark to advise him in matters of instrumentation. Sibelius was so pleased over his association with Goldmark that he immediately wired the news to friends in Finland, who took care to see that it was mentioned in the local newspapers.

Although Goldmark was extremely courteous to his new pupil, he apparently had neither the time nor the inclination to help him in mastering the difficult art of orchestration. Their meetings were limited to a few consultations at which the teacher suggested alterations in compositions. During this period, Sibelius completed his Piano Quartet in C major, an Overture in E major (the A minor Overture dates from a later period), and a Ballet Scene for orchestra. The last two were promptly sent to Kajanus, who conducted them the following spring.

Sibelius's debut as a composer of orchestral music occasioned no special words of praise in Helsinki musical circles. The critics dutifully observed that the new compositions displayed promising indications of what might be expected from him in the future. Both the Overture and the Ballet Scene have been preserved in manuscript in spite of the composer's attempts to destroy them. They contain no traces of the unique style that emerged later. At this stage in his career, Sibelius had only vague and confused notions concerning his future "way."

The gay life in the Austrian capital was even more to his liking than the one he had experienced in Berlin. In later years, he recalled his thrill at finding himself seated near Bruckner in a concert hall and also upon hearing Johann Strauss conduct his waltzes. He was stimulated by the heated musical arguments, especially between the partisans of Wagner and Brahms. It is little wonder, then, that Vienna witnessed the very beginning of creative efforts that would soon mark Sibelius as a composer of great stature in his own country. He worked on the first sketches for his *Kullervo* and an octet for woodwinds and strings which later provided motifs for *En Saga,* and completed several songs.

The young Sibelius of this period was in appearance a far cry from the forbidding portraits that have become so famous throughout the world. He was, in fact, an extremely good-looking man with an impressive head of unruly hair. Upon close contact, he gave the impression of being exceptionally nervous and lacking in self-confidence, especially in public. In the presence of an intimate friend, however, he could appear quite poised, conceited, cynical, and even arrogant. He greatly prized those objects associated with living in the "grand style" which he could ill afford—costly wines, food, cigars, and clothing.

The picture is best given in the words of Adolf Paul, who, in *A Book About a Man,* sketches the young Sibelius with clinical precision. When Paul went to Berlin, he had every intention of continuing his music studies in order to become a piano virtuoso. His autobiographical novel, in which he himself appears as Hans, deals principally with his own inner struggles and his ultimate decision to become a writer. When the book was published in Stockholm in 1891, it was affectionately dedicated to Jean Sibelius, who figures as one of the principal characters under the name Sillén. Here is our introduction to Sillén:

> A strange fellow this Sillén. Even though they had been comrades for two years Hans still couldn't make him out. He finally came to the conclusion that in spite of a thousand or more caprices and an equal number of contradictory actions, he was not mad. Nor was he given to airs. If he was, he soon lost the urge to be so, thanks to the intentional sarcasm and pitiless taunts of his comrades, who wished to educate and make a man of him. Consequently he had to be a genius.

For that reason Hans simply rejected his honest Christian name of Sillén and baptized him "Boy Genius." It was both convenient and characteristic, for his many whims were the most childish imaginable and, far from being brilliant, belonged more to a spoiled brat than to a full-grown man. He was a great gourmet and liked good cigars more than himself—which is to say, not a little. For him, all his fellow men were a necessary evil, little more than casual acquaintances in this vale of tears. He was a polished egotist. If he craved anything—a cigar costing two crowns, for example—he suffered unspeakably and was the most miserable man in the world until he had the desired object in his hand. Then he would become quite indifferent and throw away his expensive cigar without thinking about it. He derived his pleasure not from the ownership of something but from the longing for it. And his naïveté!

He always gave the impression of having suddenly dropped from a distant planet or of having made his entry into this world in some other impossible way, for everything endowed his imagination with the most peculiar qualities and nothing could proceed naturally.

Ideas came to him glimmering on a ray of sunshine reflected in the water—falling like a dead leaf—hopping like a bird. . . .

For him there existed a strange, mysterious connection between sound and color, between the most secret perceptions of eye and ear. . . . For this reason he spoke of this only in the strictest confidence and under a pledge of secrecy. "For otherwise they will make fun of me."

At times Sillén's aloofness infuriates Hans, who shouts:

"You! The worst egotist in the world! You always pretend to be so genial and absent-minded! You walk around in such deep and ingenious thoughts! You would sooner kill one of your nearest relatives than answer one of his everyday questions! And as for the people to whom you are not related closely enough in order to be impolite, you have only phrases, a whole magazine of ready-made phrases in the most beautiful order. They put their questions in the slot and they get their answers wrapped and labeled. And you need not interrupt your thoughts! The whole world could turn over rather than one of your thoughts be disturbed!"

Sillén then describes the difficulties he experiences in composition and outlines his ambitions:

"Hell, how little I get done! I haven't the courage to tell people how lost I am. You will probably not believe me, but it's true that I stay in bed until noon and then I'm absolutely lazy the rest of the day. It's impossible for me to work. I don't call that work, the exercises I dash off for my teachers. And I have ideas, great ideas that ought to occupy me all the time, but which I cannot force my lazy body to start on seriously.

"Criticism is the only thing that sustains me—

especially criticism directed against others, because it has opened my eyes for things other than blind admiration. Beethoven and Wagner—they are no longer any gods to me, but human beings, great and incomparable human beings, but with great faults. And the fact that I see that even they have faults gives me courage. It has killed the schoolboy in me, taken away the fear of what the teacher is going to say, and awakened my ambition to even greater merits and greater faults. And then I feel that my ideas are worth something and are equally if not more entitled to live. And thus to create on an even greater scale, to continue where my predecessors have finished, to make the art of my own time—all this becomes not only my right—no, it becomes my duty." Sibelius's love for expensive cigars has become well known. Here the youth explains how it came about:

"The odor of cigars reminds me so much of my childhood. When my father died and I took possession of all his things I was struck with the strong cigar odor clinging to them. His books, his papers, they were all permeated with this same odor, which became sacred to me. And now when I smoke my childhood returns and my world of ideas becomes such as it was then, completely pure and untouched by foreign elements with which it has been mixed. And that is why the aroma of cigars is for me the memory of happy times. Only a good cigar is needed to take me back. And you want to deny me this pleasure!"

Chapter III

Hundreds of stories, many of which have appeared in print, concerning Sibelius's love for strong spirits circulate through Helsinki even today. Collectively they are known as the Kämp stories, named after a famous restaurant that he used to frequent, and which still exists. They are, for the most part, amusing and harmless little jokes not unlike those told about any great public figure. For Sillén, however, alcohol provides an escape from reality, and he discusses his problem in seriousness:

"But sometimes I have another habit which I am almost ashamed to tell you about. It's to go alone to a tavern, sit down, and have one drink after another. And gradually I produce a mood in which I think in absolute earnest: 'Now you are a genius, a great genius perishing! Feel how you are sinking, how the deep is pulling you down more and more!' This is my present life. It becomes absolutely clear only when I drink spirits. But then when I leave, Reason stands at the door and whispers in my ear: 'That you can be so foolish!' "

Finally Sillén gives his credo as an artist:

"Yes, being able to give, and *give to everybody,* is the true mark of aristocracy. Inheritance and ancestry make a person noble only in the eyes of fools. It is only a sign of poverty to talk about 'art for art's sake.' All have a right to it—the shabby fellow as well as the over-refined, well-educated *salon* type. It must not be only mathematical riddles to help the latter pass their time. It must be Nature—more of the Nature that has produced both of them. For both need it and both have a right to be justly treated. And Art is the third person who dispenses this justice. And even more—to cast light on the great, the commonly human, that unites these two extremes is art's greatest task. That is why it is an unnatural crime to produce well-made, and well-dressed art works that can be understood only by a privileged few. Away with clothes! They hide frailty, and frailty must not be concealed—it must be destroyed!"

Many years later, Paul wrote to Sibelius: "I have just reread *A Book About a Man* for the first time in twenty years. I was happy and surprised at meeting you again. Fancy that even then I understood your caprices and your talent."

Paul's portrait of the young Sibelius rings with the conviction, exuberance, and unashamed truthfulness associated with youth. It is not the image of a famous composer, but of a fellow student seen with all his faults. Sibelius's later self-isolation at Järvenpää, his stock answers to interviewers (e.g., comparing his compositions to the wings of a butterfly), his frequent periods of prolonged depression, his at times charmingly urbane exterior before visitors, his fastidiousness in matters of dress, the Kämp stories—all of these expressions of his personality, and others, become understandable and take on fresh meaning in the light of Paul's portrait.

Most important of all, Paul casts valuable light on the first stage of the famous "way" his friend was seeking. Within one year after the novel was published, Sibelius made his real debut with a composition that was certainly not designed to be understood only by the privileged few: *Kullervo*.

*"The score contains some very fine things side
by side with feeble and detestable ones. But
the splendor of the show will
make everything pass muster."*
                    Berlioz on Meyerbeer's
                    Le Prophète

●
Upon returning to Finland, Si-
belius spent the summer of 1891 with his family in Loviisa.
In July, a singular honor came his way. He was invited to
participate as a judge at a music festival held in Tammisaari.
The other judges included Faltin, Wegelius, and Flodin.
Clearly his student days were over, now that his elders were
willing to accept him as their equal. During the course of
the festival, the Loviisa Septet performed an Andante for
wind instruments which Sibelius had recently completed.

More and more the public was becoming aware of
the name of Sibelius. Two short pieces for violin, later revised as opus 2, were published in local journals. Adolf Paul's
A Book About a Man appeared in Stockholm. During October, the Music Association of Helsinki presented a concert in
which the baritone Abraham Ojanperä sang some of the
songs that Sibelius had written in Vienna. Flodin liked them,
and concluded: "This much is certain—Jean Sibelius is one

of our composers who most truly captures the Finnish spirit in his music without seeming to force matters."

The peaceful years under the first two Alexanders were at an end, and their successors, Alexander III and Nicholas II, were far less appreciative of Finnish sensitivity. Russian tampering with local regulations, the appearance of Russian-born civil servants, and the declaration that the Russian language was official in certain branches of the government brought forth angry protests. Many artists and intellectuals banded together in a group known as the "Young Finns." Their leader was the writer Juhani Aho, their official voice the newspaper *Päivälehti*. Sibelius became associated with this group, and in December 1891, *Päivälehti* sponsored a gala concert in which Kajanus and his orchestra participated. Music by Sibelius, Kajanus, and the pianist-composer Oskar Merikanto was featured.

Sibelius was now ready to make his real debut with a gigantic work. He hoped to ride high on this swelling wave of Finnish nationalism with his *Kullervo* for soloists, male chorus, and large orchestra. Although he was completely inexperienced in such matters, he had to hire the musicians and, in accord with tradition, rehearse them himself. At the first performance, which took place on April 29, 1892, copies of the text in Finnish and in Swedish translation were given to the bilingual capacity audience.

On the original program, Sibelius designated *Kullervo* as a symphonic poem in five movements. In his later years, he frequently referred to it as an "independent symphony." Furuhjelm calls it an epic drama with an intermezzo and two preludes, in which the plot actually begins with the third movement, the fifth constituting the final act. One could with equal justification consider it a secular cantata.

After the first movement, which is merely designated as Introduction, the musical narrative begins with *Kullervo's Youth*. This was undoubtedly inspired by all or part of runos XXXI to XXXIV in the *Kalevala,* in which we are introduced to the unhappy hero. After being sold by his uncle as a slave to the smith Ilmarinen, Kullervo escapes and wanders throughout the land until at last he rejoins his family. Here he learns that his sister has been lost while gathering berries.

In the third movement, *Kullervo and His Sister,* the youth is sent by his father to pay the taxes. The chorus sings:

Kullervo, Kalervo's offspring,
With the very bluest stockings,
And with yellow hair the finest,
And with shoes of finest leather,
Went to pay the taxes,
And he went to pay the land dues.   (xxxv, 69–74)

On his way, he spies a beautiful maid, "with her yellow hair all flowing," on the heath of Väino and invites her to ride in his sleigh. There follows a lengthy section in which the chorus narrates the action and the two soloists interpolate bits of dialogue. When the maid spurns his repeated invitations, the exasperated youth drags her to his sleigh and wins her affection with gifts of gold, silver, and precious fabrics. After all passion is spent, the lovers identify themselves. In a long solo, the maid reveals her horror upon learning that she is his sister, and then jumps to her death in a foaming cataract. Kullervo laments:

"Woe my day, O me unhappy,
Woe to me and all my household,
For indeed my very sister,
I my mother's child have outraged!"   (xxxv, 271–4)

In the fourth movement, entitled *Kullervo Goes to the War,* the youth sets off to destroy the people of Untamo. There are no voice parts in this section, but Sibelius included on his program the following verses from the legends:

Kullervo, Kalervo's offspring,
With the very bluest stockings,
Went with music forth to battle,
Joyfully he sought the conflict,
Playing tunes through plains and marshes,
Shouting over all the heathland,
Crashing onwards through the meadows,
Trampling down the fields of stubble. (xxxvi, 155–62)

In the fifth and final movement, *Kullervo's Death,* the hero returns victorious from the war and finds his home deserted. He wanders unhappy through the forest until he arrives at the very spot where he seduced his sister. In anguish he asks his noble sword whether it would be disposed to slay him. When the sword answers in the affirmative, he falls upon it. The chorus concludes:

Even so the young man perished,
Thus died Kullervo the hero,
Thus the hero's life was ended,
Perished thus the hapless hero.   (xxxvi, 343–6)

The audience applauded the composer-conductor after each movement, and when, after one hour and a half, the last note sounded, there was a "never-ending explosion of enthusiasm." Robert Kajanus was among the first to present a floral tribute to his young friend. It bore a prophetic quotation from the final verses of the *Kalevala,* in which Väinämöinen sings to the people:

"This way therefore leads the pathway,
Here the path lies newly opened." (L, 15–16)

The new work was such a success that Sibelius repeated it four times before the orchestra's season was over. The poet J. H. Erkko was so impressed that he wrote verses entitled "To Janne Sibelius—after hearing his Kullervo Symphony." In a newspaper article, Adolf Paul hailed his friend as the "Finnish Grieg" and predicted that the day would come when he would be world-famous. "He's really quite a personality," Paul added, "even though he is something of a gypsy."

In later years, Aino Sibelius recalled that there was considerable danger in staking one's reputation on a work with a Finnish text at a time when most of the people attending and supporting symphony concerts were Swede-Finns. But *Kullervo* was deliberately created in order to appeal to the Finnish majority—not the "privileged few," to quote "Sillén"—and certainly this was the effect it had. Statements by Ekman and Ringbom that the critics, though failing to comprehend the significance of *Kullervo,* rivaled the audience in voicing their enthusiasm, if only because they did not dare to show their ignorance or run the risk of running against public opinion, are not correct. Praise was mingled with criticisms aimed at the very weaknesses with which foreign critics were to charge Sibelius's symphonies several decades later.

In *Päivälehti*, the composer's colleague Merikanto wrote: "One thing is certain—with this work Sibelius has taken a big step forward and at the same time brought Finnish art toward a more promising future." But he added that the performance had been ragged and the orchestra far too loud for the soloists, and he noted that the over-all structure of the work seemed confused. The following day, after hearing *Kullervo* for a second time, Merikanto elaborated on this last observation. He noted that it contained a superabundance of musical ideas that seemed to crowd one another out because they were imperfectly developed. There were moments when he felt that the orchestration was "odd." But for the rest he had nothing but praise, especially for the "magnificently realistic" role of the orchestra in the third movement and the "steady, melancholy Finnish spirit" that prevailed throughout.

Flodin had even greater reservations. "Mr. Sibelius," he wrote, "has unquestionably associated himself with the national musical trends that in our day find such pregnant spokesmen among the Scandinavians and Russians. . . . He wanted his music to be Finnish from beginning to end. In the strange character of the runo song, in the rhythms of the folk dances, and in the horn calls of the shepherd he found the mood he needed. . . . In the monotonous whole-tone progressions [he may have meant pentatonic] and in the use of five-four rhythm, he has completely followed the ancient runo songs. . . .

"In the purely orchestral parts of *Kullervo* one feels a lack of concentration and development to a genuine climax. . . . But that is just the way the composer wants it. By extraordinary means he arrives at extraordinary results." And then Flodin suggests prophetically: "If Mr. Sibelius were to write a new symphonic poem—a Lemminkäinen portrait, for example—he would be obliged to create a completely different setting for the new Finnish milieu so as not to repeat what he has said once and for all in *Kullervo*."

Flodin clearly understood why Sibelius wrote *Kullervo* and the extra-musical considerations that contributed to its success. He wanted the composer to write Finnish music, but not quite that Finnish. He did not want to see him follow the well-worn path of the national composers who were busy writing in the folk idiom. Sibelius heeded this advice to the letter. After 1893, *Kullervo* was never again heard in its entirety during the composer's long life, and one year after Flodin had written his critique, Sibelius began work on his *Lemminkäinen Suite*.

Sibelius refused to permit the performance of *Kullervo* on the grounds that it needed extensive revision, and yet, as he told Gray, he believed that to make these revisions would destroy its true character. The third movement, *Kullervo and His Sister*, was heard in Finland during the mid-thirties, and *Kullervo's Lament* (the final measures of the third movement) during the Sibelius Festival of 1957—but only after the composer had exacted assurances that it would be designated on the official program as dating from 1892.

Kullervo will be something of a disappointment for those who expect to discover early signs of the mature Sibe-

a. Portrait of Sibelius by Eero Järnefelt, his brother-in-law, 1892

b. Portrait of Sibelius by Akseli Gallén-Kallela, 1894

Gallén-Kallela's *Symposium* (1894). From left to right:
Gallén-Kallela, Oskar Merikanto, Robert Kajanus, and
Jean Sibelius

lian style. It is a grandiose, heavy-handed work, an assimilation of the many prevailing styles in music of the era. In it may be found the influence of Kajanus, Wagner, and especially Bruckner.

But it must be remembered that *Kullervo* dates from 1892, a fact that makes it easy to understand why the Finns hailed it as a masterpiece. Here at last was music that seemed rooted in Finland's recently "discovered" culture. In the third and final movements when the chorus intones *"Kullervo Kallervon poika"* ("Kullervo, Kalervo's offspring"), we can understand why Flodin suspected that the composer sought his inspiration in the folk songs of his country.

"Kullervo is, for its time, an extraordinarily daring and powerful work," Furuhjelm wrote in 1916. "In its contempt for the conventional *bon ton* and public taste, it can measure swords with the most audacious works written by European masters during the nineteenth century. It is the most extreme of Sibelius's works in a certain direction, in the same way, for example, as the Fourth Symphony is in another direction. It is a work of gigantic but fascinating proportions, and set against the European musical background at the time of its creation, it must be viewed as epoch-making. It is not the most harmonious of Sibelius's mythological works. There are many rough, unpolished passages in it. But it is the most imposing and interesting of its type."

Such reservations as General Järnefelt may have entertained concerning his daughter's marriage to a penniless musician were completely dispelled by the success of *Kullervo*. Janne and Aino were married the following June and spent their honeymoon in Karelia. Sibelius's remark at the age of seventy that on his honeymoon he heard the *Kalevala* runes from the lips of the people for the first time in his life was obviously intended to refute Flodin's charge that *Kullervo* was influenced by such melodies.

It is frequently impossible to evaluate justly the importance of a wife in shaping her husband's career. Aino Sibelius is no exception. She refused to share the spotlight with her famous husband and was content to bear him six daughters (one died in infancy) and create a home environment in which he would be undisturbed. Aino undoubtedly possessed the strength of character which he lacked, and she showed great understanding in tolerating his caprices.[1] It was not always an easy task, she once admitted in a rare interview, but for her, life with Jean Sibelius brought rich personal rewards.

After the honeymoon, the young couple set up house in Helsinki with cast-offs from members of the family. During November, one relative wrote: "Aino and Sibba are now as though engaged again. They are so wrapped up in each other that they don't even notice the world." A few weeks later, however, Sibelius was compelled to grapple with reality. He begged his uncle to act as a co-signer for a thirty-five-hundred-mark loan—a tidy sum in those days—in order to pay off old debts. In December, he signed a contract with the Otava Publishing Co. for his first published opus, *Seven Songs of Runeberg*, later designated as opus 13. It is notable that the title did not read *Seven Songs of Sibelius*, for such modesty as

---

[1] *For example, the children were forbidden to sing or practice music in the home.*

may have prompted him to place his own name beneath that of the famous poet soon vanished.

Sibelius had to settle down and serve as the bread-winner for a family in which a first child was expected the following March. He had few qualifications for earning a living except the ability to play violin in Kajanus's orchestra or teach music. Sibelius chose the latter way. Fortunately, Wegelius was willing to hire him as a teacher of theory, composition, and violin in his Music Institute. Sibelius served in this capacity—with several interruptions—until 1900. Kajanus thoughtfully provided him with additional income by giving him similar duties in his own Orchestra School.

Many flattering things have been said about Sibelius as a teacher by his former students. Most of them, however, were birthday tributes paid to a retired national hero. Sibelius, who as a student thoroughly disliked the academic disciplines, could hardly be expected to enforce them as a teacher of younger men. Furthermore, he was far too occupied with his own compositions to entertain any great interest in helping others. In 1921, when he broke a contract with the Eastman School of Music, he described himself as an "impossible" teacher. Even more than Haydn, Sibelius needed an Esterházy.

Around his seventieth birthday, Sibelius told Karl Ekman: "After the success of *Kullervo*, Robert Kajanus once pointed out to me how desirable it was to have a piece by me in the regular repertoire of the orchestra written for the general public and not making too great demands on their powers of concentration and comprehension. This would be an advantage both for the orchestra and for my popularity as a composer, Kajanus said. I was not at all disinclined to write a piece in a more popular style. When I got to work, I found that some notes I had made in Vienna were very suitable for adaptation. In this way *En Saga* appeared."

Twelve years later, the composer told a different story to Ringbom. "But nothing came of it [the invitation]," said Sibelius. "Instead I completed the orchestral work that I had started and to which I gave the name *En Saga*. This tone poem was by no means the result of Kajanus's request to write 'a popular *da capo* piece'! I did not comply with his request." Sibelius at eighty-two contradicts what a seventy-year-old Sibelius had said about a work he had composed at the age of twenty-seven!

This, as we shall see, is not an isolated example of the composer's very human attempt to "correct" certain earlier impressions. It should not be attributed to advancing senility, but rather to the rose-colored glasses through which a national symbol saw his early struggles and wanted others to see them. In this particular case, Sibelius obviously felt that in his earlier account he had rated his famous tone poem too low when he described it as a work that would not tax the powers of concentration and comprehension of audiences. Furthermore, his complete *volte-face* is one of the many indications that in his final years he no longer relished stories dealing with the influence of Kajanus.

Sibelius conducted *En Saga* at a concert in Helsinki on February 16, 1893. It followed Grieg's Second Suite from the music to *Peer Gynt*. The critics found it original, but they were not overgenerous in their praise. Wegelius dubbed it a "Pyrrhic victory," and others slyly suggested that on the strength of this work the composer was qualified to become an organist in Porvoo. Sibelius promptly withdrew his new composition for revision.

"It makes me impatient when people talk about orchestration," he told Olin Downes in 1936. "I don't think orchestration. I think music. It comes to me in that form. I write it down as I hear it." Although this may hold true for a few of the composer's later compositions, not one word of it applies to the first version of *En Saga*. *As orchestration* it is undoubtedly one of the worst things Sibelius composed. It is replete with passages so clumsily scored that each instrument succeeds in canceling out another. This results in colorless masses of sound.

Sibelius evidently entertained serious doubts as to whether a revision of *En Saga* would be worth while, for the second version was not heard in Helsinki until nine years later. In a very fine comparative study of the two versions, Ringbom understandably refrains from placing too great an emphasis on the obvious weaknesses of the first: Sibelius was alive at the time. Although the two versions are substantially the same in thematic content, the second indicates that during the nine intervening years Sibelius had learned a great deal about orchestration. The second version is shorter and contains fewer modulations and tempo changes and a greater number of pedal and held notes. It is a thrilling and brilliantly conceived musical narrative that has won many admirers.

En Saga is frequently cited as the prime example of Sibelius's early maturity as an instrumental colorist. This is an error if the work is associated with 1892. Properly speaking, it should be regarded as contemporary with the Second Symphony. Finally, it should be noted that *En Saga,* in spite of its title, has no program.

How, one may properly ask, did Sibelius learn to orchestrate? Partly by trial and error, as he later confessed to Ekman: "It was of immense importance to me that [Kajanus] placed his orchestra so completely at the service of my art, partly by himself so industriously performing my works, partly by placing his orchestra at my disposition whenever I cared to try the effects of combinations of sounds and generally see how my new scores sounded in reality. Kajanus's encouraging attitude furthered my development as an orchestral composer during the 1890's in a great measure and was of value to me, too, in other respects at a time when our musical life was led more or less by amateurs."

Thus, Sibelius enjoyed the rare privilege of being able to employ a symphony orchestra as a laboratory in order to experiment and correct faulty orchestration. It also follows that Kajanus was present and provided him with many valuable suggestions—the superiority of one key over another, the limitations of the several instruments in their respective registers, and the infinite possibilities available in scoring for instruments in combination. In an interview with a German newspaper correspondent during 1942, Sibelius described Kajanus as *"mein Lehrmeister."*

Not very many years before his death, however, Sibelius emphatically—one might even say angrily—denied that Kajanus had helped him to master orchestration. Yrjö Suomalainen's biography of the conductor (1952) quoted Kajanus as saying: "Our influence on each other lasted until the Fifth Symphony [1915]. But after that [Sibelius] never asked me for advice in matters of orchestration." Sibelius was furious. He hounded the biographer by telephone and attempted to find another writer willing to publish a "scholarly" denial.

When the composer's private secretary, Santeri Levas, published the first volume of his own Sibelius biography in 1957, he assured his readers that the earlier reference to a Kajanus influence was completely without foundation. When Sibelius read it, Levas continued, "tears formed in his eyes." Hoping to settle the matter, he quoted the composer as saying: "I have never asked for advice from him nor, for that matter, from anyone else. I composed, and he conducted. That was the extent of our co-operation."

Kajanus had died in 1933.

*"I believe that music alone—that is to
say, absolute music—cannot by itself satisfy."*
                    Sibelius to J. H. Erkko,
                    July 8, 1893

•

Two months after the failure
of *En Saga*, the University Chorus, better known as the Y.L.,
performed a short *Kalevala*-inspired piece that Sibelius wrote
especially for them. It was entitled *The Boat Journey (Venematka)*, later opus 18, no. 9, and based on verses from
runo XL, telling how Väinämöinen, "old and steadfast," sets
off for Pohjola in the company of Ilmarinen and Lemminkäinen in order to steal the magic Sampo, the Finnish equivalent of the Holy Grail. During the course of their journey,
they sing joyous songs to the entertainment of maidens standing on the shore. "One can see elements of folk-song rhythms
in *Venematka*," Sibelius later admitted. "Such a composition
had the effect of a bomb at that time because the general
practice was to sing serenades."

During the summer of 1893, Sibelius drew up plans
for a much greater "bomb." It was to be an opera entitled
The Building of the Boat (Veneen luominen), in which
Väinämöinen would once again be the central figure. In a let-

ter to J. H. Erkko, he revealed his project and requested the poet to collaborate in the preparation of the libretto:

But first I must tell you of the conclusion I have been forced to reach concerning the role of music—and not without considerable pain. I believe that music alone—that is to say, absolute music—cannot by itself satisfy. It arouses feelings and emotions, but there is always something left unsatisfied in our souls. Music is like the wife who needs the husband in order to become pregnant, and music's husband is poetry. Music can reach its true power only when it is guided by poetic meaning—in other words, when music and poetry are united. Then the obscure atmosphere that the music has aroused becomes clear, and the words, even though magnificent in themselves, take on greater meaning.

This surprising confession from the architect of seven "absolute" symphonies must be understood in terms of his experiences up to the time he wrote it. *Kullervo,* which had been "guided by poetic meaning," had scored a phenomenal success. *En Saga,* with no program other than its vague title, had not. Thus his "way" at that time seemed to lie in the direction of an expanded *Kullervo,* or opera.

His own outline of the libretto for *The Building of the Boat* follows:

Scene 1: Väinö, who is as young as possible without offending a Finn, is resting on the shore during his journey. It is evening. The sky is getting red. The Queen of the Moon is seen knitting and singing on a cloud. Väinö falls fiercely in love and asks her to be his own. The Queen promises to agree if Väinö will sing a boat together out of the splinters of her spindle.

Scene 2: It is a bright day. Väinö is constructing the boat by singing. Sampsa Pellervoinen (silent) gives him the wood. Väinö is missing three words.

Scene 3: Runo xvi, lines 148–370. Väinö goes to Tuonela to seek the words. The end is changed so that when Väinö is half awake, the Goddess of Tuonela says those three missing words.

Scene 4: We see the surface of a great lake. The sky is black. Väinö is sailing in his new boat and expressing the fire of his love in song. The sky is getting red. The Queen of the Moon, knitting and singing on a cloud, descends slowly so that Väinö, who is standing in the bow of the boat, is able to embrace her as the curtain falls.

Sibelius estimated that Erkko would not have to write more than one hundred lines, the rest to be taken directly from runos viii and xvi of the legends. "This subject overpowers me so that I cannot get any peace," he confessed. Around his seventieth birthday, Sibelius recalled that the fate of the opera was sealed when the producer, Kaarlo Bergbom, pronounced it "too lyrical." In all events, Sibelius never lost interest in the subject. It provided the inspiration for his tone poem *Pohjola's Daughter*, opus 49, which appeared in 1906.

Upon abandoning his project, Sibelius decided to follow the lines suggested by Flodin. He began work on a cycle of four tone poems based on part of the legends in which the adventures of the hero Lemminkäinen are described. The prelude to the unfinished opera became *The Swan of Tuonela,* the third tone poem in the cycle.

During 1893-6, Sibelius worked intermittently on his new suite, which he described as his "great task." One of the more important interruptions was an invitation to compose for the Student Corporation of Viipuri a lengthy score that would net him five hundred marks. The occasion was an evening's entertainment given in Helsinki on November 13, 1893, to raise money for education in eastern Finland. The high point of the evening was a series of seven tableaux representing important moments in the history of Karelia. The members of the audience were able to purchase elaborate souvenir programs containing reproductions of pertinent historical documents. It was essentially a patriotic gathering, one of the many manifestations of what has been called "Karelianism." A description of the tableaux follows:

1. The interior of a Karelian home in the year 1293. A runo singer [imported for the occasion] performs an ancient folk melody. News arrives that war has broken out.

2. Torkel Knutsson is seen as the founder of Viipuri Castle.

3. The Lithuanian Prince Narimont collects tribute from the Karelian people.

4. Karl Knutsson, surrounded by his courtiers in Viipuri Castle, listens to a ballad singer.

5. Pontus de la Gardie is seen as the conqueror and burner of Käkiholma [Kexholm] in 1580.

6. The siege of Viipuri Castle in 1700.

7. Viipuri's union with greater Finland in 1811.

Sibelius's score included an overture (later to constitute opus 10), preludes to the tableaux, background music,
and one song. Because of the special nature of the occasion,
he concluded the music to the final tableau with his own arrangement of the national anthem. The audience rose and
joined in with the orchestra.

"There was such shouting that the music couldn't be
heard," Sibelius reported to his brother. Extra-musical considerations prevented most of those attending from appreciat-
ing the significance of the composer's contribution. Among
the exceptions was Flodin, who wrote: "The music was
Finnish. Even those who understood little about music sensed
the breath of the Finnish spirit—the Finnish folk spirit."
Later, after hearing a slightly shortened concert version, the
critic added: "The second number [the Ballade that originally accompanied tableau 4] is one of the best things the
composer has done to date. Sibelius has given us some of Finland's history in music."

For several years, Sibelius remained undecided as to
what to do with his complete score. For some time, he regarded it as a suite for orchestra in seven movements. Not until 1896 did he finally reduce it to the Overture and the
Karelia Suite, which later became opus 11. The published
Suite consists of three numbers: 1. Intermezzo, originally for
tableau 3, and known as March in the Old Style; 2. Ballade
from tableau 4, the vocal solo being rescored for instruments;
and 3. *Alla marcia,* from tableau 5, the early performing parts
reading "March on an Old Motif."

Sibelius undoubtedly selected the most attractive numbers for publication. The Overture is a trifle too long and repetitious, not without a few "muddy" moments in its orchestration. The Suite deservedly enjoys a far greater popularity. Here Sibelius stands revealed as a superior craftsman in the realm of popular music. The sprightly *Alla marcia* appears to be the perfect model for the sort of music the English composer Eric Coates devoted a lifetime to writing. The notation that it is based on an "old motif" should tempt some scholar familiar with the vast collection of Karelian folk tunes to search for the original—if it exists. Sibelius insisted that all of his melodies were of his own invention. This insistence may help to explain an amusing incident. When, some time after Sibelius's retirement in 1926, a member of his family discovered the original *Karelia* score, he was astonished to find that it concluded with the composer's own arrangement of the national anthem. When this was brought to the attention of Sibelius—he had completely forgotten about it—he quickly tore out the final pages and destroyed them.

During 1893, Sibelius took advantage of another opportunity to supplement his income. The Y.L. sponsored a prize competition for original compositions for male chorus. The first prize was awarded to Emil Genetz (1852–1930), a well-known Finnish composer of choral music, for his *Hakkapeliitta*, which was based on a seventeenth-century Finnish cavalry march and the chorale *A Mighty Fortress Is Our God*.[1] Sibelius won the second prize with his *Rakastava* (*The*

[1] Hakkapeliitta *defies translation. It is derived from a Finnish cavalry yell popular during the Thirty Years' War, meaning "Chop them down!"*

 CAMROSE LUTHERAN COLLEGE LIBRARY

Lover), the text of which was taken from three runos in the first book of the *Kanteletar:* [2] 1. "Where Is My Beloved?"; 2. "My Beloved's Path"; and 3. "Good Evening, Little Bird." Kajanus orchestrated the Genetz composition and requested Sibelius to do the same with his own. Both were first heard in the Y.L.'s concert given in Helsinki on April 28, 1894.

Flodin was incensed over the decision of the judges. He pointed out the unoriginal character of the Genetz work and added that the accompaniment had been written by "another composer." "Mr. Sibelius," he continued, "stands unquestionably above the other as far as originality is concerned. His composition is Finnish—Finnish through and through—as is most of Mr. Sibelius's music." Within a short time, *Rakastava* became rather popular in Finland in the original version for unaccompanied male chorus, even more so in the composer's own arrangement for mixed voices.

In 1911, Sibelius rewrote ("arranged" would be misleading) *Rakastava* for string orchestra, triangle, and tympani. It was subsequently published as a suite in three movements as opus 14. This final version has become well known outside Finland and has led such Sibelius scholars as Ralph Wood to suspect that it is closer in kinship to the Fourth Symphony (1911) than to anything the composer wrote around 1893. This is correct, but it should be added that *Rakastava* really belongs to both periods. It is an excellent illustration of Sibelius's development as a composer. After eighteen years, he employed the same melodies and, to a certain degree, the same harmonies, but in the suite for strings

[2] *The* Kanteletar *is a collection of folk songs of ancient Finland which Lönnrot had taken down from oral tradition and issued in 1840.*

the melodies undergo an almost magic transformation in terms of rhythmic and contrapuntal subtleties. Contrary to what one might suspect, the "middle" version for male chorus with string accompaniment contains no hint of what Sibelius wrote in 1911. It is, in fact, an extremely crude and unoriginal affair. The composer probably dashed it off in great haste.

In Finland, university graduation exercises—they are known as "promotions"—have always been conducted with great pomp and ceremony. For such occasions, it was customary to commission cantatas. Sibelius was honored by an invitation to compose a cantata for the ceremony to be held in Helsinki on May 31, 1894. The text selected was by Kasimir Leino, who has been described as one of the composer's *Päivälehti* friends. Their friendship must have been stretched to the breaking-point: when a newspaper announced five weeks before the ceremony was to be held that Sibelius's cantata was almost ready, he wrote a prompt denial and insisted that he had not even seen the text. Leino then wrote an indignant letter stating that Sibelius had been given most of the text many weeks before and had had the complete text in his possession at the time the letter was written.

In all events, the cantata was completed in time, and Sibelius conducted the performance without attracting any attention in the press. This long and not very interesting work for mixed chorus and orchestra has remained unpublished and without opus number. Although it is generally believed to be an independent composition, one part of the middle section, *Alla marcia,* has been published in several editions in Finland under the title *Festive March (Juhlamarssi)* .

During June 1894, "all Finland was in the city of

Vaasa," according to one contemporary report. The occasion was an elaborate music festival at which Finland's grand old man of letters, Zachris Topelius (1818–1898), was the guest of honor. Compositions by Faltin, Kajanus, and Wegelius figured on the programs. Among the younger musicians, Armas Järnefelt was represented by his tone poem *Korsholm* and Sibelius by his *Improvisation* for orchestra, both works having been composed especially for the festival. Local reviewers praised the new Sibelius composition for its "simple, beautiful melodies and the extremely tranquil orchestration."

In 1895, Sibelius conducted his new work in Helsinki under the title *Spring Song (Vårsång)*. When it was published seven years later, it was given the French subtitle *La Tristesse du printemps*. Although Cecil Gray found this to be the more "correct" title, Sibelius in his later years declared it to be the invention of his German publishers. Gray's theory that *Spring Song* is remarkably similar to ancient Provençal melodies and consequently constitutes a problem for aestheticians to solve appears a trifle far-fetched.

Spring Song was frequently performed in Europe and the United States during the first decade of this century. Since then, it has been forgotten almost everywhere except in Finland, where it is still regarded with affection as a seasonal work. It is pleasant and at times rather obvious—Wood refers to its *"Kapellmeisterish* layout"—and not without some awkward scoring in the middle section. Many writers have wondered how Sibelius could have composed it after the infinitely more original *En Saga*. We have already seen, however, that the *En Saga* dating from 1892 is quite different from the score published in 1903.

When Sibelius conducted his *Spring Song* in Helsinki, he also included on the program six numbers from his *Karelia Suite*, a *Serenade* for baritone and orchestra, and a tone poem entitled *The Wood Nymph* (*Skogsrået*). Although Flodin found the *Serenade* the best thing on the program, it soon vanished and has remained unlisted by the Sibelius biographers throughout the years.[3]

The Wood Nymph was originally written for piano and a small ensemble to accompany the recitation of verses by Rydberg. Only a short time earlier, it had been given in this form at a lottery soirée for the benefit of the Finnish Theater. Rydberg's poem deals with a subject that especially appealed to Sibelius—a young man lured into the forest by a beautiful but deadly nymph, the legendary *Skogsrå*. Little Janne had seen the *Skogsrå* in the forests surrounding Hämeenlinna, and now he was able to describe her in music. Four years later, when *The Wood Nymph* was heard at the *première* of the First Symphony, it was pronounced a product of the composer's *Sturm und Drang* period. Sibelius immediately lost all interest in it.

> Working people, arise!
> Work is the will of the all highest,
> But misery the shackles of a slave,
> These we break.

This is not an excerpt from the celebrated Communist *Internationale* written in 1871 by Eugène Pottier with music by Adolphe Degeyter. It is taken from the second

[3] *In 1910, Sibelius employed a motif from the* Serenade *in the first of the songs constituting opus 61, "*Långsamt som kvällskyn.*"*

verse of a *Workers' March* by the Finnish poet J. H. Erkko and published in a musical setting by Jean Sibelius. In 1893, a woman social worker and temperance leader named Alli Trygg decided that the Finnish working class needed a song that would stress the happiness found in hard toil, and at the same time would reflect the deep spiritual values of the Christian religion. She prevailed upon Erkko and Sibelius to write what she hoped would prove to be a national hymn, but which was soon discarded as being too "revolutionary."

Although Sibelius's *Workers' March* is without any musicial significance, it establishes the fact that during these years the composer was sensitive to the social and political trends in his own country. At the age of seventy, he told Ekman: "Politics have never interested me in themselves. That is to say—all empty talk on political questions, all amateur politicizing I have always hated. I have tried to make my contribution in another way." He was, of course, thinking of his symphonies, not of the *Workers' March,* which was published in an obscure labor journal in Viipuri during 1896 and promptly forgotten—so much so that it has never been listed among his compositions up to now.

Sibelius has called these years, 1892–5, his *Symposium* period. The name is taken from the title of a painting by his friend Akseli Gallén-Kallela, considered by many to be one of Finland's greatest artists. When Gallén displayed his painting in Helsinki during the fall of 1894, it was called *The Problem.* It immediately evoked a storm of disapproval. One wit dubbed it *The Mistake,* and there were numerous sly references concerning the real nature of the "problem."

Gallén wished to represent a group of artists in a

moment of profound concentration. As his subjects, he selected three well-known musicians and himself. Seated at one end of a table littered with glasses and empty liquor bottles we see Kajanus and Sibelius. They appear to be somewhat disarranged, and are staring into the distance with glazed eyes. Near the center, the composer-pianist Oskar Merikanto has apparently fallen asleep with his head on the table. Standing and peering out of the canvas from under the wing of an Egyptian sun god is the painter himself.

All Helsinki knew at this time that Gallén, Kajanus, and Sibelius formed the nucleus of a group of artists who frequently gathered in the more popular restaurants. There they engaged in long, heated discussions about the meaning and function of art while enjoying their cigars and drinks. Many people were scandalized that one of these sessions should be made the subject of a painting for public display. Gallén was too much of a realist for the Finland of the time.

These *Symposium* years had a stimulating effect on the rising young Sibelius. "The waves rolled very high," he later recalled. With Kajanus, who by virtue of his age and position was the acknowledged leader of the group, Sibelius was able to analyze his musical problems along technical lines. Gallén brought to these discussions a fresh point of view, that of the painter preoccupied with color and spatial relationships. They were all ardent nationalists eager to place their art at the service of Finland's aspirations.

At that time, Sibelius and Gallén were both drawing on the *Kalevala* for their inspiration. The painter was completing his highly stylized conception of *Lemminkäinen's Mother* and Sibelius his *Lemminkäinen Suite*.

"*[Jean Sibelius] is in his* Sturm und Drang
period."   *Imperial Alexander University
protocols for 1897*

•

By the spring of 1896, Sibe-
lius had completed his *Lemminkäinen Suite,* later designated opus 22, and was ready to present it to the public.
Compared with the tragic hero Kullervo, Lemminkäinen figures in the *Kalevala* as a comical character—a combination
of a Nordic Don Juan and a "mother's boy." Many writers
have ventured to describe the incidents depicted in the music, not knowing that Sibelius himself prepared an elaborate
program of carefully chosen excerpts from the legends for
distribution to the first-night audience. We quote them in
part, not only to correct the somewhat misleading "interpretations," but also to show why the influential critic Flodin
became so violently opposed to the music.

The first tone poem is entitled *Lemminkäinen and
the Maidens of the Island.* Here it is told how the young
hero seduces an entire community of women:

Then the lively Lemminkäinen,
Roamed about through every village,
For the island-maidens' pleasure,
To delight the braidless damsels.   (xxix, 223–6)

So great is his success that when he announces his intention to depart:

Wept the island girls already,
Damsels at the cape lamented:
"Wherefore goest thou Lemminkäinen,
And departest hero-bridegroom?"   (357–60)
These concluding lines are clearly represented in the final
measures of the score, in which repeated woodwind figura-
tions are heard over a sly, mocking passage played by the
violins.

The title of the second tone poem, *Lemminkäinen
in Tuonela,* is misleading in that the central figure in the
original program is the hero's mother. Fearing that her son
has met with misfortune, she descends into Tuoni's murky
regions in search of him:

Met the sun upon her pathway,
And before the sun she bowed her.
  "O thou sun, whom God created,
Hast thou seen my son pass by you?"   (xv, 179–182)
When the sun tells her that Lemminkäinen has been slain
and his fragments thrown into the river, the mother rakes
together the remains of the wretched youth and by means of
magic joins them together and gives them life. Overjoyed at
having her son alive, she asks him what he most desires.
Lemminkäinen replies:

  "There is something greatly needed,
For my heart is fixed forever,
And my inclination leads me
To the charming maids of Pohja."   (612–15)
In the final measures of the published score, this frivolous
ending in a predominantly tragic work is unconvincingly
represented by a short passage for solo cello.

The Swan of Tuonela, the third in the series, is given
no program other than its title. In the *Kalevala*, the legendary bird serves as little more than a bit of décor.

In the published score for the final tone poem, *Lemminkäinen's Homeward Journey*, the following extracts from
canto xxx are printed:

> Then the lively Lemminkäinen,
> He the handsome *kaukomieli*,
> From his care constructed horses,
> Coursers black composed from trouble,
> Reins from evil days he fashioned,
> Saddles from his secret sorrows,
> Then his horse's back he mounted, (481–7)
> And he rose upon his journey,
> At his side his faithful Tiera,
> And along the shores he journeyed,
> On the sandy shores proceeded,
> Till he reached his tender mother,
> Reached the very aged woman. (489–94)

In the original program, only the first four lines of the above
text appear. There are no references to Tiera and the mother.
Instead, Sibelius continued with excerpts from another canto,
in which a different homeward journey is described:

> Starting on his homeward journey,
> Saw the lands and saw the beaches,
> Here the islands, there the channels,
> Saw the ancient landing-stages,
> Saw the former dwelling-places. (xxix, 454–8)

Although the differences between these two versions of the
program may appear unimportant, it seems significant that

in the original one Sibelius selected his text from two separate cantos. In doing so, he obviously intended that the sights greeting Lemminkäinen be general rather than specific.

The new work met with difficulties from the very beginning. During rehearsals, the musicians disliked it so much that they quarreled violently with the young composer-conductor. At times there were serious doubts as to whether the performance would take place. It was an especially distressing moment for Aino Sibelius, who wept in the lobby while her husband alternately threatened and pleaded with his hostile orchestra. The performance, however, did take place on April 13, 1896, as scheduled.

The new suite met with a far cooler reception from the critics than had *Kullervo*. Neither *The Swan of Tuonela* nor *Lemminkäinen's Homeward Journey*, two works that later brought Sibelius fame throughout the Western world, appeared to attract any special notice. In fact, Flodin regarded the final number as a rather unoriginal affair, being little more than a restatement of what Sibelius had already said in *Kullervo* and the *Karelia* music. The obvious implication was that he had taken a backward step in the creation of music that was purely "Finnish" in feeling.

Flodin found the first tone poem the best of the four, but he detected in it the marked influences of Tchaikovsky, Liszt, and Wagner. Another critic noted the Wagnerian influence, and asked: "But what composer can avoid it?"

These early charges of Wagnerian influence are especially interesting in the light of Sibelius's later attempts to deny it. What is even more interesting is that Flodin has been described as "an enthusiastic and orthodox Wagnerian."

That contemporary critics were correct in pointing out this influence cannot be questioned. *Lemminkäinen and the Maidens of the Island* is remarkably close to the Wagnerian idiom in both its thematic content and its development. Even so, it deserves inclusion among Sibelius's finest tone poems. One hearing should convince the most skeptical listener that Sibelius was capable of creating music charged with passion. The melancholy English-horn solo in *The Swan of Tuonela* suggests that the young Finnish composer had been deeply moved by exposure to *Tristan und Isolde*. When about 1947, Ringbom pointed out to Sibelius the close relationship between motifs in two of the tone poems, Sibelius admitted the resemblance, but added that it was neither intentional nor conscious because the leitmotif technique was always foreign to his mode of thought. The *Lemminkäinen* music, however, was composed by the young "Sillén," who once described the German master as "a great and incomparable human being," and not by the world-famous Finnish master living in retirement at Ainola, where on innumerable occasions he told visitors: "I do not like Wagner."

Sibelius conducted a revised version of his suite during November 1897, opening the concert with a new work entitled *The Rapids-Shooter's Brides* (*Koskenlaskijan morsiamet*) for baritone (or mezzo-soprano) and orchestra, opus 33.[1] The text tells how the rapids-shooter, Vilho, takes his bride, Anna, out to witness his prowess. The river nymph,

[1] *Until recently,* Koskenlaskijan morsiamet *has been translated as* The Ferryman's Brides.

who is in love with him, becomes jealous and hurls a rock from the depths of the stream, killing them. According to one contemporary report, the members of the orchestra were so used to playing their parts without the soloist that they actually resented his appearance during the final rehearsals. Sibelius dedicated the work to Maikki Järnefelt, the wife of his brother-in-law Armas.

Flodin, after acknowledging the new piece with a few brief comments, proceeded to attack *Lemminkäinen* even more violently than before. "I'm no Hanslick," he thundered, "but I say frankly that such music as 'Lemminkäinen' represents disheartens me, makes me troubled and pained. Is it music's task to evoke such moods in life?" Flodin's curious new turn can be accounted for only by his disgust over the moral tone of the first two poems. After one repeat performance, Sibelius withdrew the two offending sections. They were not heard again until thirty-seven years had elapsed.

When the conductor Georg Schnéevoigt revived them as novelties in 1934, he told the attractive but completely false story that they had been discovered among the effects of Robert Kajanus after his death in 1933. Actually, Sibelius had guarded them in his home throughout the years and had donated the original manuscripts to the Kalevala Society in 1921.

When *Lemminkäinen and the Maidens of the Island* was performed in 1934, it was known as *Lemminkäinen and the Maidens of Saari*. Although the difference between these two titles is rather marked in Swedish, in Finnish it involves the subtle distinction between *saari*, which means island, and *Saari*, a particular island mentioned in canto XI of the legends. The confusion probably occurred when the Kalevala Society, the supreme authority in such matters, carelessly acknowledged receipt of the manuscript of *Lemminkäinen ja Saaren neidot.* As a result of this error, the tone poem was published with the incorrect title, and writers of program notes concluded that the music described an entirely different series of adventures, in which the hero visits the Saari maidens and abducts one of their number, the beautiful Kyllikki. By 1954, when the manuscript was prepared for publication, Sibelius was so confused that he dictated a new program (which was never used) combining the two adventures.

All of this might appear trivial if we did not know that during his early years Sibelius truly believed that "his way" led in the direction of program music. His two attempts to create large works in this idiom had failed, but for different reasons. Flodin had pronounced *Kullervo* too "Finnish," and, furthermore, because of the linguistic barrier, it was not likely to attract the attention of foreign conductors. As for the *Lemminkäinen Suite,* the critic's chief objection was that he did not like the program. Almost against his will, Sibelius found himself driven in the direction of the only large form that he had not tried—the symphony.

Work on the *Lemminkäinen* revision was interrupted by an odd assortment of new compositions, many of them minor occasional pieces. Among them is a hymn for unaccompanied male chorus entitled *Natus in curas,* opus 21, with a Latin text by a Professor Gustafsson. It was composed for the unveiling of a monument to a Professor Pippingskjöld. The academic background of this work is especially interesting because, as we shall see presently, Sibelius entertained high hopes of being elected to the faculty of the Imperial Alexander University.

Another occasional piece that Sibelius completed by November 1896 has been given far greater attention than it deserves. It is the short one-act opera entitled *The Maid in the Tower* (*Jungfrun i Tornet*), composed for a lottery soirée for the benefit of Kajanus's orchestra and Orchestra School. Both Furuhjelm and Gray, who have examined the score, dismiss it as inconsequential, and in his later years the composer evidently shared this opinion. Once when the English conductor Warwick Braithwaite asked Sibelius whether his little opera would be published after his death, the latter replied dryly: "She will remain in the tower and not come out."

The public's reception of the *Lemminkäinen* music in 1896-7 must have been a bitter blow to the young Sibelius in his struggle for recognition. He experienced a second defeat during this same period which was all the greater because it was completely unexpected.

In 1896, the aging music teacher at the University, Richard Faltin, announced his intention to retire. Sibelius, who had served as his temporary substitute a few years earlier, was appointed to replace him until a permanent successor could be elected according to existing rules and regulations. By virtue of these temporary appointments, it was obvious that the young composer was the leading contender, and Faltin made no secret of the fact that he wanted him as his successor. For Sibelius, who had only part-time employment, the University position was a prize greatly to be desired, bringing with it a guaranteed yearly income, fairly light duties, and considerable social prestige.

Such advantages were bound to attract other qualified candidates, and Faltin's nominating committee decided
that three had met the professional requirements and had a
sufficient knowledge of both Finnish and Swedish. Sibelius
undoubtedly felt somewhat less certain of his chances when
he learned that one of his rivals was Robert Kajanus, the
influential founder and conductor of the Philharmonic Society, his senior in years and reputation, his superior in the
Orchestra School, and his friend. The third and youngest of
the candidates was Ilmari Krohn, an organist in Tampere
who had already earned his Master's degree and was working on his doctoral dissertation.

In submitting his *curriculum vitæ,* Sibelius included
a most impressive list of thirty-one compositions, most of
which had been performed and a few even published locally.
This hitherto unknown document is valuable in that it contains five early works that escaped his biographers. He was
naturally most eager to impress his judges, and consequently
included almost everything that he had written, though if he
had completed his *Workers' March* (*Työkansan Marssi*),
which was published during this same year, he did not include it.

Kajanus presented a much more modest list of compositions, but was more than able to compensate for this de-
ficiency by stressing his years of experience as conductor,
teacher, and administrator. Neither he nor Sibelius was required to deposit scores for examination by the committee.

Krohn was not altogether a stranger in local musical
circles, and could point to the fact that he had conducted a

public concert of his own works even before Sibelius. His compositions, though numerically inferior to those of the other candidates, were substantial. He was the only candidate who could present definite proof of musical scholarship. Any impartial judge would have awarded the position to Krohn, for he was obviously the best qualified from the academic point of view. Sibelius, in spite of glowing testimonials that appeared later, had shown himself an extremely indifferent teacher. Kajanus, with the demands made upon him by his conducting and his Orchestra School, already had more than enough to occupy his time.

As part of the examination, each candidate was required to deliver a lecture on some appropriate topic of his own choosing. Krohn discussed Robert Schumann's activities as a music critic and, incidentally, was the only candidate to lecture in Finnish. Kajanus, taking the University professors for greater fools than they actually were, made the mistake of trying to pass off as his own another's published study of the life and works of the Finnish-born composer Bernhard Henrik Crusell (1775–1838). The ruse was detected during the heat of the debate that followed.

Sibelius, in the only lecture he was to deliver during his long lifetime, discussed the influence of folk songs on art music and the special problems encountered by composers attempting to harmonize the pentatonic Finnish folk melodies. In view of the many remarks concerning the relationship between his own music and folk song, it may appear surprising that he once posed as an expert in this particular field. He had, however, actually served as a folklorist when he recorded in musical notation a number of regional and ceremonial runos which the Finnish Literary Society published in 1895 (not to be confused with the *Six Finnish Folk Songs* published for piano in 1906). In all events, the committee found Sibelius as a lecturer somewhat inferior to Sibelius as a composer, and charitably pronounced his talk as "original" but rather "mosaic" in quality. Krohn was judged the best in this area.

Faltin and his committee, in making their recommendations to the faculty, stressed that each candidate possessed qualities lacking in the others and nominated them in the following order: Sibelius, Kajanus, and Krohn. The last-named was quickly placed *hors de combat* with the usual academic platitudes. It was clear, however, that Kajanus could not be dismissed so lightly. After much praise for his services to the cause of Finnish music, the committee emphasized that his duties were so great as to compel him to regard the teaching post as secondary, which was essentially correct. As for Sibelius, it was said that he was already Finland's greatest composer, from whom much more could be expected were he spared financial worries and given adequate time for composing. The faculty confirmed the committee's recommendation with the following vote: Sibelius, 25; Kajanus, 3; Krohn, 0.

The small minority of three supporting Kajanus was quick to point out the fallacy in the committee's reasoning. To create an atmosphere in which Sibelius could continue to compose was well and good, but hardly acceptable as the prime reason for qualifying him as a teacher. Without saying it in so many words, they intimated that if Sibelius were given the post, he would be what has come to be known as a "composer in residence."

The debate that followed became extremely bitter. As an example of Sibelius's immaturity, the minority referred to the poor performance under his baton of the *Coronation Cantata* given as part of the University ceremonies honoring Tsar Nicholas II in November 1896. There was even an "anonymous letter" stating that the composer was still in his *Sturm und Drang* period, and consequently unfit for so important a position. Kajanus lodged a strong protest, in which he accused Faltin of lacking impartiality in the choice of his successor. His sympathies for the Music Institute as opposed to the Orchestra School were well known, Kajanus insisted.

Sibelius was in a delicate position, and he wisely declined an invitation to appear before the faculty in his own defense. To antagonize Kajanus openly would have made it a personal battle in which he could lose much. Kajanus was not only his friend and unofficial teacher, but also the most powerful musical voice in Finland. His was the power to close the doors of the Philharmonic Society to Sibelius and thus deprive him of a hearing. Furthermore, Sibelius was confident that he would be given the post. The wisdom of his decision to remain silent was confirmed when a second and final faculty vote was taken. Kajanus played the last act of this academic comedy alone—swiftly and decisively. Setting the protégé over the master had injured his pride, and he had to save face. He made a direct appeal to higher authorities to have the faculty decision reversed; as Professor Ilmari Krohn whispered nervously to me, "Kajanus went to

St. Petersburg!" In the spring of 1897, the faculty was con-
vened in order to learn that the position had been awarded
to Kajanus.

Sibelius was a defeated man. The *Lemminkäinen
Suite*—his "great task"—had been pronounced a step in the
wrong direction. The guaranteed annual income that the
University position would have afforded had been snatched
from his grasp. The future was not exactly reassuring for a
man given to extravagant tastes and at the same time the father of two children.

By the following winter, both of these defeats were
turned into stunning triumphs. On November 29, Sibelius
conducted a concert of his own music in Turku. On the program, he included the two shorter sections of his suite, *The
Swan of Tuonela* and *Lemminkäinen's Homeward Journey*.
They met with great success, and within a few years Kajanus
featured them on his orchestra's tour that included Paris.
They were subsequently published by Breitkopf & Härtel
and attracted considerable attention in both Europe and the
United States.

One day after the Turku concert, the composer's supporters petitioned the Senate to grant him a yearly stipend
of three thousand marks (not two thousand, as reported by
Ekman) to compensate him for his loss of the teaching position. The request was granted. Ten years later the stipend
was made into a life pension.

Although the original grant was a modest one
(roughly $2,400), it was equal to the salary Sibelius would
have earned in the University post. He still had to supplement his income for a few years by part-time teaching, until

Sibelius at the time he composed the *Lemminkäinen Suite*

a. Robert Kajanus   b. Karl Flodin

royalties and financial aid from sympathetic friends relieved him of these burdens. It was an extraordinary moment in Finland's cultural history. Government assistance to young artists previously had been limited to travel grants and prizes, and now a new precedent had been established. For Sibelius, who had not yet composed his First Symphony, *Finlandia,* or the *Valse triste,* the pension represented public recognition of his role as a national artist and the beginning of a new life.

Chapter VII   1898–1899

*"I cannot understand why my symphonies
are so often compared with Tchaikovsky's. His
symphonies are very human, but
they represent the soft part of human nature.
Mine are the hard ones."*
                    Sibelius

•

Early in 1898, Adolf Paul went
to Helsinki to supervise the Swedish Theater's production of
his new historical drama, *King Kristian II*, a long, rambling
account of the life and loves of the sixteenth-century Danish
monarch. He found his friend Janne gay and confident in
his new role as a government-sponsored artist and most willing to compose some incidental music on extremely short notice. According to Paul, the score was completed in less than
one day.

"Here's your 'Fool's Song,'" Sibelius said while playing the piano and singing. "And this is 'Dyveke's Dance'
[*Musette*]. It should be for bagpipes and reeds, but I have
scored it for two clarinets and two bassoons. Extravagant, isn't
it? We have only two bassoon-players in the entire country,
and one of them is a consumptive. But my music won't be
too hard on him—we'll see to that. And here's an overture
in the bargain—an Elegy for strings. . . . Tell me, couldn't
you use a little ballet music? I have also written a Minuet for
you."

The *première* of *King Kristian II* took place on February 28, 1898, with Sibelius conducting a small ensemble (two clarinets, two bassoons, harp, and strings) behind the scenes. The public reception was so cordial that the drama was given twenty-four times before the spring season ended. The music dealer and critic K. F. Wasenius sold a piano arrangement of the music printed by Breitkopf & Härtel of Leipzig. Later in the year, Sibelius added three new pieces (Nocturne, Serenade, and Ballade), and both Wasenius and the German publishers promptly issued the full score. It was the first orchestral music of Sibelius to appear in print.

The music to *King Kristian II* was probably the composer's first music for orchestra to be played outside Finland: it is said that Hans Winderstein conducted it in Leipzig during 1898. It was also the first Sibelius music heard in the Anglo-Saxon world: Van der Stucken played it with the Cincinnati Symphony Orchestra during December 1900, and Henry Wood included it in a London Promenade program during October of the following year. In Finland, the music soon became very popular as a concert suite, especially the lyrical and Grieg- (and Wagner-) like Elegy for strings.

The score for *King Kristian II* marked Sibelius's debut as a composer of theater music, and during the years that followed, he revealed on several occasions an exceptional talent for such work. The original pieces are both simple and unpretentious. The three pieces added later are not cut from the same cloth—they are scored for a much larger ensemble—and they suggest that the composer's primary interest was to expand his suite to a more impressive length. This accounts for the unbalanced character of the published suite, an inevitable consequence when an artist undertakes to expand a charming miniature into something more grandiose. With the extra money earned from the Swedish Theater and royalty advances from his publisher, Sibelius immediately obtained a leave of absence from his teaching duties in order to spend the rest of the winter in Berlin. These sojourns abroad were to become increasingly frequent, and on several occasions Sibelius stressed that they served to stimulate his creative work. Popular notions concerning the "isolated" composer writing his nature-inspired masterpieces in some remote corner of Finland are without foundation. He worked on many of his most famous compositions, from *Kullervo* to *Tapiola,* while living abroad.

During this second Berlin winter, Sibelius probably completed *Sandels,* which he later designated as an "improvisation" for male chorus and orchestra. It was entered in a prize competition sponsored by the Swedo-Finnish choral society known as the M.M. (*Muntra Musikanter—Merry Musicians*). One of the rules of the contest attempted to avoid a problem that was to haunt Finland for decades. It specified that the text could be either Swedish or Finnish as long as it did not deal with the touchy language quarrel. The judges included Faltin, Kajanus, and Wegelius.

Sibelius selected a Swedish text by Runeberg, and, using the pseudonymn *Homo,* won a first prize of seven hundred marks. No entry was deemed worthy of a second prize, but Armas Järnefelt received a third prize of three hundred marks for his *Suomen Synty* (*The Birth of Finland*). An unknown second-year music student named Selim Palmgren won honorable mention for *Drömmen* (*The Dream*), which he entered in the contest without telling his teacher, Wege-lius.

When the M.M. performed *Sandels* for the first time during March 1900, Flodin described it as "the greatest and most important setting of a Runeberg text which has been written." Wasenius, critic for a rival paper, wrote: "It really is Sandels portrayed in sound. . . . But it is more than that, for both Runeberg and Sibelius are to be found in this noble music."

Evidently Sibelius had learned an important lesson from the earlier contest in which his *Rakastava* had won a second prize—namely, that it is advantageous to employ a popular patriotic poem as a text. Runeberg's stirring verses from *The Tales of Ensign Stål* commemorate the defeat of the Russians by the Finns under General Johan August Sandels at the Battle of Virta Bridge.

The poem opens with a description of the aristocratic general enjoying rare wines and viands with a clergyman. Sandels appears unconcerned as the battle reaches its crucial stage, and is even annoyed when a messenger with progress reports interrupts his conversation. Finally, when the messenger relates that the Finnish troops are accusing their leader of cowardice, Sandels roars heartily and then orders that his charger, Bijou, be saddled. Against the advice of subordinates, he rides at the head of his soldiers and leads them to a stunning victory.

Sibelius's music matches the he-man atmosphere of Runeberg's poem. The superficial tone of the opening dinner scene, the anxiety of the messenger, the discontent of the soldiers, the growing din of battle with the inevitable booming of cannon (bass drum), and the Finnish victory, culminating in a rousing "Hurrah" for the general—all have clear and even obvious counterparts in the score. Nowhere does Sibelius divert the attention of the listener with prolonged orchestral interludes or attempt subtle effects. The mannerisms later to be associated with the mature Sibelian style are completely absent here. *Sandels* is almost unknown outside Finland. The full score, still unpublished, is the exclusive property of the M.M. Society.

Another important result of Sibelius's visit to Germany was contact with Breitkopf & Härtel in Leipzig. Although it has been said that Adolf Paul inspired this visit, it is likely that Wasenius had a hand in it. Ultimately it proved to be of great financial advantage for both Sibelius and the publishers. Breitkopf & Härtel became interested in this new Finnish music at the turn of the century, and until World War I they left no stone unturned in helping to make the name of Sibelius known to the Western world.

Upon returning to Finland in the spring, Sibelius completed several minor compositions, including the six songs that constitute opus 36. The first of these, *"Svarta rosor"* ("Black Roses"), is one of the small number of his many art songs which have become known outside the Scandinavian area. Around this time he also wrote what has been styled a "tone piece" entitled *Tiera*, which is a curiosity, being the only one of his four known compositions for band which has been published. It was obviously inspired by some or all of the sections in the *Kalevala* describing Lemminkäinen's comrade-in-arms, Tiera.

But Sibelius was putting the finishing touches on a

far more ambitious project that was to be the successor to *Kullervo* and the *Lemminkäinen Suite*. With it he hoped to avoid those defects which Flodin had ascribed to these earlier works. On April 26, 1899, he conducted the world *première* of his First Symphony in Helsinki.

The critics and the general public were unanimous in their enthusiasm. For Flodin it was an occasion for great jubilation, and he enjoyed it like a mother rejoicing in her child's first steps. He noted with satisfaction that until this moment Sibelius had followed the free form of the symphonic poem (*Kullervo*) and the symphonic suite (*Lemminkäinen*), in which there had been only a superficial connection between the movements. He felt that in adopting the symphony as a form of expression, Sibelius had taken a great step forward without placing any restrictions on his powers of imagination.

Evaluating the significance of the First Symphony in the light of the composer's total production, Gerald Abraham points out that it was written when Sibelius already had thirty-eight opus numbers to his credit, including *En Saga*, *The Swan of Tuonela*, and *Lemminkäinen's Homeward Journey*, all of which he finds more characteristic of the Sibelian style. Cecil Gray is also of this opinion, adding that the First Symphony was written after the composer had attained "complete mastery" in other forms. These judgments have resulted from comparisons based on opus numbers rather than on dates of composition.

As late as 1915, Sibelius had only hazy notions concerning the opus numbers of his compositions, and the lists we have today are most misleading. For example, *Cassazione*

(1904) is opus 6, the incidental music to *The Lizard* (1909) is opus 8, whereas the First Symphony (1899) is opus 39. Furthermore, *En Saga*, opus 9, and the two shorter *Lemminkäinen* tone poems, opus 22, were all revised after the *première* of the First Symphony, which rightly belongs with the music to *King Kristian II, Finlandia*, and the other pieces composed for the "Press Celebrations."

That the First Symphony is far from earth-shaking becomes quite understandable when it is placed in its proper chronological position. Cast in the traditional four-movement form—each in its "proper" position—it presents no radical departures from its Romantic predecessors. One does not create a first symphony out of thin air with no model in mind. Many feel that Sibelius wrote his with Tchaikovsky in mind, but others have suggested that Borodin was the model. One must begin somewhere, and in 1898 a Finn could not have chosen better models than Tchaikovsky and Borodin. Unfortunately, many of Sibelius's later critics have employed the Russian label to describe his style in general. This is both unwarranted and incorrect. "What is Russian is not borrowed," Bernard Shore has observed.

It is comparatively easy to select individual passages in which one may detect the influences of Liszt, Wagner, Tchaikovsky, Borodin, etc., but as this is a *first* symphony, the differences merit greater attention than the similarities. The first movement opens with a long, rather unorthodox introduction scored for solo clarinet which leads immediately to a first theme of amazing strength and originality. The third movement is a scherzo whose rhythmic foundation recalls some of the elemental power found in the Beethoven and Bruckner symphonies. On the other hand, the saccharine second movement and the finale, with its brassy cadences accented by cymbals, never escape the shadow of Tchaikovsky, who is, to quote Olin Downes, "an obvious fellow, alas."

Much of the brassy sound in the First Symphony results from Sibelius's unrestrained use of the tuba. In his later years, he told Törne that he felt a composer could do without the tuba. If a composer considered the tuba indispensable, Sibelius continued, then he should soften it by doubling it with the string basses, bassoons, and perhaps even a bass clarinet. True to his word, the composer dispensed with the tuba after his Second Symphony, but in both his first symphonies it constitutes a noisy foundation that frequently dominates the scene unless held in check by watchful conductors.

Also included on the program with the First Symphony was a composition for boys' and men's chorus with saxhorn septet entitled *The Song of the Athenians*, opus 31, no. 3. Rydberg's stirring poem begins:

Splendid is death when thou fallest
    courageous,
Leading the onslaught,
Fallest in war for thy land,
Diest for birthright and home.
Rise with thy strong arm furious,
Rise to fight for thy country,
Hasten to yield up thy life,
Life for the races to come!

There was no need to spell out the secret meaning of this bellicose text for an audience that resented Russian rule

more than ever. Only two months earlier, Governor General
Bobrikov had published the February Manifesto, which virtually nullified Finnish civil rights. Sibelius could not have
selected a better moment to offer his own war song to his
countrymen.

The following October, Sibelius presented another
"improvisation" for male chorus, recitation, and orchestra
entitled *The Breaking of the Ice on the Uleå River (Isloss-
ningen i Uleå älv)*, opus 30, based on a text by Zachris Topelius. The occasion was a lottery evening for the benefit of the
Savo-Karelian Student Corporation. "This work can hardly
be said to be among the best of Sibelius's compositions, but
still it bears the sign of his spirit from beginning to end,"
wrote the critic of *Hufvudstadsbladet*. Also on the program
was an unusual presentation of *The Song of the Athenians*
during which the audience witnessed a specially designed
tableau depicting ancient Greeks in authentic costumes.

It is difficult in an age of super-screen talking pictures
and television to understand this passion for static historical
tableaux. They were, however, in vogue in Helsinki, and Sibelius was busy putting the finishing touches to a gigantic
score to accompany six tableaux.

*"Sibelius sober was like the rest of us when
we were drunk."*   *Robert Kajanus*

•

Under Alexander I and II, the Grand Duchy of Finland had enjoyed an extraordinary amount of self-government. With the advent of Nicholas II in 1894, however, these happy days came to an end. In order to implement plans for the complete Russianizing of Finland, the St. Petersburg government sent a new governor to Helsinki, the hated General Bobrikov, who had earned the reputation of a ruthless administrator in the Baltic provinces. With the publication of the February Manifesto in 1899, Finland lost her political autonomy.

Sullen and unwilling Finns were conscripted into Russian military units; Russians replaced Finns as provincial governors, civil servants, and police; the teaching of Russian as the principal foreign language in the schools became compulsory. Bobrikov abolished all rights of freedom of speech and assembly, and secret-service agents were everywhere to apprehend violators.

The people responded to these outrages by holding a series of "Press Celebrations," November 3–5. Bobrikov did not prohibit these public meetings because on the surface they were similar to the many lotteries and other entertainments conducted for charitable purposes. There appeared to be nothing "political" in a fund-raising campaign for the benefit of the Press Pension Fund. The high point was a bilingual soirée in the Swedish Theater, during which the audience witnessed six historical tableaux depicting landmarks in Finnish history. The tableaux were described in the press as follows:

1. The hero Väinämöinen is seated on a rock and accompanies his song on the kantele to the delight of the legendary *Kalevala* folk. In the sky we see the Maid of Pohjola working at her golden spinning-wheel.

2. The Swedish King Eric IX witnesses a mass baptism of the Finns by Henry, Bishop of Uppsala, during the twelfth century. An inspired Finnish virgin beholds signs in the heavens which are interpreted as omens of good fortune.

3. Duke Johann's court in the Castle of Turku. The sixteenth-century Swedish ruler expresses his love for Finland and his intention to work for her well-being. In this gay and festive scene we see the Duke's beautiful wife, Catharina Jagellonica, surrounded by cavaliers, ladies-in-waiting, pages, etc.

4. Finland in the Thirty Years' War [1618–48]. Four allegorical figures representing Austria, Germany, Sweden, and Finland border the tableau. Gustavus Adolphus II presides at a ceremony in which young Finnish peasants who have joined the struggle are given a banner of religious freedom.

5. "The Great Tribulations" [1700–21]. The Rus-

sians under Peter the Great have ravaged Finland from Lake Ladoga to the Gulf of Bothnia. Before the charred remains of homes, "Mother Finland" sits among her freezing children and their cattle. Cold, hunger, and war threaten them with death.

6. "Finland Awakes." The Grand Duchy faces a bright future under the enlightened rule of Tsar Alexander II during the nineteenth century. The poet Runeberg listens to his muse, Snellman addresses the country's youth with nationalistic fervor, and Lönnrot is busy collecting legends for his *Kalevala*. In the background, we see such signs of material progress as the first folk school and the first locomotive. A young lady representing "The Spirit of History" recited the following verses by Eino Leino:

> Plow! Seed!
> This is the time for seeding and hopes.
> Wishes are sometimes fulfilled,
> Sometimes eaten by the frost.
> Now is the May of Finland,
> Now to plowing and seeding;
> Cutting and binding—all else,
> May that be with God!

For this spectacle, Sibelius composed and conducted a *Preludium* for wind instruments, orchestral preludes for each of the tableaux, and some appropriate background music to accompany the reading of texts that had been written by Eino Leino. As in the earlier Viipuri celebrations, the last tableau was the grand climax. Instead of bringing the evening to a close with the national anthem, Sibelius wrote his own patriotic music for "Finland Awakes." Once again, extra-musical considerations conspired against any widespread appreciation of the composer's role in this undertaking, but some critics bothered to note that the final prelude was "singularly realistic," "quite dramatic," and "so full of hope with its folk-like simplicity."

Several weeks later, Kajanus presented four of the preludes as a concert suite under the following titles: *All'-Overtura* (tableau 1), *Scena* (tableau 4), *Quasi Bolero* (tableau 3), and *Finale* (tableau 6). During the following spring, a slightly different selection was heard in Turku, with titles taken from the tableaux: *Preludium, Heathendom, Bishop Henry Baptizes the Finns, Duke Johann's Court, Gustav Adolf II,* and *Finland Awakes.* Only the music for tableau 5 was omitted.

In a letter to Kajanus dated February 21, 1900, Baron Axel Carpelan, a wealthy musical amateur, referred to a mysterious "commissioned overture" and suggested that it be given the title *Finlandia.* He felt that the Finns should have a composition to match Rubinstein's *Russia* and Liszt's *Hungary.* It happened that when Carpelan wrote this letter, he was not familiar with the tableau music. What probably happened was that Kajanus decided that the prelude to the final tableau, "Finland Awakes," was ideally suited for this purpose, and thus suggested the title *Finlandia* to Sibelius. During the same year Fazer & Westerlund published it in the composer's own arrangement for piano under this title.

One of the most widespread myths concerning *Finlandia* is that in Finland it was regarded as "the forbidden work" for many years. For this, Sibelius is largely responsible. At the age of seventy, he told Ekman: "It was actually rather late that *Finlandia* was performed under its final title. At a farewell concert of the Philharmonic Orchestra before my departure for Paris, when the tone poem was played for the first time in its revised form, it was called *Suomi* [*Finland*]. . . . In Finland its performance was forbidden during the years of unrest."

It is true that at the concert to which the composer alluded the tone poem was officially listed on the program as *Suomi,* a title that had no meaning for the Russians. But in all the newspapers it was listed as *Finlandia.* Just how late is "rather late" we cannot say. It is a matter of record, however, that *Finlandia* was performed under that title in Helsinki during November 1901 and throughout the remaining years when Finland was still a part of the Russian Empire. Had Governor General Bobrikov been interested, he could have purchased a copy of *Finlandia* from a local music store.

Many have wondered whether Sibelius borrowed the famous hymn-like tune in *Finlandia,* and among them was Mrs. Rosa Newmarch. "The thematic material employed in *Finlandia* . . . is my own invention," Sibelius assured her. Although there is no reason to question the composer's sincerity in this assertion, the opening measures are a note-for-note duplication of a composition that Emil Genetz had written for male chorus eighteen years earlier. It is the well-known *Arise, Finland!* (*Herää Suomi!*), composed in 1881 and performed in Helsinki during April of the following year for the ceremonies celebrating Lönnrot's eightieth birthday. *Arise, Finland!* soon became extremely popular, and it is likely that Sibelius heard it many times during his student years in both Hämeenlinna and Helsinki.

If *Finlandia* has brought its creator fame, it has also produced much hostile criticism from those who object to what are styled its obvious and even cheap qualities. The composer's stanchest defenders often pass over it nervously in order to dwell on the merits of what they consider to be his more important works. What is ignored is that *Finlandia* is a first-rate example of hack writing by a composer who happened to be in a highly exalted patriotic mood. Sibelius understood the function of these tableau soirées, and he wrote the sort of music which was expected for such gatherings. There was no room in his prelude for subtleties. We should remember that *Finlandia* honored not only Runeberg, Snellman, and Lönnrot—there was also a locomotive on the stage!

It is evident that, as late as 1905, Sibelius planned to publish the complete score for the "Press Celebrations": Breitkopf & Härtel issued *Finlandia* as opus 26, no. 7, indicating that six other numbers were to be added. But as its fame spread throughout the world, the composer decided to keep it as a detached work. In 1911, he revised three other numbers from the complete score. These were published as *Scènes historiques I*, opus 25: *All'Overtura, Scena,* and *Festivo* (formerly *Quasi Bolero*). The *Preludium* and the remaining two preludes have been preserved in manuscript.[1]

---

[1] *The suite* Scènes historiques II, *opus 66, was published in 1912. The three numbers are entitled:* The Chase, Love Song, *and* At the Drawbridge. *Although Furuhjelm claims that one motif in* At the Drawbridge *is derived from the original music to tableau 3, the rest of the music in this suite has nothing to do with the "Press Celebrations" of 1900.*

Finlandia's companion pieces have never enjoyed its popularity. They are, however, extremely effective examples of theater music. The *Scena*, for example, with the strings playing *sul'ponticello* to suggest the approaching conflict, the trumpet calls, battle music, and triumphant ending, is superior to most scores of similar pretensions which have been produced by the Hollywood alchemists.

By 1900, Sibelius was ready to attempt a conquest of Europe. He had to his credit several tone poems, a full-length symphony, and numerous shorter pieces. Breitkopf & Härtel were interested in him and would be more interested, given a little public curiosity. Sibelius faced the age-old problem of trying to secure a hearing, and at the time his prospects did not look promising. Once again, and almost as if by magic, outside help came at just the right minute. Sibelius's conquest of Europe, such as it was, began with clock-like precision.

The Paris Exposition of 1900 gave Finland her opportunity to make known her achievements in the arts. Robert Kajanus, who felt that the time had come for Finnish music to take its place beside his country's achievements in the visual arts, proposed that the Philharmonic Society tour Scandinavia and northern Europe and finally give two concerts in the French capital. The plan was daring. If Finland could demonstrate independence and distinction in the realm of art, she could also convince outsiders that her aspirations for political independence were legitimate.

The issue was too delicate to merit official approval. "The Senate has refused money," Carpelan wrote Kajanus, "and even if we obtain it from private sources, we can be sure that Bobbin [Bobrikov] will refuse to give us passports." But money was obtained from private sources, and Carpelan and Kajanus carefully planned each and every detail.

Non-regulars were added to the orchestra, swelling the total to over sixty-five musicians. The soprano Ida Ekman was invited to accompany them in order to render songs by Mielck, Merikanto, and Järnefelt. At the final Paris concerts, the singers Aino Ackté and Maikki Järnefelt, the wife of Armas, were to appear as soloists. Sibelius was officially carried on the books as "assistant conductor," though his duties were restricted to sharing the applause with Kajanus. The principal compositions in the repertory for the tour were limited to three composers: Järnefelt was represented by his Andante for strings, a Prelude for orchestra, and *Korsholm;* Kajanus by his *Aino Symphony,* a suite entitled *Summer Memories,* and two Finnish Rhapsodies. But the lion's share went to Sibelius, with his First Symphony, *Finlandia* (now revised), the music to *King Kristian II, The Swan of Tuonela,* and *Lemminkäinen's Homeward Journey.*

The first lap of the tour covered Sweden, Norway, and Denmark. It was a rousing success. The rendition of national anthems and other patriotic songs resulted in standing ovations that revealed the undisguised Scandinavian sympathies for Finland in her struggle for independence. When Sibelius acknowledged the applause of the Norwegians, one Christiania critic described him as follows: "Jean Sibelius reminds us a great deal of Strindberg. . . . Mongoloid features [*sic*], fuzzy hair, a defiant expression, a sarcastic touch about the mouth, and flashing, sharp eyes. He wore a flower in the lapel of his frock coat and bowed in a reserved manner."

After Scandinavia, the orchestra played in Lübeck, Hamburg, Berlin, Amsterdam, Rotterdam, the Hague, and Brussels and finally presented two Paris concerts on July 30 and August 3. As they proceeded south, all did not go well. At times, the advance publicity was far from adequate, and the failure of some musicians to appear at the proper times resulted in unfortunate delays and last-minute changes in the program. In Paris, the warm seasonal temperature resulted in disappointingly small audiences. Yet the consensus was that the tour had been a great success and well worth undertaking.

The main result of the tour was a mild German curiosity about Sibelius's music. The two short *Lemminkäinen* pieces and, especially, *Finlandia* earned him a reputation as a significant new voice from the North and the successor to Grieg. If the First Symphony did not always meet with unqualified approval, it did indicate that Sibelius was willing to grapple with the larger forms that Grieg had avoided. Within a few years, the Helsinki papers were jubilantly reporting each new German performance. Sibelius's future looked bright.

But it was a promise without fulfillment. What, one may ask, happened in Germany? It is a question that the composer later attempted to answer. "When Busoni died [1924], I knew where I stood," he told a Swedish critic. "Busoni was the only person in Germany who was really interested in my music. He was my friend." One of the composer's biographers, Ringbom, denies the statement that Sibelius never attained any great renown in Germany. As proof, he points to the frequency of performances during the first decade of this century, the composer's relationship with Breitkopf & Härtel, a German biography by Walter Niemann (1917), Busoni's friendship, etc.

The Germans, however, soon began to evince signs of wearying of the new Finnish music, and by 1917 their interest dropped almost to the zero point. If the tour appeared to herald the conquest of Germany—a conquest that ended in defeat—a more lasting interest in Sibelius was soon to spring up in an unsuspected quarter, the English-speaking world.

When Kajanus returned to Finland, he learned that the Paris tour had netted not only valuable publicity but also a large number of unpaid bills. In an effort to raise money, he organized a lottery evening. For this occasion, Sibelius presented another of his "improvisations," a work for mixed chorus, recitation, and orchestra entitled *Snöfrid*, later designated opus 29. As late as his fiftieth birthday, he regarded *Snöfrid, Sandels,* and *The Breaking of the Ice on the Uleå River* as three companion pieces belonging to opus 28.

Rydberg's romantic text deals with one of the composer's favorite subjects and bears many similarities to the program he wrote for *Florestan* and the text for *Skogsrået*. The nymph Snöfrid urges a handsome youth named Gunnar to live dangerously and exchange his soul for worldly treasures that the trolls offer him. Presumably the youth heeds the voice of his conscience and manages to resist temptation.

Sibelius's setting borders on the operatic. It opens with some rather obvious storm music; many of the passages for chorus remind one of a nineteenth-century folk opera. *Snöfrid* is about as close as Sibelius ever came to writing in the Wagnerian style, and it contains several passages that seem to have been lifted bodily from *Tristan und Isolde* or the *Ring*. Although it is generally regarded as having been composed in 1900, Sibelius indicated that it dates from 1896.

Wagner—how many composers educated in Germany during the final years of the nineteenth century attempted to escape his influence! And how few succeeded! With his First Symphony, Sibelius had given proof of a willingness and an ability to strike out in new directions. The results had been so gratifying that he soon decided to work on another symphony.

*"A composer born in Finland who goes to
Italy had better be careful. If he doesn't,
he'll find that he has composed* Il Trovatore.
*The men who discuss his symphonies had
better go slow, too. . . ."*
          Olin Downes

●

Baron Axel Carpelan, who
had worked so hard to make the tour a success, now began to
show a personal interest in Sibelius's career. The warm and
intimate friendship that soon developed between the two
men lasted until Carpelan's death in 1919. In the fall of 1900,
he offered Sibelius enough money to permit him and his
family to enjoy the winter in Italy. "I am really not myself
when thinking of the journey," the composer wrote his
benefactor. "You have really put air under my wings."

Once again Sibelius obtained a release from his teaching duties at the Music Institute and proceeded to Berlin,
where he was invited to conduct his two *Lemminkäinen*
pieces at the Heidelberg Festival during June 1901. After
spending several months in the German capital, the family
moved on to Rapallo, where Sibelius installed his wife and
children in a pension and rented a small villa for himself in
order to work undisturbed on his Second Symphony and

other projects. "I am now composing for the piano, and I feel lost," he wrote his brother, Christian, in February. "Let's see how the symphonies go. Barking, of course. But perhaps something good also."

This period of intensive creative activity was not untouched by moments of nostalgia for Finland. In a postcard to Kajanus dated March 2, 1901, he wrote in part: "The Mediterrannean in storm! All the small birds are here! They shoot at them. They place snares for them. Even poisoned cakes. Nevertheless, they sing and wait for the spring. Finland! Finland!! Finland!!! . . . Do you still like my music? Write. The almond trees are in blossom."

"Now I am again completely a man of imagination," he wrote Carpelan. "Nothing disturbs me. I could initiate you, my comprehending friend, into my work, but I do not do so from principle. To my mind it is the same with compositions as with butterflies: once you touch them, their essence is gone—they can fly, it is true, but are no longer so fair." This comparison between his work in progress and butterfly wings became one of the ready-made "wrapped and packaged" answers that so irritated Adolf Paul. During his later years, Sibelius delighted in repeating it when parrying questions concerning the much-awaited Eighth Symphony.

Sibelius returned to Finland with the birds, and after a short stay departed once again for Germany, this time to conduct at the Heidelberg Festival. Such an invitation was a signal honor for any non-German composer, and the Finnish press proudly drew attention to it. Adolf Paul wrote home that he was astounded by Sibelius's energy and mastery as a conductor, and that the tumultuous applause immediately prompted one impresario to fix a date for a Berlin concert. Faltin noted that his protégé occupied a difficult place on the program between Richard Strauss and Wagner. In spite of inadequate rehearsals, the excessive heat, and "many adverse circumstances," he felt that Sibelius had scored a great success.

Near the end of 1901, Flodin wrote a flattering article entitled "Jean Sibelius, a Finnish Composer," in which he concluded: "With pride we here in Finland note that Jean Sibelius is also beginning to win ground in greater Europe." [1] By this date, the local papers had reported numerous performances in Germany as well as a few in such distant cities as Cincinnati and Chicago. At all of these concerts, the music involved was either *King Kristian II* or the two *Lemminkäinen* tone poems, which had been published by Breitkopf & Härtel. *Spring Song, En Saga,* the *Karelia* pieces, and *Finlandia* were still in manuscript and thus not available.

On March 3, 1902, the Second Symphony was given its world *première* in Helsinki with the composer conducting. It was dedicated to Axel Carpelan in gratitude for his financial assistance. This time, Sibelius decided against filling out the program with earlier compositions that might be attributed to his *Sturm und Drang* period. Instead, he wrote two shorter works. The first was Impromptu for women's chorus and orchestra to a text by Rydberg; it was based in part on a string trio dating from around 1885. In 1910 it was revised and published as opus 19. Flodin admired its simplicity and

[1] *Earlier that year, Flodin sharply criticized the Swedish composer Peterson-Berger for writing that Sibelius was "the very much talked-about composer—quasi-genial madness—artistic bohemianism—trumpery, enlarged by local patriotism and political considerations."*

refined atmosphere. The second was designated on the program as Overture. According to one report, Sibelius wrote it during one night in a Helsinki hotel shortly before the concert.

This is the Overture in A minor that Ekman erroneously concluded was the composer's first attempt to write for orchestra while studying with Goldmark. During the winter of 1957, I chanced upon a complete set of parts for this overture among some unclassified material in the Sibelius Museum in Turku. After comparing the music with Flodin's review of 1902, I was able to establish that it was contemporary with the Second Symphony. Flodin found it "a very casual work," and continued: "It rests upon two pillars between which there is an airy and amusing bridge. But it is as if different architects had built the bridge and the pillars. In itself the section for brass which opens and closes the overture is beautiful and unusual, but the rhythmic motif of the allegro [middle] section sounds like an accompaniment. This is not enough to produce a real and logical connection between the serious introduction and the finale. The work, however, is effective as it stands."

The extended chorale-like and chromatic fanfare for four trumpets with which it begins is unusual for Sibelius. The weakest section is certainly the middle one, which Flodin described as sounding like an accompaniment. It contains a lively theme that later appeared in the final movement of the string quartet *Voces intimae* and, in slightly altered form, in the opening movement of the Third Symphony. It even has a few measures from *Finlandia*. Sibelius soon lost all interest in his improvised overture, which was not heard again until after his death.

The chief attraction, of course, was the new symphony. Flodin's first reaction was that it was less "Finnish" than the First Symphony and betrayed the influence of Tchaikovsky. One year later, however, his enthusiasm increased, especially after hearing it paired at a concert with *Death and Transfiguration* by Richard Strauss. The German, Flodin conceded, was the more eclectic composer, and without doubt a supreme master of orchestration, but he insisted that Sibelius was by no means inferior as an orchestrator. As for the symphony, he hailed it as "an absolute masterpiece . . . one of the few symphonic creations of our age that point in the same direction as the Beethoven symphonies."

Early foreign reactions to the Second Symphony were less enthusiastic. When Hans Richter conducted the first English performance in Manchester during 1905, the reviewer for the *Musical Times* observed: "The Second Symphony—in D—of the Finnish composer Jean Sibelius was played without creating any pronounced impression." A St. Petersburg critic, P. Kovalev, heard it in Vienna during 1910, and reported to his readers: "Sibelius's Second and Brahms's Fourth were played. The program was purposely set up in order to show the high qualities of the one and the deficiencies of the other. Sibelius's symphony lacks unity and is made up of shreds. As soon as he reaches a peak, something else attracts his attention. There is almost a complete lack of polyphony . . . something permissible only in the case of Schubert. In his Second Symphony, Sibelius is little more than a great talent approaching dilettantism."

As late as 1923, when Sibelius conducted this symphony in Rome, a critic named De Rensis observed: "Sibelius finds himself at great disadvantage before a work of grand proportions. . . . While he is an unsurpassed composer in his shorter compositions, he becomes loquacious and inarticulate when he has to develop his ideas over a large field, and the musical phrase loses all its efficiency and drags itself heavily and uselessly along, whereas, were it limited to a few measures, it would prove full of emotional power."

Like the First Symphony, the Second is in four movements, with the slight difference that the scherzo and finale are joined together. Gray finds the first movement a "veritable revolution" because of the application of what he considers to be an entirely new principle in symphonic form. What happens, he says, is an inversion of the so-called first-movement "sonata form," in which the themes ordinarily are stated in the exposition, taken apart in the development section, and then put together again in the recapitulation. Sibelius, he maintains, presents detached melodic fragments in the exposition, builds them into an organic whole in the development, and then disperses his material back into fragments in the recapitulation.

Upon close analysis, Gray's widely quoted theory amounts to nothing more than a play on words. If a composer writes an exposition based on a few broad themes, then it follows that in his development section he will divide them into smaller units. If, however, he decides to base his exposition on two or more groups of thematic fragments, then further thematic subdivision can hardly take place later on. What Gray is really saying is that, whereas other composers develop fairly long themes, Sibelius prefers to employ extremely short ones.

The remaining movements are perhaps more interesting and original than those of the First Symphony. The titanic struggle between the forces unleashed in the second movement assumes such proportions that the listener doubts that even the composer could have kept matters under control. "I am a slave to my themes and submit to their demands," Sibelius later wrote. The curious little oboe melody in the trio of the scherzo, with its incessant repetition of B flat, is frequently cited as the classic example of the composer's ability to create a theme out of almost nothing. Even without the benefit of cymbals, the impressive, heroic finale creates the desired effect. Here comparisons between Sibelius and Tchaikovsky are unavoidable. But the Finnish composer is no servile imitator. In the Second Symphony, he displays a strength and power of imagination which have rarely been equaled.

In the Second Symphony, Sibelius dispenses with harp, cymbals, and bass drum. Although the tuba remains, it is handled less obtrusively than in the First Symphony. Only on rare occasions does it betray what the composer later described as its *Schwerfälligkeit*. The Second Symphony dates from the same year as the revised version of *En Saga*, and these two compositions show how far Sibelius had progressed in mastering orchestration. The consultations with Kajanus and the use of his orchestra as a laboratory were beginning to produce results.

Although Sibelius ridiculed attempts to attach programs to his symphonies, some Finnish musicians have been unable to resist the temptation. During 1945–6, Professor Ilmari Krohn, Finland's leading musicologist, a composer in his own right, and a contemporary of Sibelius, published a study entitled *Die Stimmungsgehalt der Symphonien von Jean Sibelius*. In it, he claims to have discovered programmatic leitmotifs in all seven symphonies. He is convinced that in the Second Symphony, Sibelius wished to depict "Finland's struggle for political liberty." I vividly recall a meeting with Professor Krohn during which he designated one theme in the slow movement as "the Russians" and another as "a Finnish prayer to God."

Twenty years before Krohn published his study, the Finnish conductor Georg Schnéevoigt directed the Second Symphony in Boston. According to the program notes for that concert, Schnéevoigt said: "The first movement depicts the quiet pastoral life of the Finns undisturbed by thoughts of oppression. The second movement is charged with patriotic feeling, but the thought of brutal strife over the people brings with it timidity of the soul. The third, in the nature of a scherzo, portrays the awakening of national feeling, the desire to organize in defense of their rights, while in the finale hope enters their breasts and there is comfort in the anticipated coming of a deliverer."

Obviously there is more here than meets the eye. Schnéevoigt, a close friend of the composer, was one of his most famous interpreters both in Finland and abroad. As we have already seen, Sibelius's early interest in program music was so great as to lead him to the conclusion that music unguided by poetic meaning could never be completely satisfying. Years later he completely reversed this stand and denied that he was a "literary" musician. The truth probably lies somewhere between these extremes. Later we shall see how the composer once outlined the "program" to his Fourth Symphony to some intimate friends and then indignantly denied its validity in a letter to the press.

One month after the *première* of the Second Symphony, Helsinki celebrated the inauguration of the Finnish National Theater. It was an important moment in the development of native dramatic art and the crowning achievement of its most devoted missionary, Kaarlo Bergbom. Music by Melartin, Merikanto, Armas Järnefelt, and Sibelius was heard during the ceremony. The high point of the evening was a new Sibelius composition that Bergbom had commissioned, *The Origin of Fire (Tulen synty)*, opus 32, for baritone, male chorus, and orchestra. The baritone Ojanperä sang the solo part, and Sibelius conducted the Philharmonic Society and a special chorus of over three hundred voices.

The Origin of Fire—in England it is known under the amusing title *UKKO the Firemaker*—is based on canto XLVII in the *Kalevala,* in which Louhi, "old and gap-toothed dame of Pohja," hides the sun and the moon in a mountain and steals the fires from the homes in Väinölä. As darkness envelopes the earth the soloist sings:

> Therefore was the night unending,
> And for long was utter darkness,
> Night in Kalevala forever,
> And in Väinölä's fair dwellings,
> Likewise in the heavens was darkness,
> Darkness round the seat of Ukko. (XLVII, 41–6)

Ukko, the supreme god, ponders this mystery and finally decides to investigate for himself. In a dramatic recitative the soloist relates:

> And he went the moon to seek for,
> And he went to find the sunlight,
> Yet he could not find the moonlight,
> Nor the sun he could discover.   (63–6)

The chorus now tells how Ukko created fire and light:

> In the air a light struck Ukko,
> And a flame did Ukko kindle,
> From his flaming sword he struck it,
> Sparks he struck from off the sword-blade,
> From his nails he struck the fire,
> From his limbs he made it crackle,
> High above aloft in heaven,
> On the starry plains of heaven.   (67–74)

Ukko entrusts his creation to the Maiden of the Air, who carelessly lets it drop to earth. The work comes to a close as the chorus describes the consequences:

> Then the sky was cleft asunder,
> All the air was filled with windows,
> Burst asunder by the fire-sparks,
> As the red drop quick descended,
> And a gap gleamed forth in heaven,
> As it through the clouds dropped downward,
> Through nine heavens the drop descended,
> Through six spangled vaults of heaven.   (103–10)

The Origin of Fire is conceived along the general lines of the earlier "improvisations"—*Sandels, The Breaking of the Ice on the Uleå River,* and *Snöfrid.* Just as the opening measures of *Sandels* admirably convey the mood of preciosity which dominates the general's intimate dinner party, so here they immediately establish the prevailing mood of darkness and despair. Sibelius, it must be admitted, possessed the uncanny knack of knowing how to begin his compositions on just the right note. The solo and choral parts are completely divorced. After a very short introduction, we hear the baritone solo, then his recitative, and finally the chorus. Just before the chorus relates how Ukko created the fire, Sibelius indulges in a brief moment of "fire music" which is strikingly effective in its simplicity.

Where, we may properly ask, was Sibelius headed in 1902? The Second Symphony pointed in the direction of absolute music, but *The Origin of Fire* revealed him as the same "literary" musician who had written nine years earlier that absolute music could not by itself satisfy.

In May 1902, Sibelius wrote to his brother: "This damned marriage with Mrs. Musica! As you know, she is quite a passionate lady and fairly 'strong-willed.' . . . Enjoy life and stay gay and merry. But don't do it for seventeen (!!) years as I have done. Isn't it strange, this business about *Man lebt nur einmal?*"

Caricature of Sibelius by Albert Edelfelt

a. Portrait of Sibelius, 1904, by Albert Edelfelt
b. Aino Sibelius, about 1910

"Lauri: *I'll say something. Let's move into
the forest, and to Hell with the din
of the world!*"   *Aleksis Kivi's*
                      The Seven Brothers

●

In 1903, Sibelius's brother-in-
law, Arvid Järnefelt, completed a new Finnish drama in three
acts entitled *Death* (*Kuolema*). No great contribution to
either Finnish or world literature, *Death* failed as a stage
piece and would have been completely forgotten had Sibelius not composed some music for it. The loosely knit plot
revolves about the hero Paavali's obsession that "there is no
death." After his mother, wife, children, and mother-in-law
all die, Paavali sadly concludes that death is a reality.

The opening scene actually requires appropriate
background music. Here we see the mother upon her death-
bed. In a semi-lucid moment, she tells Paavali that she has
just dreamed of attending a ball. The son falls asleep, and
Death enters to claim his victim. The mother, mistaking
Death for her deceased husband, joins him in a waltz, after
which the two depart. Paavali awakes to find her dead.

For six scenes in the play, Sibelius wrote music for
a small string ensemble, bass drum (played with timpani
sticks), and a church bell. Because the music was not ready

in time for the scheduled production date, the *première* of *Death* did not take place until December 2 in the new Finnish National Theater. Sibelius conducted the small ensemble behind the scenes, as he had for his music to *King Kristian II*. The first-night audience vigorously applauded both the author and the composer, and several of the critics expressed admiration for the music. One thought the waltz for the opening scene especially effective. It was an unpretentious little affair marked *tempo di valse lente* in which the word "dance" was written over the second section.

For more than five years, the music house of Fazer & Westerlund had been publishing compositions by Sibelius and paying him rather handsomely. For example, the *Karelia Suite* in a piano arrangement by Karl Ekman, Sr., netted the composer eight hundred marks, a collection of songs for mixed chorus from his University Cantata for 1897 five hundred, a piano version of *The Song of the Athenians* four hundred and fifty. A few months after the first performance of *Death*, Sibelius sold Fazer & Westerlund two arrangements of his music for the opening scene, one for piano and the other for small orchestra, under the title *Valse triste*. He was paid one hundred marks for each arrangement and advanced an additional three hundred for the complete score to the drama. As the complete score failed to materialize, the cash advance was later deducted from future royalty payments.

Apparently no one attached any importance to the publication of this little waltz. Certainly not Sibelius, who cheerfully pocketed his two hundred marks, feeling that he had been well rewarded for his effort. Over thirty years later, he declined to discuss *Valse triste* with his biographer

Ekman other than to say that he had written it in one week. Although some may feel that Sibelius's reluctance to discuss his most widely played composition resulted from a bad artistic conscience, the true explanation is more amusing.

The sale had been an outright one, and Sibelius never received a penny of the enormous royalties his *Valse triste* must have earned through the years. In 1905, when the Finnish publishers sold all Sibelius rights to Breitkopf & Härtel—to their later regret—*Valse triste* was included in the transaction. The enterprising German firm soon issued it in arrangements for everything from military band to solo flute. In 1910, the Finnish papers reported that *Valse triste* had become so well known that it was featured prominently in a new German novel by Ludwig Gattermann, *Über die Heide.*

Sibelius, a poor businessman, as he later admitted, had unwittingly deprived himself of a small fortune. Yet *Valse triste* earned him rich rewards in terms of free publicity throughout the world. Thanks to its phenomenal popularity, audiences were attracted to his less-known compositions. The composer recognized its great drawing power and frequently included it on his programs "by popular request" when conducting abroad.

Valse triste soon became even more maligned than *Finlandia.* Many have been at a loss to explain why it should have made the composer's name known to the many and injured his reputation in the eyes of the few. No system of musical analysis has yet been devised which will enable publishers to estimate in advance a new work's true market value, as the manufacturers of present-day "popular music" well know. *Valse triste* just happened to capture the public's fancy. Taken for what it is, background music to accompany the dream waltz of a dying woman, it is singularly effective. Later we shall see how Sibelius attempted to write another *Valse triste,* only to meet with failure.

The rest of the music to Järnefelt's play is less suited for adaptation as concert numbers. For example, the music to the final scene is written for church bell tolling over string arpeggios. In 1906, Sibelius combined the music for the third and fourth scenes, conducting the result in the city of Vaasa as *Scene with Cranes (Scen med tranor).* Here he added two clarinets to the string ensemble in order to create a very realistic imitation of the screeching of the birds. Although this delightful little mood piece is frequently performed in Finland and has even been recorded there, it remains unpublished to date.

Shortly after the *première* of *Death,* the German violinist Willy Burmester, formerly the concertmaster in Kajanus's orchestra, announced to the press: "Sibelius has written a violin concerto that he has dedicated to me. I am coming to play it here in Helsinki next year. Sibelius . . . do you know him? They say he's becoming known as a very great composer." Sibelius, however, did not wait for Burmester's return. On February 8, 1904, he presented his concerto in Helsinki, and the difficult solo part was entrusted to the less competent hands of Viktor Novacek. Whatever the difficulties between Burmester and the composer may have been, when the former returned to Finland he played the Tchaikovsky Concerto. When Sibelius published the revised version of his concerto as opus 47, he dedicated it to the young Hungarian virtuoso Franz von Vecsey.

Many years later when Sibelius discussed the problems involved in writing concertos, he gave the following advice to his pupil Törne: "You must not forget the incredible stupidity of most virtuosos—of course, I do not mean the great and glorious exceptions. And bear this in mind not only in writing your solo passages, but also and perhaps still more in elaborating the purely orchestral parts of your score. I warn you especially against long preludes and interludes. And this refers especially to violin concertos. Think of the poor public!"

No better illustration of this advice could be found than his own violin concerto, in which all of the ingredients common to a virtuoso piece meet in harmonious combination. It presents no radical innovations in matters of form. An orchestra of classical proportions remains, for the most part, a respectful and discreet pace or two in the shadow of the soloist. Designed to exploit Burmester's reputedly fabulous technique, it abounds in the necessary bravura passages that a composer who once had planned to become a violin virtuoso could be expected to write with authority. It is an appealing composition full of fetching melodies. To associate it with the Finnish landscape, or with anything Finnish, for that matter, would be difficult. It sounds as though its creator had spent most of his life along the banks of the Danube.

Flodin did not like the Concerto. Sibelius, he felt, had had two alternatives: he could have written a symphonic work with an *obbligato* for solo violin or a pompous concerto of the traditional type in which the soloist would be the sovereign master. Having selected the second alternative, Flodin insisted, the composer had not been able to say anything new. Again Sibelius heeded the advice of this influential critic, who was determined to chart his "way": he immediately revised the Concerto.

In its revised form, it was first heard during October of the following year at a concert in Berlin. Karl Halir was the soloist, and Richard Strauss the conductor. It was a generous gesture on the part of Strauss, and Sibelius justifiably felt flattered. Before his death, Strauss is reported to have said: "I know more about music than Sibelius, but he is the greater composer." Even if this statement is apocryphal, it does contain a few grains of truth. Strauss, incontestably the greatest master of orchestration of his generation, must have regarded Sibelius's growing fame with keen interest and noted that his original ideas triumphed in spite of an inferior technical knowledge. Sibelius, for his part, probably observed that the aging Strauss was still a master skilled in the art of saying things, but who, alas, had little to say.

In Turku during March 1904, Sibelius conducted a new composition entitled Andante for Strings. It was dedicated to the conductor of the local orchestra, José Eibenschütz. One local critic found the new work very much in the style of Tchaikovsky, and suggested that a more appropriate title would be Romance or Nocturne. When it was published five years later, Sibelius renamed it Romance in C Major, opus 42. The ability to recognize musical styles after listening to or seeing unidentified compositions is generally included in examinations for graduate music students. The

Romance in C Major is guaranteed to evoke a spontaneous "Tchaikovsky, of course."

By the spring of 1904, Sibelius and his wife had decided to live in the country and had purchased some property in the village of Järvenpää (Lake's End), near Lake Tuusula, a short distance northeast of Helsinki. One lady refused to sell him any land because she recognized him as one of the four men depicted in Gallén-Kallela's *Symposium*. But the chief difficulty for Sibelius was that of obtaining the sizable down payment, for which he had to fight "tooth and nail." He could not obtain enough money for waterfront property, but had to be content with permission to cross a neighbor's land in order to bathe in the lake. Järvenpää was becoming known as an artists' colony, and some of the composer's friends, including the writer Aho and the painter Halonen, had already built homes there.

In the fall, the Sibelius family, which now included three daughters, moved into the new log house, which had been named "Ainola" for the composer's wife. "It was necessary for me to get away from Helsinki," Sibelius later explained to Ekman. "My art demanded another environment. In Helsinki, all melody died within me. Besides, I was too sociable to be able to refuse invitations that interfered with my work. I found it very difficult to say no. I had to get away."

The legends concerning the solitary Finnish genius living in self-imposed isolation at Järvenpää have become so widespread as to give a completely distorted picture of Sibelius's personality. He continued to frequent Helsinki's popular restaurants and hotels. He also continued to visit Germany, France, and Italy whenever he could afford it. "I have come here—to Paris—for a while," he wrote Mrs. Newmarch in 1911. "Give me the loneliness either of the Finnish forests or of a big city." A few months later, he told the critic Wasenius: "I work best in the large forests or in the great cities such as London or Paris."

The move to Järvenpää was really a happy compromise. It served as a convenient brake on the composer's love of big-city luxuries, which he could not always afford. In the forest surrounding his home, he was able to renew the contact with nature which had so stimulated him as a child. Once again he could hear the "wood-sprites in the gloom weave magic secrets" which he later mentioned in describing his last great composition, *Tapiola,* composed in 1926. Yet the convivialities that Helsinki afforded were but a few minutes away by train.

No sooner had Sibelius settled in his new home than he was off to Berlin. Thanks to his friend Busoni, he had been invited to conduct his Second Symphony there. Whereas the composer of Finnish national tone poems had been cordially received as a novelty by the Germans, Sibelius the symphonist was quite another matter. In their polite reviews, the critics displayed considerable skepticism concerning the symphony's merits. To them, it seemed to lack continuity and a mastery of the problems of form.

Hard on the heels of Busoni's invitation came one from an unexpected quarter, England. There Sir Henry Wood and Granville Bantock had already performed his music. Sibelius had to decline the invitation in order to complete incidental music for Maeterlinck's *Pelléas et Mélisande* which had been commissioned by the Swedish Theater. The *pre-mière* took place on March 17, 1905, with the composer conducting. It was his most ambitious undertaking in this genre up to this date. The complete score consists of seven interludes, two "melodramas" (to accompany dialogue), and a song for Mélisande to sing in the third act.

Flodin had only words of praise for the new music. In part he wrote: "Without degenerating into the pianissimo mannerisms of the Frenchman Debussy's illustrative music to the same play, Sibelius has been able to clothe his own tone pictures in a subdued, gentle, and restrained atmosphere. Beneath this, however, we find a veritable torrent of thoughts, motifs, melodic ideas, and rhythmic patterns—and all this with the powerful (though bridled), blazing, and ardent passion of youth."

The comparison with Debussy, of course, was inevitable. Earlier, Flodin had placed Strauss in an unfavorable light, and now he felt that a comparison between his favorite and Debussy, with his "pianissimo mannerisms," was appropriate. He must have found the "Finnish" music he had been seeking among these pages. Interestingly enough, it is for precisely the same reason that such an ardent Sibelius admirer as Cecil Gray finds this music somewhat out of tune with Maeterlinck's fantasy. In a volume of piano pieces entitled *Sibeliana: Scenes from the Land of a Thousand Lakes,* published in 1910, several arrangements of selections from the *Pelléas et Mélisande* music appear under different titles. For example, "The Death of Mélisande" is renamed "The Sun Sinks." Gray feels that the new titles are more descriptive of the true character of the music than the original ones.

Before 1905 was over, Sibelius published his incidental music as a concert suite, omitting only one interlude. Once again the striking thing about the composer's theater music is its variety and suitability for the particular play in question, all achieved within a remarkable economy of means. As admirable specimens of what Wood calls "pattern work," these little mood pieces are about as far removed from Debussy as Finland is from France: we should perhaps remember that Maeterlinck's drama was presented by the Swedish Theater in a Swedish translation by Bertel Gripenberg.

"Which foreign country has shown the greatest sympathy for your art?" Sibelius was once asked. "England," came the answer, "the country without chauvinism." Behind this observation, one detects a barbed shaft aimed in the direction of Germany.

Breitkopf & Härtel, now beginning to publish this new Finnish music in considerable quantities, had a representative in London, and they wasted no time in bringing the name of Sibelius to the attention of English conductors. The earliest English performance on record appears to have taken place during October 1901 when Sir Henry Wood presented the music to *King Kristian II* at a London Promenade Concert. The composer's name was so unknown that it appeared on the program as "Siebelius"! Two years later, Wood gave the first English performance of the First Symphony, and in 1905, Hans Richter introduced the Second in Manchester.

During this same year, Granville Bantock, Principal of the Birmingham and Midland Institute of Music and the permanent conductor of the Liverpool Orchestral Society, invited Sibelius to conduct several of his compositions in Liverpool during March. Sibelius declined. Bantock paid him a visit in August and persuaded him to come to England the following December. The composer accepted this second invitation, and conducted his First Symphony and *Finlandia* in Liverpool at a "Ladies' Concert."

Because he was unable to converse with his Finnish guest, Bantock invited Mrs. Rosa Newmarch, an accomplished linguist and lecturer on music, to act as interpreter. In 1939, Mrs. Newmarch recalled her first impressions of the composer in a nostalgic little volume of memoirs entitled *Jean Sibelius: A Short History of a Long Friendship:*

"My fellow-guest proved to be a striking and characteristic example of a man from the North—a Viking type. I remember that with his hair the colour of oats in sunshine, his ice-blue eyes, his well set-up figure, neat and admirably tailored, he presented a complete contrast to the unkempt *Musikant* with whom one associated the apparition of a 'new genius.' I was put next to him at dinner with a vague idea that, as nobody knew the language he spoke, a little Russian might come in handy. I had been long enough in Russia and over the Finnish borders to know that the Finns were not too keen to speak the language of their big neighbour, but we soon effected a compromise: a sort of sandwich between French and German, to which, looking over our correspondence which has lasted over thirty years, I find to my amusement we always adhered."

Mrs. Newmarch became not only a lifelong friend, but also one of the composer's greatest champions in England. Two months after meeting him, she gave an illustrated lecture to the London Concert Goer's Club on "Jean Sibelius, a

Finnish Composer." As phonograph records were not available at that time, the illustrations were limited to a few songs and a piano rendition of *Finlandia*. Also there was no Sibelius *Wissenschaft* in English in 1906, and her source material was limited to a few scraps of information the composer had given, plus a handful of published scores. Much of her lecture consisted of an introduction to Finland and the Finnish people. After checking in the libraries, she discovered vague references to the Finns being related to the Magyars, and this gave her the justification for claiming that Sibelius and Liszt had a common ancestry! Breitkopf & Härtel, delighted with this free publicity, promptly printed her lecture in both English and German editions, adding at the end a catalogue of their own Sibelius publications.

Both as lecturer and as author of much-admired program notes, Mrs. Newmarch continued to support the cause of her friend in England. She prepared English translations for many of his songs, and on numerous occasions acted as his intermediary in arranging hearings for his new compositions. In 1913, Sibelius expressed his appreciation in a letter: "How can I thank you for all that you have done for us in Finland? Your dear name is inscribed forever in letters of gold in the history of our culture."

During this first visit to England, Sibelius met Sir Alexander Campbell Mackenzie, Principal of the Royal Academy of Music, and Ernest Newman, at that time music critic for the *Manchester Guardian*. Newman was to take an active part in the rise of an English Sibelius cult in the 1930's. In 1905, however, Sibelius was but one of the many foreign novelties invited to visit England. Perhaps the one person most responsible for helping to establish the Finnish novelty as a classic was Sir Henry Wood,[1] conductor of the London Promenade Concerts from 1895 until his death in 1944.

In his autobiography, Wood wrote: "Granville Bantock and I have always been champions of Sibelius, but now that I have performed all his seven symphonies in one season [1937] I look back with pride and satisfaction when I remember that I was the first to have helped popularize the music of this deep and original thinker. Since those days we have been able to devote whole concerts to his works and be sure of appreciative audiences. . . . [Mrs. Newmarch] was directly responsible for my interest in Sibelius. She had told me so much about him." Bantock later recalled: "Sincerity—that seems to be the essential nature of the man and the artist; and you can hardly be with him long without feeling it."

[1] *Sibelius dedicated his song "Jubal," opus 35, no. 1, to Olga Oroussova, Lady Wood in private life.*

*"Never pay attention to what the music critics
say. Remember, a statue has never been
set up in honor of a critic."*
               Sibelius to a student

●

After conducting in England,
Sibelius was in no hurry to return home. He relaxed in Paris
for a while in order to hear the French orchestras, which he
admired greatly. He was flattered by the respect Frenchmen
showed for the Legion of Honor that he had been awarded a
few years earlier. En route to Finland, he stopped off in Berlin, where he undoubtedly started to compose *Erloschen* and
the six songs to German texts, opus 50, which he completed
during 1906.

On returning to Finland in February, he was busy
with many projects. The approaching May 12 was to mark the
one-hundredth anniversary of the birth of J. V. Snellman. Although "Snellman's Day" was given scant coverage in the
Swedish-language press, the Finnish papers devoted complete
issues to it. They proudly listed the names of thousands of
citizens who on that day had changed their names from Swedish to Finnish.

For the University's contribution to this celebration,
Sibelius conducted a new "cantata" entitled *There Sings the*

Queen (*Siell'laulavi kuningatar*). Oddly enough, he had composed it to a German translation of a Finnish text by Paavo Cajander entitled *The Liberated Queen* (*Vapautettu kuningatar*). It was necessary to conceal this from the Russian rulers, who were in no mood to tolerate references to a "liberated Queen," or a liberated anything else, for that matter. When the score was published the following year, the false Finnish title *Siell'laulavi kuningatar,* opus 48, was used and most inaccurately translated in German, English, and Russian as *The Captive Queen.*

But no amount of juggling with titles and translations could conceal the true meaning of Cajander's text, which is literally a *pièce de résistance.* It tells how a great lady, once a reigning queen, is imprisoned in a gloomy castle. There, every evening, she sings her mournful song. A youth passing beneath her window hears these plaintive strains and repeats her story throughout the countryside. A Deliverer appears from the ranks of the people and restores his Queen to her former glory. The chorus rejoices:

> And from all hearts and from all lips,
> A song of gladness broke,
> A glorious hymn of thankfulness
> As Day and Freedom woke.

There was no need to explain to a Finnish audience who was being liberated from what or by whom!

Sibelius's musical setting is a perfect counterpart to the text. It opens with a choral recitative in the minor describing the Queen's plight; there follows a march in a major key to herald the coming of the Deliverer; and the work concludes with a hymn of rejoicing. The over-all layout is obvious, and there are parts that do not sound very original. For example, the march tune seems to be based on the one Liszt employed so extensively in *A Faust Symphony*. But *The Liberated Queen* must be regarded as patriotic music and a worthy companion piece to *The Song of the Athenians* and *Finlandia*. It was never intended for export. Relatively unknown abroad, it is still heard in Finland with great pleasure and pride.

During this same year, Sibelius completed another commissioned work of a different order. It was the incidental music to the drama *Belshazzar's Feast* written by his friend Hjalmar Procopé. The plot deals with an intrigue in the palace of the last king of Babylon. In an effort to gain control over Belshazzar, the Jews present the beautiful Leschanah as the lure. The King immediately succumbs to her charms, and promptly loses interest in his current favorite, Khadra. This rejected lady commits suicide after performing a Dance of Life and a Dance of Death. Belshazzar suffers pangs of remorse. Leschanah kills him in a fit of jealousy and then kills herself.

Sibelius conducted his music at the *première* given by the Swedish Theater on November 7, 1906. Scored for a small orchestra, it includes an Oriental march, a song that Leschanah sings in the second act ("The Jewish Girl's Song"), Khadra's two dances, and four preludes. Once again the composer was rewarded with ovations and floral tributes. One critic reported that the music greatly heightened the mood of the drama, and a cartoonist depicted Procopé being held aloft by Sibelius.

The following year, five of the numbers were published as a concert suite, opus 51: 1. Oriental Procession; 2. Solitude (the accompaniment to Leschanah's song) ; 3. Night Music (the prelude to Act III) ; and 4. Khadra's Dance (the two dances now made into one *da capo* piece) . Little revision was needed except enrichment of the orchestration with a second flute and an oboe. The latter is so effective in the final number that one wonders why Sibelius did not think of it in the first place.

Belshazzar's Feast is the composer's only attempt to write pseudo-Oriental music, and it is a remarkably successful one. The Oriental Procession, with its interesting treatment of the percussion, and Khadra's Dance, with its solos for oboe and clarinet, indicate that Sibelius could have enjoyed great success as a composer of music for Hollywood. Adolf Paul was shrewd enough to recognize his friend's unusual abilities in this genre. Some years later, he made Sibelius many tempting proposals to contribute music to the growing motion-picture industry, all of which were declined.

"I never felt that Sibelius would be successful with a commissioned work," Mrs. Newmarch noted in her memoirs. Evidently she had forgotten about his music for the theater—fourteen works in all, if we include the one-act opera and the lengthy scores for the historical tableaux—and among these commissioned works we find both *Finlandia* and *Valse triste*.

In 1893, Sibelius had planned to write an opera, *The Building of the Boat*, based on cantos VIII and XVI from the *Kalevala*. Although he abandoned this scheme and turned to other sections of the legends for his *Lemminkäinen Suite*, the original idea still tempted his fancy. By 1906, the tone poem *Pohjola's Daughter*, opus 49, was ready, and he conducted it at a Siloti concert in St. Petersburg on December 29. It was dedicated to Robert Kajanus.

The title page of the original manuscript describes it (in German) as "a symphonic fantasy freely based on the famous *Kalevala* epos." When the full score was published during 1906, it contained a paraphrase of canto VIII, in which it is told how the aged hero Väinämöinen attempts to woo the Maid of Pohjola as she sits on a rainbow, weaving a fabric of gold. She craftily agrees to yield on the condition that he perform a series of difficult tasks to prove the power of his magic. The final one is to construct a boat from the splinters of her spindle and launch it without touching it. The old man's magic fails him at the crucial moment. He wounds himself with his ax and gives up in despair to seek a magic cure that will stanch the flow of blood.

Flodin felt that a program for *Pohjola's Daughter* could not be determined with any accuracy. Such enthusiastic writers of programmatic analyses as Gray, Newman, and Ringbom do not agree with this, but concur in providing their readers with "the names and numbers of all the players." For those who like to engage in this harmless though futile game, a brief glance at the composer's own outline for the plot of *The Building of the Boat* may provide some new ideas.[1]

The St. Petersburg critics were interested in the new tone poem and pronounced it a highly successful attempt to treat the *Kalevala* as Wagner had treated the Teutonic legends. In fact, some professed to find in it the strong influence of Wagner; others attributed the brilliant instrumental coloring to Rimsky-Korsakov. When Armas Järnefelt conducted it

[1] *See pages 55–6.*

a few months later in Stockholm, some Swedish critics detected shades of Tchaikovsky. Whatever the individual merits of these observations may be, the consensus of opinion was that in *Pohjola's Daughter* Sibelius had produced a magnificent piece of orchestration. In addition to the regular orchestra, he calls for piccolo, English horn, bass clarinet, double bassoon, two cornets, tuba, and harp.

During April 1907, a special concert of Hungarian and Finnish music was presented in Helsinki. The guest of honor was the Hungarian composer Ferdinand Rékay, who shared the podium with Kajanus, Järnefelt, Selim Palmgren, and Sibelius. For his own contribution, Sibelius selected what he called a "dance intermezzo," *Pan and Echo*, opus 53, which he had composed and conducted the previous year in Vaasa. Later he slyly confided to a friend: "There was not one note of Finnish music in it!"

Pan and Echo interested the critics less than its conductor. In spite of many later testimonials to the contrary, Sibelius was never famous as a master of the baton. Musicians found it difficult to follow his jerky, wooden beat. In attempting to correct this, Sibelius resorted to gestures that one critic found "exaggerated." Flodin thoroughly enjoyed the unexpected choreography. After noting that Sibelius made an elaborate motion to the audience for complete silence, Flodin continued: "He swung with his body, fenced with his arms, crooked his back, and fingers flew through the air—just as though he were Schnéevoigt."

In November, a composer who enjoyed an enviable reputation as a superior conductor visited Helsinki—Gustav Mahler. He led the Philharmonic Orchestra in a program of music by Beethoven and Wagner. Mahler was at that time a well-known—some have said tragic—figure in music and but a few years away from a heart attack that would prove fatal. Unlike Sibelius, he had been a child prodigy, and at the time of his visit to Finland he already had eight symphonies to his credit. It was inevitable that the two composers should meet, and Sibelius later recalled their exchange of opinions concerning the essence of the symphony as a form. For Sibelius, it was "the severity of style and the profound logic that created an inner connection between all of the motifs." Mahler's reply was: "No, the symphony must be like the world. It must embrace everything." Much can be found in Mahler's music to prove that he practiced what he preached. Several years after this meeting, Sibelius described his own Fourth Symphony as "a protest against the compositions of today." Mahler's "world-embracing" symphonies undoubtedly helped to stimulate this "protest."

According to Ekman, the environs of Järvenpää proved so stimulating that no sooner had Sibelius settled in his new home than he began work on his Third Symphony. It was not completed, however, until 1907, when he presented it for the first time in Helsinki at a concert given on September 26. Also on the program were *Pohjola's Daughter* and the suite from *Belshazzar's Feast*. Although the new symphony was cast in three movements, Flodin immediately pointed to the scherzo-cum-finale form of the last one. "Sibelius stands without doubt at the height of his art," he wrote. "He has cast all mannerisms aside and, whereas he used to repeat himself, he now reaches down into a new reservoir." Two months later, when Sibelius conducted his new symphony for a St.

Petersburg audience, one Russian critic styled it "a suite in the style of Mendelssohn . . . as monotonous as the Finnish landscape. It is full of sad melodies, depressing even for our ears."

However absurd the comparison with Mendelssohn may seem to some readers, it is worth noting that there were no references to Tchaikovsky. Indeed, the Third may be regarded as the beginning of Sibelius's attempt to break away from the style of the heavy-handed "Romantic" symphony. A more pastoral style of writing, in which the strings predominate, prevails. Gone are the grandiose effects requiring tuba, bass drum, and cymbals. Two of the composer's favorite devices, horn pedals and short fragments for woodwinds playing in thirds, are found everywhere. The binary form of the third movement suggests an attempt at greater concentration. The first movement especially contains some of his finest and most original themes.

In spite of its many undeniably fine qualities, the Third Symphony rivals the Sixth as Sibelius's least-popular work in this form. Even Rosa Newmarch and Olin Downes pronounced it his "weakest" symphony. In the United States, Karl Muck planned to perform it with the Boston Orchestra, but later changed his mind. Pierre Monteux actually rehearsed it with the same ensemble, but the performance never took place.

The Third Symphony was dedicated to Granville Bantock, and the original plan was for Sibelius to conduct its world *première* with the Royal Philharmonic Society in London during March 1907. Because it was not ready by that date, the composer's visit had to be postponed until February of the following year. At that time the critic for the *Musical Times* recorded his reactions: "One merit of the new symphony is its conciseness, an attribute for which one is thankful in these days of dreary debilitating diffuseness. This three-movement work, which occupies only twenty-seven minutes in perform-ance, is constructed on themes that are Scandinavian in char-acter and not without attractiveness."

During this second visit to England, Sibelius saw Mrs. Newmarch almost daily, and she noticed that he was suf-fering from a painful throat infection. Upon returning to Fin-land, he submitted to an unsuccessful exploratory operation, and in desperation consulted a German specialist. What Sibe-lius secretly feared to be cancer ultimately proved to be a malignant tumor, which was eventually removed. "Dear Brother," he wrote Christian from Berlin, "As far as my voice is concerned the doctor said that it will be good. . . . For the rest of my life I am forbidden alcohol. 'Alcohol hurts you.' As for tobacco, he didn't mind a small amount. But I will probably have to give that up too. I have now abstained for about a month. Life is quite another thing without this stimu-lant. I had never thought that such a thing would happpen."

It is futile to attempt to guess what passed through Sibelius's sensitive mind as he faced the possibility of a slow, painful death at the very prime of life. His despair must have been aggravated by the knowledge that he was the father of three children, with a fourth expected shortly. Furthermore, he possessed no tangible assets of any importance to provide for his family's future security.

Some have suggested that this crisis produced a con-siderable amount of soul-searching and self-evaluation—

Downes talks of relinquishments, abnegations, and purifications. It has also been said that their tragic and even morbid musical utterances are to be found in the string quartet known as *Voces intimae,* and especially in the Fourth Symphony. There are, however, no hints of such utterances in the incidental music to the play *Swanwhite,* which he conducted for the first time in the Swedish Theater on April 8, 1908.

Swanwhite is a fairy tale by August Strindberg, who completed it in 1901 while under the influence of Maeterlinck. He intended to write incidental music for it himself, but abandoned the idea when he learned that Sibelius had accepted a commission from the Swedish Theater. The central character is Swanwhite, a young girl who lives in a castle in which there are roses, doves, and a peacock. As a child, she was betrothed to a king whom she had never seen, and now she has a stepmother who is a sorceress. One day a young prince arrives in order to arrange for Swanwhite's marriage to the king. The inevitable happens—the two fall in love. After much *jeu,* the course of true love triumphs.

For the theater production, Sibelius composed fourteen numbers scored for the small ensemble he had employed in his original *Belshazzar* music. The critic Wasenius found it admirably suited to the mood of the play and observed with satisfaction that the composer had avoided writing for an orchestra of Straussian proportions.

The following year, Sibelius published his music to *Swanwhite* as a concert suite, opus 54. It consists of seven numbers completely revised and scored for an ensemble almost double the size of the original one. Much of the revision consists in an expansion of the original melodic ideas. For example, the wistful little waltz theme in "The Maid with the Roses" is sustained for twenty-five measures in the original score, while in the published suite it is stretched to a monotonous sixty-six measures.

During January 1909, St. Petersburg concert-goers heard another world *première* of a Sibelius composition. This time it was the tone poem *Night Ride and Sunrise*, opus 55, which Alexander Siloti conducted at one of his concerts. According to Sibelius, it was based on a motif that occurred to him while spending the winter of 1901 in Italy. The Russian critics were unimpressed by the new work; all agreed that it was monotonous. "This time there is no orchestral attraction," one wrote. "The contents of the piece do not correspond with its title. It is difficult to understand who is riding where, and why. Sibelius has not provided us with a cabby [*izvoschik*] in order to give his work direction."

The composer was evidently worried about the impression it would create. Mrs. Newmarch recalls: "Sibelius often spoke to me of this work; he regretted that I had no opportunity of hearing it. I remember that he once asked me whether it might lead people to expect in it a reflection from the older romanticism of Raff's day, whereas the music is concerned with the inner experiences of an average man riding solitary through the forest gloom; sometimes glad to be alone with nature; occasionally awe-stricken by the stillness or the strange sounds which break it; not filled with foreboding, but thankful and rejoicing in the daybreak." A solitary figure surrounded by the mysteries of nature was one of Sibelius's favorite subjects.

Night Ride and Sunrise is divided into two clearly

recognizable sections. After a short introduction, the "ride" begins, a galloping trochaic rhythm sustained by the strings for over three hundred measures. This rhythm moves constantly from one section of the strings to another, thus producing a singularly realistic impression of the horse's change of pace as it rounds a turn or encounters a hill. Over this we hear the "strange sounds"—sudden and unexpected outbursts by the woodwinds and brass, with held notes breaking off into little figures. The second section is a highly personalized "sunrise" in which the somber shades of night retreat ever so slowly before the approaching northern dawn, and it is accompanied by the inevitable bird calls.

In spite of its many undeniably fine qualities, *Night Ride and Sunrise* is one of Sibelius's most-neglected tone poems. His worry about the impression it would create was justified. Superficially it appears to be one of the most conventional and hackneyed works ever written, and anything less than a first-class performance only tends to heighten this first impression.

*"If this sort of thing continues, there will be
no such thing as correcting mistakes in
parts at a rehearsal—the composer will have
to furnish an affidavit with every
individual note. As modern ears become
accustomed to these things all standards will
be swept away."*   W. M. Humiston,
    on the Fourth Symphony

●

As interest in Sibelius began to
decline at a rapid rate in Germany, the opposite seemed to be
happening in England. At the beginning of 1909, the composer felt well enough to pay a third visit to "the country
without chauvinism." On February 13, he conducted *Finlandia* and *En Saga* at a concert given in Queen's Hall, London. Although Wood had given the first English performance
of *En Saga* three years earlier, it was considered the evening's
novelty. A critic for the *Musical Times* wrote: "It is a long
work and displays the composer in a serious mood. The thematic material is not striking, but the colour and unexpected-
ness of the orchestration and the eerie treatment fascinate the
attention and send the mind romancing. The strings are much
divided and the timpani are not employed—a reticence not
usual with modern composers."

During these years, Alfred Kalisch, a musical journalist, presided over the Music Club, which has been described as "a dressy concert-cum-supper affair." Its avowed purpose was to permit members to meet well-known composers and performing musicians in an informal atmosphere. The honored guests for 1909 were Claude Debussy, Vincent d'Indy, Arnold Schönberg, and Jean Sibelius. Many years later, Sibelius recalled meeting the two French composers in London and hearing some of their music, as well as compositions by Elgar and Bax. "All I heard confirmed my idea of the road I had traveled and had to travel," he commented. According to Törne, he said: "Debussy himself knew very well that he was neither grand nor profound. I know, because I have met him." It is unlikely that Debussy ever made such an admission. Perhaps Törne missed the point of a joke.

Sibelius, condemned to total abstinence, was anything but a convivial guest as he glumly watched the members of the Music Club enjoy their wine and cigars. Arnold Bax remembers the impression he created on this occasion: "Of all the human beings with whom in the course of my life I have become acquainted none, I should say, has altered more, during the last thirty years, than Sibelius. Physically he has changed much, but this apart, comparison of my impression of him in 1909 with that of 1936 might be of two totally different men. . . . The earlier Sibelius gave one the notion that he had never laughed in his life, and never could." Eugene Goossens, Jr., who also met him at this time, recalled in 1950: "Sibelius did not impress me at first sight, as did, for instance, Debussy. I recall him as a military figure with a chokingly high collar and a close-clipped, greying moustache

—the antithesis, in fact, of the rather benign figure of his recent pictures."

Sibelius remained in London during February and most of March, and was a frequent visitor at the homes of Henry Wood and Rosa Newmarch. In her memoirs, the latter has reproduced a letter from Aino Sibelius expressing her anxiety over her husband's state of mind. "I am glad that you are in London at this time," she wrote. "He is badly in need of such friends as you, and just now it is still more necessary for him when his life is going to take another course. This last year has been of great importance to him, and I hope, as you do, that it will show influence on his art also." Before leaving London for another visit to Paris and Berlin, Sibelius completed his String Quartet in D minor, opus 56, *Voces intimae*.

Voces intimae is Sibelius's only published work in this form. If, as it would appear, his life was taking another course, it is significant that he sought chamber music as the means of expressing his art in a more personal and concentrated form. Shortly after he returned to Finland, it was announced in the press that he was working on two other string quartets. These never saw the light of day—at least, not as string quartets.

Voces intimae is in five movements, and the subtle connecting links between these, plus the marked linear style that prevails throughout the entire work, have led students of Sibelius's music to associate it most closely with the Fourth Symphony. The undeniable similarity is strengthened by the over-all mood of tragic despair common to both works.

Yet, in spite of its many virtues, this quartet has never become solidly established in chamber-music literature. Some have claimed that this is because of its "modernity," but that seems rather far-fetched when we recall the current vogue of the six quartets of Béla Bartók. More than likely the reason why chamber-music groups do not play it or music-lovers request it is to be found in the fact that *Voces intimae* neither plays nor sounds like a string quartet. The impression produced on both players and listeners is that Sibelius wrote it with the strings of the symphony orchestra in mind.

Among the many minor compositions completed during this year we find eight songs to Swedish texts by Josephson, opus 57, the ten small piano pieces constituting opus 58, two songs for the Swedish Theater's production of *Twelfth Night,* opus 60, a new Ballet Scene (not to be confused with the one dating from Sibelius's student days in Vienna), and a funeral march for orchestra entitled *In Memoriam,* opus 59.

Referring to this last work, based on a motif that occurred to him while he was in Berlin in 1905, Sibelius later told Ekman: "The title may give the impression that I was thinking of the death of a particular person when I wrote it. This is not the case, however." Perhaps this was intended as an answer to Gray's previously published assertion that the composer had been impelled to write *In Memoriam* as the result of "a genuine bereavement, a personal loss, a great affliction." Why, one wonders, did Sibelius insist that he had nothing in mind when he wrote it? After his death, his eldest daughter, Mrs. Eva Paloheimo, assured me that it was written in memory of Eugen Schauman, the young Finnish patriot who assassinated Governor General Bobrikov on the steps of the Senate building in Helsinki in 1904. Sibelius's original intention in 1904 had been to write a Requiem Mass in memory of Schauman.

It is difficult to understand Gray's enthusiasm for this noisy, pretentious march for a large orchestra including tuba, bass drum, and cymbals. His countryman Ralph Wood finds it a blend of Beethoven's *"Eroica"* and Wagner's *Götterdämmerung,* but a blend that has lost the virtues of either. It was, of course, played at the composer's state funeral in 1957.

In addition to the works listed above, Sibelius composed incidental music to the Swedish drama *The Lizard* (*Ödlan*), by his friend Mikael Lybeck. For years, a certain amount of mystery has surrounded this music, which until recently was believed to have been lost. In 1915, the composer listed it as opus 29a; fifteen years later, he changed it to opus 8. It rightly belongs near opus 60. Interest in it was heightened when Sibelius later described it as "among the [compositions] most full of feeling I have ever written."

In the fall of 1908, Lybeck sent his friend a copy of his recently published play with the request that he compose music required in two scenes in the second act. Unlike the dramas of Adolf Paul and Arvid Järnefelt, which were cluttered with unnecessary action and quasi-philosophizing, *The Lizard* has a simple plot of the standard triangle variety:

Alban, the new master of the Eyringe estate, is deeply in love with a girl named Elisiv. The third member of the triangle is Alban's amorous and ghoulish cousin, Adla. Adla delights in wearing a masquerade costume representing a lizard, in order to terrify Elisiv.[1] In the first scene of the second act, Alban declares his love for Elisiv and serenades her on his violin. In the third, she imagines that her fiancé's parents have

[1] *The similarity in pronunciation between Adla and Ödlan was probably intentional.*

returned from the grave to warn her that the marriage can never take place. In the final act, Elisiv dies of a broken heart and the gloating "lizard" meets her death at the hands of Alban.

In an enthusiastic letter accepting the commission, Sibelius praised the play for its style and poetry. After numerous delays, including the trip to England, he started to work on it in July of the following year. The result was forty-three pages of music for string quintet and solo violin. The first part, thirty-seven measures in all, accompanies Alban's violin serenade. In the second part, however, Sibelius "spreads out," as he wrote Lybeck, in the musical background for the heroine's hallucinations.

The *première* took place in the Swedish Theater on April 6, 1910, with the composer conducting. "Nowhere does the music stand still," Wasenius wrote, "but it undergoes psychological transformations constantly, and at a tempo that gives it tremendous importance within the literature of theater music. And all this with a small string orchestra, and not the mass effects of present-day ensembles. This circumstance alone places the art of Sibelius in an even greater light."

It is far from coincidental that the music for *The Lizard* is scored for a chamber-music ensemble. As we have seen, it was written during a time when Sibelius's musical thoughts were proceeding along such lines, and he may well have employed in it some of the material from his two unfinished string quartets. As the music follows the pantomime on the stage closely, it is less effective as a detached concert piece. In spite of its warm first-night reception, the Swedish Theater soon dropped the play from its repertory. Sibelius presented his manuscript to Lybeck and promptly lost all interest in it.

In March 1910, a printed document marked "not for the public" began to circulate among the wealthy Finnish families. It was a petition signed by ten prominent citizens, including a banker, a publisher, a government official, and several University professors. The reader was informed that, though Sibelius had completely recovered from his illness, he was in sad financial straits. In view of his growing international reputation, the undersigned requested that the recipients of the letter help the composer in his hour of need. It is not known how much money this solicitation yielded, but it must have been considerable.

Two months later, the composer announced to the press that he had declined an invitation to compose a ballet entitled *The Bear Hunters* (*Karhun Tappajaiset*) for the Palace Theatre in London because he was working on a new symphony. "Perhaps I am too much of a hypochondriac," he confessed in a private letter. "But to waste on a few *pas* a motif that would be excellently suited to symphonic composition!"

Sibelius did, however, attempt to write another money-making *Valse triste,* and this time he took care to protect his royalty rights. When the Finnish National Theater presented a revised version of *Death* on March 8, 1911, two new numbers were added to the instrumental music. They were published during the same year as *Canzonetta* for strings and *Valse romantique* for small orchestra, both opus 62. Breitkopf & Härtel advertised them as "companion pieces to the celebrated *Valse triste*" and this may have induced Sir

Henry Wood to program them at a Queen's Hall concert in London. Their reception was distinctly on the cool side, and the critic for the *Musical Times* pronounced them "delicately scored and mildly fanciful, but otherwise not interesting."

When Wasenius asked Sibelius to comment on the report from England, the latter replied with some irritation: "Still, in the beginning didn't my *Valse triste* meet with even less success than these pieces? . . . On what grounds can I expect to be treated differently from the other great geniuses before me?" The irritation betrayed the intent. Before his retirement in 1926, he wrote many instrumental pieces of the same caliber as *Valse romantique,* and they all suffered similar fates. No more than any other composer was Sibelius able to analyze the chemistry of a "hit."

At the time when the new music to *Death* appeared, Sibelius yielded to one of Paul's many invitations to "make gold." Paul, still precariously clinging to his career as a dramatist, had written a new play in German, *The Language of the Birds* (*Die Sprache der Vögel*). It deals with one of King Solomon's many love affairs and a futile feminine attempt to wrest from him his secret in understanding the birds. Paul requested some wedding music for the third act "and, if you have time, some bird music." It is not known whether Sibelius obliged with the bird music, but the Wedding March was heard at the play's *première* in Vienna during March 1911. Neither the play nor the music produced the gold that Paul and Sibelius needed so desperately. For several years, Breitkopf & Härtel listed the Wedding March as a manuscript for rental; finally they returned it to the composer. Ten years later, Paul had ambitious schemes for an English production of his play. He wanted to use the music to *Belshazzar's Feast* and publish it in London with new titles, but the plan fell through.

Throughout the fall of 1910, Sibelius intimated to the press that his Fourth Symphony, opus 63, was nearing completion, but refused to give any clues as to its nature. By April 3 of the following year, it was ready, and he presented it at a concert of his own compositions in Helsinki. The public did not know that the composer had made extensive changes in the score after the final rehearsal, a fact that was probably responsible for a not very polished performance. Also on the program were *In Memoriam, Night Ride and Sunrise,* and an impressionist tone poem entitled *The Dryad,* opus 45, no. 1, which Sibelius had conducted earlier in Norway.

On the surface, the evening appeared to be a success. In addition to the usual floral tributes, the University Chorus serenaded the composer in the lobby. Their conductor, Heikki Klemetti, made a speech on behalf of Finland's youth and thanked Sibelius for all he had done for his country. But Furuhjelm later recalled the grimaces and head-shaking in the audience. The critics were polite, but not very enthusiastic. Kajanus said: "Things will be better for Sibelius thirty years from now."

Three days before the *première* of the Fourth Symphony, a Swedish newspaper published a preview of it by the composer's close friend and confidant, Baron Axel Carpelan. "One has nothing to compare it with . . ." he wrote, "not even among Sibelius's own works. . . . In its entirety, the symphony may be regarded as a protest against the prevailing style in music . . . above all, in Germany, the home of the symphony, where instrumental music is on its way to becoming mere technique, a kind of musical engineering that tries to cover up its own inner emptiness with an enormous mechanical apparatus." Carpelan was obviously voicing the composer's own feelings, for, one month later, Sibelius wrote to Mrs. Newmarch: "My Fourth Symphony is finished. It has twice been heard in concerts in Helsingfors. Although the work is by no means a concert item, it has brought me many friends. . . . It stands out as a protest against the compositions of today. Nothing, absolutely nothing of the circus about it." Sibelius's popularity was dwindling rapidly in Germany, and his "protest" was made especially against the music of Strauss and Mahler.

The Fourth Symphony has been many things to many people, but it has never been called a "circus." The Finnish critic Elmer Diktonius aptly called it the "Bark Bread Symphony," recalling days of famine when the poor were forced to adulterate flour with finely ground bark, the resulting loaves being rather unpalatable. The "Bark Bread Symphony" soon proved even more unpalatable abroad than at home. In Sweden, it was hissed; Sibelius recalled that a Danish audience "did nothing"; in England, the critics were "bewildered." Walter Damrosch prefaced the first American performance in 1913 with an apology from the podium! The performance, he added, was not intended to be an expression on his part of the merits of the symphony; he merely considered it his duty to give it a hearing. Some months later, Karl Muck rehearsed it eight times for a performance in Boston and then, returning the score to the Boston Orchestra's librarian, said: "I'm blest if I know what he wants." [2]

The Boston critics matched anger with stupidity, and thus they have been immortalized in Nicolas Slonimsky's *Lexicon of Musical Invective:* "Sounds like the awkward efforts of amateur composers with little or no training" . . . "ultra modern" . . . "cubist music" . . . "music of the twenty-first century" . . . "dissonant and doleful mutterings, generally leading nowhere" . . . "a mixture of musical quassia and wormwood, which suggests that the composer is dissatisfied with something—and so, probably, is the general public." When a guest conductor presented it in Berlin as late as 1933, he was informed: "No more Sibelius is wanted."

When Sir Henry Wood presented the Fourth with the Queen's Hall Orchestra in London during 1920, the critic Kalisch noted: "This work has not been heard since Sibelius conducted it before the war. It hardly proved more acceptable on this occasion. The work seems to express a sullen and unpleasant view of life in general. We were informed in the analytical programme that the *scherzo* is merry and buoyant, which causes one to wonder what sort of music Sibelius would write if he were depicting melancholy and discontent."

Those who object to Sibelius's episodic handling of his thematic material should find excellent pastures in the Fourth Symphony. But it is neither radical in form nor atonal in its use of dissonance. It is cast in four separate movements,

[2] *It should be noted, however, that no less an authority than Olin Downes later characterized the Muck performance as "a reading which I believe over the years was one of the best I ever heard."*

with the traditional positions of the second and third movements reversed. Although the interval of an augmented fourth appears throughout the work, it would be difficult to prove that the Fourth exhibits any evolutionary growth over the Third Symphony. It is scored for the modest ensemble found in the Third, with the addition of bells in the final movement.[3]

The most valid and significant observation encountered concerning the Fourth Symphony is that it does not sound like a symphony in the conventional sense of the word. There is not one honest orchestral *tutti* in it. Instead, Sibelius treats the different sections of the orchestra—woodwinds, brasses, and strings—as though they were entities unto themselves. The effect produced is one in which three chamber-music groups take turns playing, and rarely intrude upon one another's utterances. It would be a simple exercise to arrange this work for a string quintet without destroying any of the musical ideas. They would, in fact, stand revealed in the same intimate simplicity.

Can it be that in its early stages the Fourth Symphony was conceived as a string quartet? If so, then it is far less "enigmatic" than some have been led to assert. We have already seen that it was written during a period when Sibelius sought chamber music as a medium of expression. After *Voces intimae*, he wrote some chamber music for *The Lizard* and was reported working on two other string quartets. In attempting to adapt these chamber-music sketches for the needs of the symphony orchestra, Sibelius may have decided that to "spread them out" would involve obvious padding and the de-

---

[3] *Finnish conductors, with Sibelius as their authority, insist that the part written for* glocken *should be rendered on the* glockenspiel.

struction of his musical ideas. Thus, he hit upon the happy solution whereby he could preserve their essential character by regarding his orchestra as three chamber-music ensembles.

Shortly after the *première* of the Fourth Symphony, Wasenius wrote a special article in which he reproduced what he claimed to be the composer's own program to the new symphony. It was, he insisted, inspired by a trip to the Koli hills in Karelia which Sibelius had made earlier with his brother-in-law, the painter Eero Järnefelt. The specific object depicted, Wasenius continued, was the mountain known as Kolivaara, and he added that the several movements represented the composer's general impression of the mountain, the ascent, the view from the top, and the descent. The information was said to have come from "a highly reliable source." The fact that the symphony had been dedicated to Eero Järnefelt appeared to add some weight to the argument.

The following day, Sibelius published an emphatic denial of this interpretation. He had, he admitted, made some remarks to this effect in private, but they had been made on April Fool's Day. The critic insisted that Sibelius's program was no joke, and refused to make a retraction. In recent years, much scorn has been heaped on Wasenius for what he wrote, but one wonders what the true story was. Wasenius had been an enthusiastic supporter of the composer's music, and was not in the habit of printing falsehoods. Did Sibelius in an unguarded moment really tell the truth about his Fourth Symphony? Knowing his early enthusiasm for program music, which he kept to the very end of his creative years, the question merits serious consideration.

Törne once asked Sibelius whether he had a favorite

among his own works. "Be sure I have," was the answer, "but nobody will ever know which!" Törne suspected that it was the Fourth Symphony because Sibelius talked about it more than any other work. The fact that he requested that the third movement, *il tempo largo,* be played at his funeral appears to strengthen this suspicion.

Of all the Sibelius symphonies, the Fourth is most difficult to understand for both the musician and the listener. Completely lacking in surface appeal, it demands repeated hearings before becoming intelligible. For those willing to make the effort, the rewards can be most gratifying. It is, in my opinion, one of the great works in the symphonic literature of our century.

"Sibelius? Sibelius! My dear Downes,
I must tell you the truth. I prefer my music
without cod-liver oil!"

Charles Martin Loeffler

●

In January 1912, the Imperial Music Academy in Vienna offered Sibelius a position as teacher of composition. When we recall that his music had never been very highly regarded in Austria, this sudden and unexpected interest in him as a teacher is difficult to understand. "It did not cost the master a long struggle to decline it," Ekman writes. What happened was that the composer immediately made the news of the invitation known to the Finnish press, but withheld his decision for over one month. During this interval, his influential friends warned the Senate that unless his pension was increased, he would be compelled to leave Finland. When the Senate voted a yearly pension of five thousand marks (roughly $3,000), the papers joyfully announced: JEAN SIBELIUS REMAINS IN FINLAND.

During March, Sibelius conducted his Fourth Symphony at three consecutive concerts in Helsinki. Also on the program were the suite for strings entitled *Rakastava* and the *Scènes historiques II:* 1. The Chase; 2. Love Song; and 3. At the Drawbridge. A piece for unaccompanied mixed chorus entitled *People from Land and Sea* (*Män från slätten och havet*), opus 65, no. 1, was written for a Swedish music festival held in Vaasa during June. The South Finnish Student Corporation commissioned a *Song for the People of Uusimaa* (*Uusmaalaisten laulu*), and, in gratitude for it, elected Sibelius to honorary membership in their society.[1] Also completed were the three sonatinas, opus 67, which are generally regarded as his finest music for piano.

In the fall, Sibelius made a fourth visit to England in order to conduct in Birmingham, Liverpool, Manchester, Bournemouth, and Cheltenham. At the Birmingham Triennial Festival concert of October 1, he presented his Fourth Symphony and shared the podium with Sir Edward Elgar, who conducted *The Music Makers*.[2] In his introduction to the Newmarch memoirs, Granville Bantock claims that the Fourth was commissioned for this festival.

Mrs. Newmarch attended the final rehearsal of the Fourth Symphony with Frederick Delius, who drawled: "Damn it, this is not conventional music." Later he amplified his views on Sibelius for his own biographer: "A lot of his work is too complicated and thought out. I've no use for that sort of writing. I've written pages of it myself—paper music

---

[1] *As a student, Sibelius had joined its Swedish equivalent, the Nyland Student Corporation.*

[2] *Oddly enough, Elgar and Sibelius never became more than acquaintances. The Finnish composer once said: "Elgar wrote pages of magnificent music, and then, without warning, lapsed into a few bars of vulgarity, only to recover himself as though he had never written a bar below his best." It is a strange observation coming from one who wrote thousands of bars that were decidedly below his best. Elgar declined an invitation to attend a reception for Sibelius in 1921, but was delighted to welcome Richard Strauss to London some years later.*

—but I had the sense to burn them. . . . The English like that sort of thing just as they like vogues for this and that. Now it's Sibelius, and when they're tired of him they'll boost up Mahler and Bruckner." Peter Warlock (Philip Heseltine) was considerably more enthusiastic in a letter to a friend. "Sibelius's new symphony is absolutely original," he wrote, "quite in a class by itself and uninfluenced by anything, save Nature. It struck me as being genuine 'Nature Music.' It is very strange and mysterious, but at the same time a work of great beauty which one could appreciate more and more on repeated hearings."

The Fourth Symphony, however, left most of its English listeners puzzled. Among the more charitable critiques, we find the following: "Sibelius's symphony brought us into another world—one with which most of us are so unfamiliar that we stumbled in our endeavour to understand. The idiom of the music and its form—with ends that did not seem to finish—left one in bewilderment. We shall be prepared to rank ourselves with its admirers when we are more familiar with its peculiar mode of expressing temperament."

It had been a highly successful visit, and Sibelius accepted a commission to compose a choral work for the festival to be held in Gloucester the following year. En route to Finland, he presented his Fourth to an undemonstrative audience in Copenhagen. There he was asked by the Danish publisher Wilhelm Hansen to write music for a "tragic pantomime" entitled *Scaramouche* by Poul Knudsen and Mikael Trepka Bloch. Strictly speaking, *Scaramouche* is not a pantomime, for it contains a considerable amount of dialogue. The simple story tells how Blondelaine, the beautiful young wife of Leilon, is bewitched by an evil and deformed violinist named Scaramouche. After the violinist seduces her, Blondelaine kills him. Overcome with madness, she then dances until she drops dead in the arms of her husband.

Although Sibelius completed his score in 1913, Hansen did not publish it (as opus 71) until five years had elapsed. The *première* at the Royal Theater of Copenhagen took place on May 12, 1922. Unlike most of Sibelius's music for the theater, that for *Scaramouche* seems to have no particular character of its own. One suspects that he found it difficult to work up any real enthusiasm for his task. It is, however, competently written, and it follows the stage action closely. In 1921, Sibelius planned to revise his music as a concert suite, but he soon gave up this idea.

In 1909, Adolf Paul published a little comedy in the Spanish style entitled *Blue Vapor* (*Blauer Dunst*), for which he also wrote some songs and dances. Prior to its Hamburg *première*, he asked Sibelius to arrange for a small orchestra a few tunes that he himself had invented; he promised not to reveal that he had had a hand in it. Whether Sibelius complied with this request is not known. In all events, *Blue Vapor* as a play turned out to be a failure, and Paul decided to commission a Count Birger Mörner to adapt it as a comic-opera libretto in Swedish translation. "Dear Janne," he wrote in December 1912, "I am glad that I have given you a libretto you like. B.M. was quite enthusiastic about adapting it as a libretto. Please do it, Janne." The following March, Paul exulted: "With a new opera by you I shall be able to take on any first-rate publishing house. . . . Sign the contract I sent you. I am giving you sixty per cent since you ask for only fifty. You should have the text by now."

In April, the Helsinki papers announced that Mörner had completed the libretto and that Sibelius had agreed to write the music. But the composer refused either to confirm or to deny the report, stating that he had not seen the text and consequently could not say whether it was suitable. At the end of the year, Paul made one final plea: "Don't you want to write a *commedia dell' arte* with me, Janne?" Evidently *Blue Vapor* was one of the composer's "butterflies" which failed to materialize because of too much advance publicity.

The only new composition that Sibelius conducted in Finland during 1913 was a short tone poem entitled *The Bard,* opus 64, which he revised for publication the following year. The important role given to the harp as the solo instrument, with simple chords replacing the customary virtuoso passages, suggests that the composer desired to evoke the image of some legendary musician playing on a primitive instrument. His inspiration may well have been Runeberg, whose poem of the same name tells how the Bard, after performing for many years for the pleasure of noble folk, returns to his home and dies after playing one final chord.

After his fourth visit to England, Sibelius told the Finnish press: "Next September I have been requested to conduct in the Gloucester Cathedral a new work for chorus and orchestra which I shall compose this winter." But it turned out to be still another "butterfly," and by the end of the year he wrote to Mrs. Newmarch: "I cannot go to Gloucester because I have no new choral work to offer. So far I have no inspiration to write one, and cannot, and will not, force myself."

On the following September 10, 1913, however, Sibelius was represented in Gloucester by a "new" composition entitled *Luonnotar*, opus 70, described as a tone poem for soprano and orchestra. The soloist was the famous Finnish singer Aino Ackté, to whom the work was dedicated. It is likely that Sibelius had completed it by the end of 1910, when it was announced in the Finnish papers that Mme Ackté and the composer would shortly present a new tone poem in Munich. It was not heard in Finland until January 1914.

The text for *Luonnotar*—which may be freely translated as meaning *Spirit of Nature*—deals with the creation of the world according to the first canto of the *Kalevala*. The Maiden of the Air, weary of her lonely life as a virgin, sinks to the surface of the ocean, where she is made heavy with child. When, after seven long centuries, she is still unable to deliver her child, she invokes the aid of Ukko. Miraculously, a teal appears and builds a nest on her knee. The heat generated by the bird's egg becomes so unbearable that the Maiden—she has now become the Water-Mother—spills the nest into the ocean, with the consequence that the egg is shattered.

> But a wondrous change came o'er them,
> From the cracked egg's upper fragment,
> Rose the lofty arch of heaven.
> From the yolk, the upper portion,
> Now became the earth's bright lustre;
> From the white, the upper portion,

Rose the moon that shines so brightly;
Whatso in the egg was mottled,
Now became the stars in heaven.[3]   (1, 231, 235–42)

"The new Sibelius tone poem was sung in Finnish by Mme. Ackté," wrote the critic for the *Musical Times,* "but not even the English translation supplied made the subject very intelligible. . . . The orchestral undercurrent seemed more interesting than the vocal part, but, as with most of this composer's works, one has to exert faith that there is more in the music than is apparent on one hearing." Sibelius always regarded *Luonnotar* with special affection. Shortly after the Gloucester performance, he wrote to Mrs. Newmarch: "It strikes me more particularly that musicians are still writing in the post-Wagerian style—with the same laughable pose and the still more laughable would-be profundity. Perhaps you know that Mme Ackté sang a new work by me at the Gloucester Festival. Now this work is written in 'my own' style, for which, apart from my friends, I get so little recognition."

Indeed, *Luonnotar* must be regarded as one of the composer's most personal and individual expressions in music. The short wavering figure for strings with which it begins establishes the dominant mood, the "eternal silence of the infinite" which terrified Pascal. The subtle treatment of the difficult part for voice shows how far Sibelius had traveled along his "way" since writing *The Rapids-Shooter's Brides* (1897), a work of similar proportions. The text for *Luonnotar* is available in German translation, but if it is to

[3] *The text of the tone poem ends here. The child turns out to be Väinämöinen, who finally succeeds in effecting his own delivery.*

be appreciated properly, the tone poem should be performed in Finnish. Relatively unknown abroad, it is especially dear to the *cognoscenti*. Gray calls it "one of the highest pinnacles in the whole range of Sibelius's creations, and consequently in the entire range of modern music."

In the letter to Mrs. Newmarch in which Sibelius discussed his *Luonnotar,* he also spoke of plans to "work and listen abroad" and added that he might visit London as a tourist. These plans were never realized because of an unexpected and extremely tempting invitation to visit the United States. Ekman has written that "the Americans were anxious not to be behind their Anglo-Saxon brothers in Europe." Nothing could be more misleading.

By 1914, the Americans were anything but behind their Anglo-Saxon brothers. They had, as we have seen, been the first to give this new Finnish music a hearing. After Frank Van der Stucken's Cincinnati performance of the *King Kristian II* music in 1900, Frederick Stock and the Chicago Symphony Orchestra played *The Swan of Tuonela* and *Lemminkäinen's Homeward Journey*—they were known as "legends"—during the following year. In Boston, about a dozen Sibelius compositions, including three symphonies, were heard between 1904 and 1913—under the batons of Max Gericke, Karl Muck, and Max Fiedler. In New York, Walter Damrosch and his New York Symphony Society, Josef Stransky and the Philharmonic Society, and Modeste Altschuler with the short-lived Russian Symphony Orchestra helped to make the composer's name known. Altschuler conducted the Third Symphony in New York one month before Sibelius introduced it in England. Arturo Vigna conducted the first American performance of *Finlandia* in 1905 at a concert in the Metropolitan Opera House. One year later, Maude Powell played the Violin Concerto with the Philharmonic Society; she subsequently repeated it on a transcontinental tour.

Valse triste, Finlandia, and Breitkopf & Härtel had done their work well. If the American musical organizations were not exactly fighting to lure Sibelius to their shores, the Helsinki papers did report in June 1913 that the composer had declined an invitation to conduct at an international music festival to be held in New York. He had, however, accepted honorary membership in the National Music Society and had agreed to join such well-known composers as Gabriel Pierné and Max Reger in contributing songs to be used by American school children.

The inspiration for this project came from the Silver Burdett Company, who commissioned Professor Horatio Parker of Yale University to edit their Progressive Music Series. Parker visited Europe in search of original material from well-known composers, and persuaded Sibelius, among others, to be a contributor. The result was the so-called *Three Songs for American Children*—"Autumn Song," "The Sun upon the Lake Is Low," and "A Cavalry Catch."

In August, a second American invitation was extended, and was accepted. Sibelius agreed to compose and conduct a work for chorus and orchestra lasting about fifteen minutes for a music festival to be held in Norfolk, Connecticut, during June 1914. The invitation came from a wealthy music-lover named Carl Stoeckel, who had established on the grounds of his estate what he fondly called an

"American Bayreuth." Stoeckel, the son of a German-born music teacher at Yale, had become a patron of the arts thanks to his marriage with the daughter of his employer, a businessman named Robbins Battell.

It is entirely possible that Professor Parker suggested that Stoeckel invite the Finnish composer to the festival. At all events, Yale University informed Sibelius that they desired to confer on him the honorary title of Doctor of Music. This proposal was made well in advance of his departure for the United States, and the composer was requested to keep this information in the strictest confidence. Sibelius immediately wrote a letter accepting the award. Perhaps it was only a coincidence, but the Alexander University in Helsinki decided to make a similar award *in absentia* before the Yale ceremony could take place.[4]

At the end of May 1914, Sibelius arrived in New York. According to Stoeckel's unpublished account, his guest did not leave the ship until one hour after the other passengers had disembarked. Stoeckel was immediately impressed by the composer's air of distinction, and noted that his clothes, linen, and shoes were all of the finest quality. During their many visits to New York's finer restaurants, he was astonished to discover that Sibelius completely abstained from all alcoholic beverages and declined to smoke tobacco. As soon as the Finnish composer had been installed in the "blue room" of the Battell mansion, Stoeckel arranged to have a village barber shave him every morning because Sibelius had

[4] *Rather curiously, Sibelius told Ekman many years later:* "Yale University wanted to give me a pleasant surprise by informing me of its decision to confer the honorary degree of doctor on me only on my arrival in America."

said that he never shaved himself. Stoeckel had an aristocrat on his hands, and thoroughly enjoyed pampering him.

Sibelius was also impressed. "Here I am surrounded by luxury and wealth," he wrote to his brother, Christian. "I am regarded as an important person, and on many occasions it's difficult to present the correct 'profile.' I enjoy an enormous fame here in America and I think that a planned tour (a secret) of forty to fifty concerts would succeed. Then I could pay off both your debts and my own. . . . My new composition—not *Rondo der Wellen*, but *Aallottaret*—is tremendous. We all know my modesty! This Norfolk is a mixture of Finland and Italy, or Algiers. Here there are trees of all kinds, leather stockings, mountains, and rivers—Negroes and whites, Methodists, Quakers, and Lutherans! The Housatonic River is like the Rhine. It's a colossal country. The Stoeckel aristocrats are enormously wealthy and well educated. . . . Their house, one of the oldest in America (150 years). That's a lot here where all are self-made men. Madame is from a noble French family. You can imagine how large their estate is when there is one in Canada *larger* than England (minus Scotland)."

For the Norfolk concert on June 4, Sibelius was given the first half of the program. He conducted *Pohjola's Daughter*, excerpts from the music to *King Kristian II*, *The Swan of Tuonela*, *Finlandia*, *Valse triste*, and the new commissioned work—not for chorus and orchestra, but a tone poem listed on the program as *Aallottaret* (*Nymphs of the Ocean*), a title derived from the *Kalevala*. One year later, it was published as opus 73 under the title *The Oceanides* and dedicated to Mr. and Mrs. Stoeckel.

The select invited audience rose to greet the composer as instructed in the program. This touching gesture and the prolonged applause following each number—especially for *Valse triste* and *Finlandia*—brought tears to Sibelius's eyes. Stoeckel was told that he wept backstage. Years later, Sibelius recalled that this was "a high-class audience, representative of the best that America possessed among lovers of music, trained musicians, and critics. The most inspired setting for the appearance of an artist."

What apparently has not been widely known up to now is that there are two completely different versions of *The Oceanides*. The first was sent to Stoeckel before Sibelius's departure for the United States, and was never performed.[5] Sibelius carried with him the second version, which was subsequently published. Although the two are somewhat alike in their general outlines, they are different in the working out of the thematic material and in details of orchestration.

The orchestral coloring in the published version of *The Oceanides* is even richer than that found in *Pohjola's Daughter*. In addition to the regular orchestra, Sibelius calls for English horn, bass clarinet, contra bassoon, four timpani, glockenspiel (*Stahlstäbe* in the score), triangle, and two harps. The themes and orchestration, with muted string tremolos and harp harmonics and glissandos, bear more than a superficial resemblance to Debussy's impressionist style, and especially to *La Mer*. Perhaps Sibelius felt that the first title he selected for his tone poem, *Rondo der Wellen* (*Rondo of the Waves*), was too close to Debussy. He later

[5] *This manuscript now belongs to Yale University.*

told Ringbom: "The title [*The Oceanides*] has reference to Homeric mythology, and not to characters in the *Kalevala*. The Finnish title of the work, *Aallottaret*, is merely a translation." [6]

The Oceanides is not Sibelius's only venture into impressionist pastures; an earlier tone poem, *The Dryad*, is strikingly similar at times to the *Prélude à l'après-midi d'un faune*. It is, however, Sibelius's most advanced move in this direction and a work of haunting beauty. Gray refers to this stylistic departure as an example of what he calls musical "pointillism," superficially similar to the technique of the impressionists. It is an opinion that not everyone will share. Once when Sibelius met his pupil Törne in Paris, he said: "I longed for unmuted trumpets and undivided and unmuted strings! These people seem afraid of anything that is immediately given to us; their interest is practically confined to the recherché." In *The Oceanides*, he eloquently betrays that for a brief spell he, too, was attracted to the *recherché*.

At Norfolk, Sibelius was introduced to many important figures in American musical life. These included the conductor Walter Damrosch, the music critic H. E. Krehbiel, the violinist Maude Powell, who had helped to popularize the Violin Concerto, and such well-known singers as Alma Gluck, Sophie Braslau, and Herbert Witherspoon. During a visit to Boston, Stoeckel gave a sumptuous banquet in honor of his guest. To it were invited many of the critics who had recently heaped scorn on the Fourth Symphony. Also present

[6] "*The new composition written at Järvenpää early in 1914 was the fascinating* Rondo of the Waves, *which finally appeared as* The Oceanides" (*Newmarch, p. 35*).

were the composers George W. Chadwick, Henry Hadley, Frederick S. Converse, and Charles Martin Loeffler. Loeffler once remarked to Olin Downes that he preferred his symphonies without cod-liver oil. Downes later remarked: "If only friend Loeffler's music had but a drop of that same oil in it! How much less dated would it sound today!"

"Yesterday in Boston they gave a huge dinner for me at which most of the American composers were present," Sibelius wrote to his brother. "From here to Norfolk, where dinner on Friday will be given for two hundred and fifty persons (among others, Taft, former president). Then to Niagara (two hundred Finnish miles). I travel only by auto! My robe for the New Haven ceremonies is the same as that of a PhD *honoris causa*—a black robe with blue trim. A beret hat. When I become a doctor, I will receive a pink hood. . . . I am enjoying this! For once I have enough servants. . . . Negroes, whites, and maid servants of all colors."

The Yale ceremonies were accompanied by the traditional academic pomp and splendor. A special sixty-five-piece orchestra entertained the spectators with renditions of *Finlandia, Spring Song,* and *Valse triste.* After this last and somewhat inappropriate selection, there was a storm of applause. Professor Parker then read a flattering citation that stressed the intensely national character of Sibelius's music, which was "yet in sympathy with the mood of the West." Twenty years later, the composer referred to Parker as "one who had for many years been active in behalf of my art," a fact that I have been unable to verify.

Stoeckel was content to bask in all this reflected glory, and he derived great pleasure in presenting his guest with any object that caught his fancy. As the departure date, June 18, neared, he presented him with jewels and toys for Mrs. Sibelius and the children. Sibelius in turn presented his host with the first, unplayed manuscript of *Aallottaret,* and later hailed him as "a combination of Sinbad and Harun al Raschid."

There is no doubt that this visit to the United States greatly impressed the Finnish people. Here was additional proof that their national composer's art had become universal. Upon arriving in Europe, Sibelius gave glowing reports of his sojourn in the New World and announced that he had been forced to agree to return there the following year to conduct an extended series of concerts. This undoubtedly was the project he had planned in order to pay off his debts and those of his brother, Christian. The tour was canceled after the outbreak of World War I.

The composer's visit did not seem to have had any noticeable effect upon his popularity in the United States. American conductors showed no interest in playing *The Oceanides.* Two months after Sibelius had returned to Finland, *Current Opinion* reported: "Almost unheralded and unnoticed by the public at large, Jean Sibelius, Finland's greatest composer, visited the United States recently to attend the Norfolk Festival."

"The soil in which your art has its roots has already become a whole country; now the country is becoming a world—and the world yours."
                    Mikael Lybeck
                    (December 8, 1915)

•

December 8, 1915, was to mark Sibelius's fiftieth birthday. Long before the day arrived, elaborate plans were made to honor him throughout Finland. He had for many years been unchallenged as his country's greatest composer. Among his most famous contemporaries, Robert Kajanus and Armas Järnefelt were now devoting most of their energies to conducting, and Ilmari Krohn was seeking his place in the sun as a teacher and musical scholar. Sibelius's astonishing success both at home and abroad inspired younger men to follow in his footsteps —Erkki Melartin, Ernst Mielck, Selim Palmgren, Toivo Kuula, and Leevi Madetoja—but their achievements appeared insignificant when compared with those of the "Master."

By virtue of the life pension that he had been receiving since 1897, Sibelius was in fact Finland's official "poet laureate," as he later described himself. The pension imposed no duties or obligations, and Sibelius was free to supplement his income in any way he saw fit. Consequently he accepted many commissions for theater music and a variety of ceremonial pieces. His royalties from domestic and foreign publishers were increasing with every year. On at least one occasion, as we have already seen, when these failed to provide for his daily needs, his friends conducted an unofficial fund-raising campaign among wealthy Finnish citizens.

The Finnish people had invested generously in furthering the career of Sibelius, and they were content with the dividends their money had earned. In Helsinki alone, between 1892 and 1915, Sibelius conducted more than thirty concerts of his own music, and Kajanus helped to keep much of it alive on the programs of his orchestra's regular subscription concerts. Even more important were the "folk" or "popular" concerts by which Kajanus soon made the name of Sibelius a household word in Finland.

Among the compositions that soon became perennial favorites at these popular concerts we find the following: the *Karelia* music, *Spring Song, Finlandia,* the incidental music to *King Kristian II, En Saga, The Swan of Tuonela, Lemminkäinen's Homeward Journey,* and, most popular of them all, *Valse triste.* It should be noted that these same compositions were among the first to be heard abroad. They all predate the Third Symphony (1907), and consequently fall within what many writers have labeled Sibelius's early or "Romantic" period.

The mechanism of musical success is difficult enough to analyze within one country; it is even more difficult on an international level. Music is a business as well as an art, and the distance between a composer's manuscript and the living sound it represents is frequently a long and costly one. Once Breitkopf & Härtel were convinced that they could make a profit out of this Finnish composer's art, they served as his chief publisher. By 1912, their catalogue of Sibelius's music, most of which was available in a wide variety of arrangements, ran to twenty-three pages. They even acted as agents for a bust of the composer by Munsterjhelm measuring eighteen centimeters in height. A copy in bronze sold for one hundred German marks, a cheaper one in plaster for only twenty.

The Finnish newspapers were soon reporting the results of Breitkopf & Härtel's advertising campaign. Hardly a day passed without one or more notices concerning performances of Sibelius's music in such centers of culture as Heidelberg, London, Munich, Frankfurt, Prague, Brussels, Chicago, Boston, St. Petersburg, Berlin, New York, Manchester, Hamburg, Rome, Moscow, Vienna, and Paris. In 1910, many of the middle-aged citizens of Hämeenlinna must have been astonished to read that "Janne" Sibelius's *Finlandia* had been heard in Shanghai.

Although a majority of the Finns was quite willing to believe that Sibelius was a great symphonist, only a small number of them was familiar with the symphonies and pretended to understand them. As a student in Berlin, Sibelius had told Paul that his mission as an artist was to "give to everybody." In such compositions as *The Song of the Athenians, Finlandia, To the Fatherland,* and *The Liberated Queen,* he eloquently voiced the national aspirations of his countrymen. By 1915, Sibelius the composer had become Finland's unofficial First Citizen, and on December 8 the people were to acknowledge him as such.

Sibelius was busy and excited as he prepared for the great event. On June 21, he sent the choral conductor Heikki Klemetti a brief sketch of his life and a list of his compositions. "This is absolutely important," he wrote. "I will discuss my genealogy. Don't leave anything out, because up to now there has been no information concerning this at home—especially that there were musicians in both branches of my family.[1] Write if you need more details." Among his major accomplishments and honors he listed the first performance of *Kullervo*, his temporary appointment as a substitute for Faltin at the University, the Legion of Honor, his conducting at Heidelberg in 1902, membership in the Swedish Music Academy (1905) and the Music Association of North Staffordshire (1908), and his two honorary doctorates. In preparing a list of his compositions by opus numbers up to the Fifth Symphony, opus 82, Sibelius left thirty numbers unassigned. He never completed this list until after his retirement.

His own contribution to the festivities was to be a gala concert in which he would conduct his Fifth Symphony for the first time. "As you know," he revealed to Schnéevoigt, "my relations with Breitkopf & Härtel are finished, and I have now composed minor pieces (about forty!) for Nordic publishers. This has disturbed my work on the new piece for

[1] *He had obviously forgotten about the long, unsigned article in the* Finsk *biografisk handbok (Helsinki, 1903), in which his musical ancestors were discussed in great detail.*

the 8th of December. I hope that I will be able to finish it in time." It was completed in time, but, as with the Fourth Symphony, Sibelius had to make last-minute revisions during the final rehearsal.

He also included on the program for his birthday concert the tone poem he had written for Mr. Stoeckel, *The Oceanides,* and the two Serenades for violin and orchestra, opus 69, with Richard Burgin as the unnamed soloist. The concert, of course, had been sold out long in advance, and Sibelius had to repeat the program three times for the general public during subsequent weeks.

Following a standing ovation and the presentation of laurel wreaths, a select group of friends and dignitaries gave a testimonial banquet in the composer's honor. By virtue of his rank, State Senator Hjelt opened the speechmaking with an expression of gratitude on the part of the Finnish people. There followed personal reminiscences by Sibelius's boyhood friend Professor Werner Söderhjelm, Robert Kajanus, Mikael Lybeck, the singer Ida Ekman, and others. Then came the reading of several laudatory poems written especially for the occasion. For many days, the press reproduced congratulatory wishes from all corners of Finland, and even from abroad. Numerous other anniversary concerts were given in Helsinki and in the smaller Finnish cities.

One of the most important results of these 1915 celebrations was the beginning of the gigantic amount of Sibelius *Wissenschaft* which has accumulated through the years. Otto Andersson dedicated three numbers of his Swedish-language *Tidning för Musik* (nos. 14–16, December 1915) to Sibelius. With a careful eye to detail, Andersson prepared a chronological table of the composer's life, the most complete list of his compositions to that date, articles dealing with genealogy, etc. As far as factual information is concerned, this first attempt at serious Sibelius scholarship constitutes the foundation upon which all later biographies rest.

The first full-length study of the composer's life and music was originally intended to be published in time for the birthday ceremonies, but it did not appear until the following year. It is the Swedish-language study by Erik Furuhjelm entitled *Jean Sibelius: Hans tondiktning och drag ur hans liv* (*Jean Sibelius: His Music and a Sketch of His Life*), which also appeared in a Finnish translation by the composer Leevi Madetoja. In 1915, Sibelius displayed none of the reluctance to permit others to examine his early student compositions which characterized his attitude after his retirement. He cheerfully deposited with his first biographer all of the music he could find. Furuhjelm was especially interested in the compositions written before *Kullervo* (1892), and devoted half of his book to their study, all copiously illustrated with musical examples. For anyone interested in the composer's early music, this book is unique in the Sibelius literature.

Remembering that Furuhjelm published his study as a tribute to Sibelius on his fiftieth birthday, we may pardon him for the undue importance he gives the early compositions. Like most of the Finnish writers who have followed him, he is rarely critical of his subject's poorest works. What he does not like he skips over hurriedly to dwell on the merits of works that interest him. On a few rare occasions, however, Furuhjelm finds it impossible to repress sly remarks about

Valse triste which indicate that he did not have a very high regard for its musical worth.

Andersson's and Furuhjelm's studies both terminate with the first performance of the Fifth Symphony. It proved to be the composer's most troublesome work in this form, and he revised it twice—in 1916 and 1919—before it was published by Wilhelm Hansen in Denmark. It has also proved to be Sibelius's most troublesome symphony for the analysts to explain, and none of them is absolutely certain whether it should be regarded as being in three movements or four.

Although the movements are not numbered in the published score, it appears that there are three—1. *Tempo molto moderato;* 2. *Andante mosso, quasi allegretto;* and 3. *Allegro molto*—and the pauses are indicated between them. In the first movement, however, the tempo changes to *Allegro moderato* beginning with the fifth measure after the letter N, and at this point the lettering begins all over again.

Gray regards these two sections as one single, indivisible movement, with the second constituting a built-in *scherzo* somewhat similar to the final movement in the Third Symphony. As for beginning again with the letter A at the section marked *Allegro moderato,* he explains that Sibelius would have exhausted the alphabet before the end of the first movement, and that this seemed a suitable place to begin all over again. But, as Simon Parmet has noted, composers and publishers do not generally follow this practice: after exhausting the alphabet they begin again with either AA, BB, CC, etc., or A^1, B^1, and C^1.

In 1947, Ringbom attempted to settle the question by consulting the composer. "In reply to my question," he wrote, "Sibelius stated that in view of the fact that both parts are based on the same thematic material, he regarded the whole as one movement, though he did not seek to impose this interpretation, as the second part had very clearly the character of a *scherzo*." If Sibelius possessed the manuscripts of the first two versions of the symphony, he refused to permit scholars to examine them.

Whether the Fifth Symphony is to be regarded as consisting of three movements or four is an academic point, for the music remains unchanged. Furuhjelm, who was present when the first version was heard in 1915, recalled that it was in four movements with a definite pause between the first two. One year later, when Sibelius conducted the second version—"in its definitive form"—the critic Wasenius noted that the first two movements had been joined and a coda "crammed with dissonances" added to the finale. Both changes, he felt, were unfortunate.

In a letter (probably to Axel Carpelan) dated May 20, 1918, Sibelius described his work on the second and final revision: "The Vth symphony in a new form— practically composed anew—I work at daily. Movement I entirely new, movement II reminiscent of the old, movement III reminiscent of the end of I movement of the old. Movement IV the old motifs, but stronger in revision. The whole, if I may say so, a vital climax to the end. Triumphal."

The curious thing about this letter is that the composer obviously regarded his symphony as consisting of four movements at that time. Furthermore, his reference to "movement III reminiscent of the end of I movement of the old" would seem to indicate that he intended to detach the *scherzo* section of the first movement and put it in its traditional place, before the finale. Fortunately, the Helsinki City Orchestra possesses a set of manuscript parts for the second version which were altered to conform to the final one. From these we learn that the only important differences between the two consist of a rescoring of the slow movement and the addition to the finale of the grandiose closing measures that we know today.

The first movement, with its built-in *scherzo*, is by far the most interesting part of the Fifth Symphony. The slow movement, which recalls the one found in the Third Symphony, consists of variations on a short theme or rhythm, with the woodwinds in thirds enjoying the dominant role. In one of the variations Sibelius lapses into an "Italianesque" passage that seems foreign to his general melodic style. Also, on two occasions the heroic theme of the finale—frequently associated with the popular tune "Oh, Dry Those Tears"— is anticipated in the bass. When it does appear in the final movement for strings and horns in thirds, it is employed with stunning effect as one of those never-ending themes that can be brought to a halt only by resorting to a series of six crashing chords for the entire orchestra. As they do not fall upon anticipated beats, the symphony comes to an end before the listener realizes it.

The Fifth Symphony ranks among the composer's most popular works in this form. Gone is the brooding introspection of the Fourth Symphony; there is little here to suggest that Sibelius was preoccupied with a chamber-music style. Because its general mood has been most frequently characterized as bright and heroic, some writers have professed to see in it a musical prophecy of Finland's coming struggle for independence. Others have claimed that it is a profoundly moving evocation of the coming of spring and the quintessence of the spiritual mood that had dictated Sibelius's creative work in the preceding years.

Musicians generally shun the verbiage of the writers of program notes. Sibelius's good English friend Granville Bantock was an exception. Concerning the Fifth, he wrote: "In the music of this symphony we are brought face to face with the wild and savage scenery of his native land, the rolling mists and fogs that hover over the rocks, open lakes and fir-clad forests; while in the continuous rumble of the threatening storms and war's alarms we are made to feel how the iron has entered the soul of this hard land where winter holds its relentless grip for seven or eight months of the year."

The forty minor pieces that Sibelius wrote before his birthday have nothing in common with his Fifth Symphony. Nor do they convince us that, as the years advanced, the composer became more selective in seeking self-expression. Among his more meritorious smaller pieces we find two for violin or cello and orchestra entitled *Cantique* and *Devotion*, opus 77; a *Sonatine* in E major for violin, opus 80; and the five part-songs constituting opus 84, which he composed for the M.M. Choral Society.

The rest are undistinguished little solo pieces for piano or violin bearing such titles as *Humoresque, Consolation, Affettuoso, Capricietto, Pièce enfantine, Dance idyll,*

Sibelius the composer-conductor at a rehearsal, 1915

At the Festival of Nordic Music. Copenhagen, 1919. From left to right: Fredrik Schnedler-Petersen, Robert Kajanus, Jean Sibelius, Georg Høeberg, Erkki Melartin, Wilhelm Stenhammar, Carl Nielsen, and Johan Halvorsen

Aubade, and the names of trees and flowers. It is difficult to share Erik Tawaststjerna's sincere admiration for many of these miniatures for the piano. "I write piano pieces in my free moments," Sibelius told Törne. "As a matter of fact, the piano does not interest me; it cannot sing." Later he told Walter Legge: "I dislike the piano—it is an unsatisfactory, ungrateful instrument, an instrument for which only one composer, Chopin, has succeeded in writing perfectly, and of which only two others, Debussy and Schumann, have had an intimate understanding."

Tawaststjerna feels that many of these trifles were composed by Sibelius for the members of his family, and that their publication was purely accidental. He asks: "But what if Sibelius was moved one day to dedicate a little valse in Tchaikovsky's melancholy valse style to the budding pianist among his daughters, or to soothe her little sister to sleep with a berceuse, or to amuse the whole family with a rondoletto, polka, or a polonaise? And if a publisher wanted to publish these quick sketches, ought the composer to have refused the request? Even Mozart's family did not live solely on sunshine and music."

"It must be very pleasant for you to serve in a
house where you hear such lovely music."
                        A Red soldier

•

As the Great War progressed,
Sibelius resented being cut off from what he called "the
great civilized countries." His concertizing abroad was now
limited to Scandinavia, and on one occasion he complained:
"Am I no longer to experience the delight that a first-class
orchestra gives me when I conduct my works?" Yet he must
have been pleased in the spring of 1916 to learn that the Tsar
had conferred on him the honorary title of Professor. Kajanus
had received a similar award eight years earlier.

During this year, Sibelius wrote numerous minor
compositions, including a short choral work for the Y.L. entitled *In the Moonlight* (*Kuutamolla*); five pieces for the
piano, opus 85; and two sets of songs, opus 86 and opus 88.
His most ambitious project was the incidental music to Hugo
von Hofmannsthal's *Everyman* (*Jokamies*), which the Finnish National Theater presented on November 5. It is a
lengthy score consisting of fifteen numbers and calling for
mixed chorus, piano, organ, and small orchestra. "The music,"
wrote Bengt Carlson, "is so intimately associated with the contents of the play that a separate performance of even part of it

is scarcely possible." Although the music remains unpublished as opus 83, it is heard in Finland whenever the play is revived.

Near the end of the year, Sibelius conducted his troublesome Fifth Symphony in Turku and Helsinki in what was called its "definitive form," only to withdraw it almost immediately for further revisions that were not completed until three years later. Ekman has written that the composer's mind was sometimes filled with gloom as the shadows of war descended more thickly over the earth. But there were lighter moments, and among them is the amusing little story concerning the dedication of a short composition for mixed chorus entitled *Fridolin's Folly (Fridolins dårskap)*.

By the spring of 1917, food was rationed in Helsinki and alcohol unobtainable. When Sibelius met an architect from Pori named Torkel Nordman on the streets of the capital, the latter confided that he had several bottles of precious spirits in his briefcase. The two promptly repaired to the home of another architect in order to enjoy this rare treat. When a slim supper consisting of fish and macaroni was served, Sibelius declared that he had not tasted meat in ages, and Nordman promised to send him a joint of smoked mutton from Pori. The main problem was to so disguise the contents of the package that meat-hungry mail clerks would not be tempted to steal it. The architect devised the happy stratagem of sending it in a violin case labeled "One violin for Professor Sibelius, Järvenpää." Two months later, the composer sent Nordman the manuscript for *Fridolin's Folly* "with greetings and thanks for the delicious violin."

Also completed during this year were another set of songs, opus 90; the six *Humoresques* for violin and orchestra, opus 87 and opus 89; the *Scout March,* opus 91b; and the *Jaeger March,* opus 91a. The *Humoresques* are seriously written miniatures that have never achieved the popularity of the Violin Concerto, though they certainly do not deserve to be classed with the composer's other short pieces for the same instrument. The *Scout March,* originally composed for a Finnish troop known as the "Forest Wanderers," has in recent times become fairly well known under the title *The World Song of the World Association of Girl Guides and Girl Scouts.* The *Jaeger March* is Sibelius's musical contribution to the bloody civil struggle that resulted in Finland's independence.

The first Russian revolution of March 1917 had repercussions in Finland. Fear of the Russian soldiers stationed there prompted the middle class to create a variety of thinly disguised organizations which ultimately came to be known as the White Guard. Anticipating a rightist *coup d'état,* the Social Democrats and other leftist elements retaliated by forming a Red Guard. These two groups were to be the chief protagonists in a fratricidal war, and both were guilty of extreme cruelties. Even today there is a considerable difference of opinion in Finland as to whether the conflict should be known as the Civil War or the War of Independence.

Between 1914 and 1916, many Finnish students and adventurers had made their way to Germany, where they were organized into the Twenty-Seventh Royal Prussian Jaeger Battalion. They constituted an effective fighting force of about two thousand men, and their active service on the Eastern front had made them seasoned troops. As the tension mounted in Finland, the Whites, who made no attempt to conceal their sympathies for the German cause, requested that the Jaegers be sent to their aid.

Feeling the need for a marching song, the Jaegers conducted a contest among their ranks for a suitable poem, and the winner was a lieutenant named Heikki Nurmio. When the poem reached Finland, Sibelius was requested to write the music. The composer's sympathies were with the Whites, and he immediately wrote the music in "a highly exalted patriotic mood." Several hundred copies were run off in hectograph and secretly distributed. Although they bore neither the name of Sibelius nor that of Nurmio, they were dated December 8, 1917—the composer's birthday.

Events moved swiftly. On November 7, the Bolsheviks seized power in Russia. One month later, the Finnish Diet declared the country's independence. On January 19, 1918, the Whites held a rally in the University's great hall, at which time Kajanus and the Helsinki City Orchestra gave the first public performance of the *Jaeger March*. Also on the program were two other pieces of patriotic music by Sibelius—*Finlandia* and a composition for mixed chorus entitled *To the Fatherland (Isänmaalle)*, which he had written at the beginning of the century—and, prophetically, *Die Wacht am Rhein*.

Five days after the concert, Sibelius sent his march to Breitkopf & Härtel. "The composition has been a great success, and it is topical," he wrote. "That is why it would be good if it could be published as soon as possible." On the night of Sunday, January 28, the Finnish Reds seized power in Helsinki. What they intended as a *coup d'état* became a civil war.

Sibelius noted in his diary that the Reds behaved like "wild beasts," and he added: "I must be especially hateful to them as the composer of patriotic music." Later he recalled "the growing arrogance and savagery of the working classes." It should be noted, however, that the indignities to which he was subjected included a few routine searches for food and concealed weapons. During one of these, a Red soldier told the family maid: "It must be pleasant for you to serve in a house where you hear such lovely music."

By the middle of February, relatives and friends decided that the Sibelius family would be safer in Helsinki than in Järvenpää. Armed with a special pass signed by the Red commandant, Robert Kajanus effected their transfer to the Lapinlahti Central Asylum, where the composer's brother, Christian, served as senior doctor. During his stay there, Sibelius completed another patriotic work, a cantata for mixed chorus and orchestra entitled *Our Native Land* (*Oma maa*), opus 92, which the National Chorus had commissioned for its tenth anniversary. The text is based on a poem by Kustaa Samuli Berg (pen name Kallio) written in 1832 which concludes: "Dearer, more beautiful to me is the land of my birth."

Among the many Red atrocities in Helsinki had been the murder of a young medical intern named Gösta Schybergson on February 2. Sibelius was so deeply shocked that he immediately wrote two compositions for male chorus based on verses by Schybergson: *One Hears the Storm Outside* (*Ute hörs stormen*) and *The Roaring of a Wave* (*Brusande rusar en våg*). Both were published during the same year with a cover photograph of the young man wearing his white student cap.

In the meantime, the Whites were grouping for a counterattack in and around the city of Vaasa on the Ostrobothnian coast. They were under the command of a seasoned General, Baron Gustaf Mannerheim, who had formerly served in the Russian Imperial Army. Early in April, Mannerheim's forces, greatly aided by the Jaeger Battalion and foreign volunteers, inflicted a crushing defeat on the Red stronghold in the industrial city of Tampere. One week later, ten thousand of the Kaiser's soldiers under General von der Goltz captured Helsinki. Victory for the Whites was assured.

On April 20, Kajanus and his orchestra presented a special concert in honor of the German liberators. Breitkopf & Härtel complied with Sibelius's request and published his *Jaeger March* in several arrangements. The impressive covers in gold and silver bear the German black cross, the Imperial eagle, and the crown of the Hohenzollerns. Oddly enough, the Jaegers were not attracted to their new song and never marched to it. Its fate was sealed by the Allied victory. So, for that matter, was that of Prince Friedrich Karl of Hesse, the Kaiser's brother-in-law, whom, in anticipation of a German victory, the Finnish Diet had asked to become king of Finland!

With hostilities over, Sibelius began work on the final version of his Fifth Symphony and also outlined two new ones. Several pressing commissions and a trip to Denmark delayed their completion. He composed an *Academic March* (*Promotiomarssi*) for the University's graduation exercises of May 1919, and a cantata for mixed chorus and orchestra entitled *Song of the Earth* (*Jordens sång*), opus 93, for the inauguration of the Swedish Åbo Academy in Turku. For the grand opening of an art shop known as Stenman's "Art Palace," he composed and conducted a *Pastorale* for two women's voices and orchestra. Later this was arranged as an orchestral composition with the voice parts *ad libitum* and published as *Autrefois—scène pastorale,* opus 96b.

For the Festival of Nordic Music held in Copenhagen during June 1919, the young Republic of Finland sent a large delegation headed by Sibelius and including Kajanus, Melartin, Madetoja, and many lesser lights. Johan Halvorsen, the grand old man from Norway, attended; Hugo Alfvén and Wilhelm Stenhammar, one of Sibelius's friends and admirers, led the Swedish contingent; Carl Nielsen stood head and shoulders above the other Danish participants.

As his contribution, Sibelius conducted his most popular symphony, the Second, with great success. Both he and his Nordic contemporaries knew that his growing international fame had automatically placed him in a class apart from the others. It is best revealed in a group photograph in which he is seen with Kajanus, Melartin, Stenhammar, Nielsen, Halvorsen, and the Danish conductors Høeberg and Schnedler-Petersen. Whereas the others are wearing street clothes, Sibelius is nattily attired in a black cutaway coat and derby. He smiles while most of the others look at him.

In November, Sibelius completed the final version of his Fifth Symphony. The following June, he conducted a new cantata entitled *Hymn of the Earth* (*Maan virsi*), opus 95, at a trade fair held in Helsinki. Six *Bagatelles* for the piano, opus 97, *Valse lyrique*, and *Valse chevaleresque* (both are included in opus 96) hardly taxed his creative powers. Undoubtedly he hoped that one of these trifles might achieve the popularity of his *Valse triste*. In Berlin, Adolf Paul planned to revive his *King Kristian II* and invited his old friend to conduct the theater orchestra. But Sibelius had too many irons in the fire to heed this invitation to make a lot of money. He had been invited to conduct in England, Finland would soon act as the host country for another Festival of Nordic Music, and, perhaps most important of all, there were prospects of earning more gold than Paul could imagine. The United States was beckoning again.

Sibelius made his fifth and last visit to England in February 1921, conducting some twelve concerts in London, Birmingham, Bournemouth, and Manchester. According to Ernest Newman, interest in his music had diminished considerably during the war years, and Sibelius had to begin his conquest of the island kingdom all over again. During the first of two concerts in London with the Queen's Hall Orchestra, he presented his Fifth Symphony.

"Whether from nervousness or not," the critic Kalisch observed, "he certainly failed to make the most of his work, and one could not help wondering how far the extreme greyness of the score was due to the music itself or to his own way of treating it. In the Fourth Symphony we seemed to be hearing a few rough sketches for a symphony rather than a symphony itself. This Fifth Symphony is not quite so sketchy. . . . Sibelius always stops when a climax is due as if to say:

'Here is where it ought to be. Let them imagine the rest.' The impression left is sometimes that he is silent because he has not really much to say."

Two weeks later, when Sibelius conducted his Fourth Symphony, Kalisch found his performance less "vigorous" than Sir Henry Wood's of the preceding year. Noting that its admirers claimed that it contained no "superfluities," Kalisch chortled: "After all, a piece of music is not a telegram. . . . But he has proved by *Valse triste* and *Finlandia* that easy rewards are within his grasp, and it is not every composer who has the strength of character to deliberately resign them." Evidently Kalisch did not attend the concert in Birmingham at which Sibelius conducted *Valse triste, Finlandia,* and his recently completed *Valse lyrique.*

At the second London concert, Sibelius shared the spotlight with Busoni, who played a Mozart concerto and his own *Indian Fantasy*. In his memoirs, Sir Henry Wood recalls his difficulties in keeping track of these two old friends: "I could generally manage Busoni when I had him to myself. My heart was always in my mouth if he met Sibelius. I never knew where they would get to. They would forget the time of the concert at which they were to appear; they hardly knew the day of the week. One year I was directing the Birmingham Festival and had to commission a friend never to let these two out of his sight. He had quite an exciting time for two or three days following them about from restaurant to restaurant. He told me he never knew what time they went to bed or got up in the morning. They were like a couple of irresponsible school boys."

Ekman writes that among the many foreign offers

that Sibelius refused was the directorship of the Eastman School of Music in Rochester, New York. As we shall see presently, during his last visit to England, Sibelius was under contract to the new American music school, not as its first director, but as a teacher of theory and composition.

A Norwegian violinist named Alf Klingenberg, one of the many Scandinavian musicians with whom Sibelius had consorted during his early student days in Berlin, was responsible for the new American invitation. After migrating to the United States in 1902, Klingenberg spent several years teaching in the Middle and Far West, and finally became the director of a small school known as the Institute of Musical Art in Rochester, New York. Shortly after World War I, George Eastman purchased the school and presented it to the University of Rochester. After a short period of affiliation, the institution was renamed the Eastman School of Music in 1921.

One year prior to the grand opening of the Eastman School of Music, Klingenberg, who retained his title as director, toured Europe in search of a well-known faculty. In answer to a letter inquiring whether he would be interested in teaching theory and composition, Sibelius wrote that the proposition was "not disagreeable." But he hastened to add: "My position here as poet laureate on an artist's pension, etc., is such that I cannot just say good-by."

In September 1920, Klingenberg visited Järvenpää, where he was staggered to learn that Sibelius demanded a salary of $20,000 for nine months of teaching. Remembering the earlier generosity of Mr. Stoeckel, and undoubtedly having more than a vague notion concerning the wealth of

Mr. Eastman, Sibelius placed a high value on his services as a teacher in the New World. Klingenberg was not authorized to negotiate a contract involving such a large sum of money, and he cabled Eastman from Stockholm for instructions. The inventor of the Kodak authorized his director to conclude a preliminary agreement, shrewdly stipulating that Sibelius must agree to conduct five public concerts of his own music and make no other appearances in America before or during his engagement with the school.

On September 30, Sibelius wrote Klingenberg: "I agree to Eastman's proposal. However, I would like to receive $10,000 immediately because I have to change my life in order to prepare myself for the new position—compose new music for the concerts, brush up my English, etc. I stick to what you and your wife said, namely that I will have time to compose, you and your wife will kindly help me in everything, and that it may be possible for me to earn some more money. Now that I have examined the matter more closely, I find that $20,000 is not so much. If all went well, the concerts alone would net me $12,500. Don't be offended by my customary frankness."

By January of the following year, all of the composer's terms had been met, and he wrote: "I have just cabled 'yes.' . . . As you planned, we will wait for the dollar to rise, and then the buying of our—I hope—bad Finnmarks will take place. What a good patriot I am!" The Rochester newspapers immediately announced that soon the famous composer of *Valse triste* and *Finlandia* would be a resident of their fair city, and within a few weeks this information was repeated by the national music journals. Jean Sibelius was listed among the faculty in the first catalogue of the Eastman school.

In April, however, the composer had a change of heart and wrote Klingenberg: "I see now that it is completely impossible for me to teach. It would be the greatest calamity for your conservatory to have me as a teacher. I can conduct my compositions tolerably well, but as a teacher—impossible. Furthermore, there are other reasons. Dear friend, act accordingly, and please understand me." Somewhat later the Eastman School announced that Christian Sinding would replace Sibelius because of the latter's "poor health" and his unwillingness to teach classes consisting of English-speaking students. Local newspapers reported that the Finnish composer had suffered a nervous breakdown.

Sibelius's decision to ask for a release from his contract was a wise one, for he had absolutely no interest in teaching. Furthermore, Eastman had the reputation of ordering his teachers around as though they were employees in his factory. Sibelius might well have undergone a genuine nervous breakdown had he gone to Rochester.

No sooner had the business with the Eastman School of Music been settled than the Scandinavian composers were welcomed to Helsinki for another Festival of Nordic Music. At the opening concert of Finnish music, Sibelius conducted *Lemminkäinen's Homeward Journey*. After Nielsen, Halvorsen, and Alfvén had shared concerts with their countrymen, Sibelius returned to close the festival with the final one, consisting entirely of his own music.

*"You may find thematic connections in my
symphonies when you study them. I myself
call these the 'symphonic necessity' because I
am more the medium than a cerebral type of
man. Especially when regarding my first
symphonies, a cerebral study would hardly
give a key to them. What is needed there is
the 'boy's mind,' as the Swedish writer
Rydberg would say." Sibelius*

•

In an undated letter (to Axel
Carpelan?) reproduced by Ekman, the composer wrote: "I
cannot become a *Vielschreiber*. It would mean killing all my
reputation and my art. I have made my name in the world by
straightforward means. I must go on the same way." Later he
told Ekman: "The demands one makes upon oneself have increased in the course of years. Greater sureness makes one
more and more prone to scorn solutions that come too easily,
that follow the line of least resistance. One is always faced
with new problems. The thing that has pleased me most is
that I have been able to reject. The greatest labor I have
expended, perhaps, was on works that have never been completed."

What purpose, one wonders, were these statements

intended to serve? A casual glance at the list of compositions at the end of this volume proves that Sibelius was a *Viel-schreiber* and that he frequently followed the line of least resistance. Ekman feels that the myriad of small compositions for piano and violin which interfered with the completion of the Fifth Symphony served as a narcotic for Sibelius during the troubled war years.

By 1920, however, World War I was a thing of the past and yet these minor pieces continued to flow from his pen. Their titles faithfully mirror their sounds: *Pièce humoristique, Esquisse, Souvenir, Moment de valse, Petite marche, Chant du soir, Scène romantique,* etc. Many of the composer's stanchest admirers have been disturbed that he should have permitted their publication and dignified them with opus numbers.

"Sibelius has produced more patently and blatantly inferior music than any composer of the first class," Walter Legge, founder of the Sibelius Society in England, observed. Sir Arnold Bax found them a source of bewilderment. In his memoirs he writes: "With undeterred hope we continue to turn over these hundreds of pages, discovering nothing with the hallmark of the master upon them. These trifles are, with scarcely an exception, entirely undistinguished and characterless, nor do we find either improvement or deterioration as the years pass and the true Sibelius of the symphonies increases in stature and power. The elegy or valse written in 1930 [*sic*] might well have been dated 1890, and vice versa. There is precisely nothing to them. They are not even bad, and never vulgar. . . . Has the composer some inexplicable regard for these banalities, and if not, why has he troubled to waste so much ink during his long career?" [1]

But, it has been argued, Sibelius is essentially a man of the orchestra, and consequently his remarks concerning a growing musical asceticism apply only to his orchestral compositions. This could hardly apply to the string of salon pieces composed between 1920 and 1922: *Valse lyrique, Autrefois —scène pastorale, Valse chevaleresque, Suite champêtre, Suite mignonne, Suite caractéristique,* and *Andante festivo.* [2]

Gray regards these works as a sort of *hommage à Johann Strauss,* and after meeting Sibelius he came to the conclusion that one could not please him more than by comparing them with the Waltz King's masterpieces. But Gray knew, and surely Sibelius must have known, that these compositions lack the sincerity, grace, and spontaneity that characterize Strauss's style. It would be simpler and more correct to say that they were written for money. But even with the magic name of Sibelius above them they have never attracted any public interest.

As early as 1918, Sibelius had outlined plans for a new symphony. "The VIth symphony is wild and impassioned in character," he wrote. "Somber, with pastoral contrasts. Probably in four movements, with the end rising to a somber roaring of the orchestra in which the main theme is drowned." Five years later, it was completed. On February 19, 1923, Si-

---

[1] *Bax, however, dedicated his Fifth Symphony to Sibelius, which prompted the latter to say: "Bax is one of the great men of our time; he has a fine musical mind, an original personal style, a splendid independence, and, thank God, he can write a melody, and is not ashamed to do so."*

[2] Andante festivo *by tradition opens each Sibelius Festival in Helsinki. It was commissioned in 1922 to celebrate the twenty-fifth anniversary of a factory in Säynätsalo. The original version is for string quartet; Sibelius later added parts for contrabass and timpani ad libitum.*

belius conducted a concert of his latest compositions with the Helsinki City Orchestra. In addition to the Sixth Symphony, opus 104, the program included *Autrefois—scène pastorale, Valse lyrique, Suite champêtre,* and *Suite caractéristique.* Surely this is the most incongruous all-Sibelius program one could imagine!

On the surface, the Sixth Symphony appears more conventional than the Fifth. It is cast in four movements that are numbered, detached, and each in its traditional place: 1. *Allegro molto moderato;* 2. *Allegretto quasi andante;* 3. *Poco vivace;* and 4. *Allegro molto.* As is so frequently the case with Sibelius, what passes for the slow movement appears to be the weakest, and the rhythmic figure upon which the third movement is almost exclusively based recalls some of the monotony found in *Night Ride and Sunrise.* The symphony could hardly be called "wild and impassioned in character." Although there are moments in the finale when this might seem to hold true, the work closes with a passage softly intoned by the strings. In addition to the instrumentation found in its neighbors, the Sixth Symphony calls for a bass clarinet and a harp. The only other symphony in which Sibelius employs the harp is the First.

Cecil Gray was apparently the first to notice that the Sixth Symphony begins with a polyphonic passage for strings in the Dorian mode. Coupling this with an interview during which the composer expressed his admiration for Palestrina, Gray concluded that the symphony was strongly influenced by the sixteenth-century Italian master. The music commentators found this concept of a "modal" symphony most attractive, and it was soon given wide distribution. Whereas

Gray felt that unity was achieved through the all-pervasive modality that he found in the four detached movements, other analysts insist that it is the result of a far more complicated and intellectualized process. The Sixth Symphony, they claim, is entirely derived from one short thematic germ.

No one appears to have been more astonished by these revelations than the composer himself. "You may analyze it and explain it theoretically," he once said, referring to the Sixth Symphony. "You may find that there are several interesting things going on. But most people forget that it is, above all, a poem."

Viewed as a "poem," it is difficult to understand why the Sixth Symphony should be admired by the few and neglected by the many. In many respects it is a more finished composition and more *echt* Sibelius than the infinitely more popular Fifth. Yet it rivals the Third as his least-appreciated work in this form. Because of its rather cold, chiseled, linear style—Gray calls it the purest and coldest water that has flowed from his fountain—it is closest in mood to the Seventh Symphony.

After the *première* of the Sixth Symphony, Sibelius once again traveled to Italy in order to conduct and to work on his Seventh Symphony. In Rome, he presented a program of his own music including *Finlandia,* the suite from his music to *Pelléas et Mélisande, Lemminkäinen's Homeward Journey,* and the Second Symphony. According to one critic, the shorter pieces fared better than the symphony. Sibelius, it was stated, was loquacious and inarticulate when attempting to develop his ideas in a large field.

As the Seventh is the composer's most-discussed symphony, it may be profitable to examine its clouded history. It is first mentioned in the oft-quoted letter of 1918 in which, after discussing plans for the Fifth (second revision) and Sixth symphonies, Sibelius continued: "The VIIth symphony. Joy of life and vitality, with appassionato passages. In 3 movements—the last a 'Hellenic rondo.'. . . . It looks as if I were to come out with all these three symphonies at the same time. . . . With regard to symphonies VI and VII, the plans may be altered according to the development of the musical ideas. As usual, I am a slave to my themes and submit to their demands." Many years later, he told Ekman: "On March 2, 1924, at night, as I entered in my diary, I completed 'Fantasia sinfonica'—that is what I first thought of calling my seventh symphony in one movement."

Accepting the letter at its face value, it is obvious that Sibelius altered his plans considerably, so much so that it would be difficult to identify the published work by this description. Neither is it in three movements nor does it contain anything even remotely resembling a rondo. The diary entry, however, is misleading. Far from *thinking* of calling it *Fantasia sinfonica*, Sibelius conducted its world *première* under that title in Stockholm on March 24, 1924. Several months later, he signed a contract with Wilhelm Hansen of Denmark for the publication of *Fantasia sinfonica,* opus 105, but when it was issued the following year, it had become the Seventh Symphony, opus 105. Oddly enough, it was not heard in Finland until three years after the Stockholm performance. During that interval, Leopold Stokowski conducted it in Philadelphia and Serge Koussevitzky in Boston and New York.

The most plausible explanation for the change in

title is that Sibelius regarded that of *Fantasia sinfonica* as a sort of trial balloon. When the Swedish critics—with a hint or two from the composer—appeared willing to regard it as a fusion or overlapping of several symphony movements into one, he felt justified in changing its title. On the other hand, we cannot exclude the possibility that Sibelius was sincere when he called his new composition *Fantasia sinfonica* and that his decision to call it Seventh Symphony was made *ex post facto*.

If this is so, we may properly ask: Is the Seventh Symphony an altered version of the work mentioned in the letter of 1918? If not, then what happened to this earlier work? The answers to these two questions might provide a clue as to the nature of the much-discussed "Eighth Symphony," which the composer ultimately destroyed.

The one-movement form of the Seventh Symphony is the principal reason for its being singled out by many writers for special comment. Some have claimed that, because of this form, it represents the grand climax in Sibelius's career as a symphonist. Although most analysts regard it as a consolidation of four symphony movements into one—the term "organic fusion" is especially popular—few agree where the divisions, if any, should be made.

Now, the word "symphony" may mean many things. Until the middle of the eighteenth century, the term was used vaguely for a variety of instrumental works. They were especially common as short instrumental interludes inserted in operas and oratorios: such is Handel's Pastoral Symphony in *Messiah*. In the hands of Haydn, the symphony became popular as an extended work for orchestra, generally in four contrasting sections or "movements." The special attraction of these "classical" symphonies is to be found in the over-all unity achieved within diversity. Each movement preserves its own identity, yet all four combine to make one work in which the element of contrast prevents the listener from being bored.

Beethoven worked within this framework while infusing it with greater power of expression and expanding it in size. He changed the order and even the number of the movements, and in his Ninth Symphony introduced soloists and a chorus. In his Fifth Symphony, he joined the two final movements and destroyed their thematic independence. After Beethoven, the symphony soon became all things unto all men.

Before long, a composer could with justification call a programmatic tone poem or series of tone poems a "symphony." Among these we find Liszt's *A Faust Symphony,* Berlioz's *Fantastic Symphony,* Goldmark's *Rustic Wedding Symphony,* and Richard Strauss's *Sinfonia domestica.* Even Sibelius referred to his *Kullervo Symphony* in a letter to Mrs. Newmarch, and near the end of his life he said that one could with justification say that he had written a *Lemminkäinen Symphony.* In the light of these developments, there is no reason why a symphony in one movement should be excluded from this all-embracing category.

The Seventh Symphony is "symphonic" in the presentation and working out of its thematic material. Yet, the Finnish conductor Simon Parmet has observed, it has nothing in common with the traditional symphony or with any one of its movements. Both Cecil Gray and Gerald Abraham go to great lengths to show that it represents an extension of what is known as orthodox sonata form, in which there is an exposition, a development, and a recapitulation. Krohn, however, feels that it is a rondo. It seems to me, at least, that the Seventh Symphony is really a *Fantasia sinfonica*, for that title describes what it really is—a work of symphonic proportions cast in no established form.

Attempts to squeeze the Seventh Symphony into sonata form have resulted in wide divergencies of opinion. For example, after a soft timpani roll there is a simple rising scale for strings which is obviously the first theme, and which plays an important role in the symphony's later development. Many writers consider this theme to be little more than an introduction: a second theme for flutes which follows seems to fit in with the concept of a first subject in sonata form. Abraham, on the other hand, discards the concept of first and second subjects in favor of "germs." The first "germ" of thematic importance, he feels, occurs in measure six, where a sustained B in the first violins drops to A. Students of comparative music analysis will find Sibelius's Seventh Symphony a rewarding subject for investigation.

Just why the Seventh should be more popular than the Sixth—to which it is extremely close in both mood and style, especially the first movement—is a mystery. Ralph Wood is one of the few who have proclaimed it the composer's weakest and most uneven work in this form, a "heroic failure" as an attempt to impose Sibelian unity in a single movement containing such diverse tempi and subject matter. Could it be that this rose by some other name—*Fantasia sinfonica,* say—might have smelled sweeter?

As his sixtieth birthday neared, Sibelius was busy putting the finishing touches to another gigantic work, the incidental music to Shakespeare's *The Tempest,* opus 109. It had been commissioned by the Royal Theater of Copenhagen, where it was given a lavish *première* on March 16, 1926. Many have insisted that the music to The Tempest was composed one year after the tone poem *Tapiola,* whereas just the reverse is true.

The Tempest is the last entry in Sibelius's long list of music for the theater, fourteen works in all if we include the tableau music and his little one-act opera. It is also one of the largest works of its kind in all music literature. The original unpublished manuscript—jealously guarded by the publisher Hansen—is more than two hundred pages in length, and contains dance episodes, interludes, songs, choral pieces, and appropriate background music for most of the scenes. Had Wood been able to examine this manuscript as well as the published concert suites, he might not have written that the music seems to be unrelated to the stage happenings.

From the original score, Sibelius published the prelude and two concert suites arranged for large and small orchestras containing seventeen numbers in all. They are uneven in character in their concert version. The prelude, an extended chromatic scale for the strings, over which the woodwinds and brass play held notes, is excellent storm music for the first scene in the play, but rather disappointing as an independent number. Such others as "Caliban," "Miranda," and "Prospero" are captivating little musical portraits that one could compare favorably with Mussorgsky's *Pictures from an Exhibition.* Wood, whose dislike for *The Tempest* music is marked, finds it lacking in "passion and soul-searching." But Sibelius was an experienced hand when writing in this idiom. Years of practical experience gave him definite notions concerning what he considered to be the true function of theater music. The "passion and soul-searching" he reserved for his last great orchestral composition, the tone poem *Tapiola.*

The year 1925 witnessed no other compositions of any stature. In addition to the five *Danses champêtres* for violin, opus 106, Sibelius composed two part-songs to texts by Larin Kyösti, opus 108, for the choral society known as Laulu-Miehet, and a short piece for organ entitled *Intrada,* opus 111a, for a special divine service held in connection with the visit of the King and Queen of Sweden to Helsinki. For General Mannerheim's Children's Fund he wrote *Morceau romantique sur un motif de M. Jacob de Julin.* Julin was a wealthy industrialist and a friend of the composer. Copies of the piece in an arrangement for piano were sold throughout Finland, and it was first heard at a gala concert in Helsinki on March 9, 1925. One paper reported: "All Helsinki society was there, with General Mannerheim and the diplomatic corps at the head. Professor Sibelius conducted the City Orchestra in several of his own compositions. The last number was a surprise—*Morceau romantique,* based on a simple theme in waltz tempo by Mr. Jacob von Julin, which Professor Sibelius masterfully arranged in a colorful and fascinating setting for orchestra." [3]

Sibelius had no new symphony to present on his sixtieth birthday, but this did not dampen public enthusiasm. Once again Finland honored him as a national hero and was even more lavish in her gifts than in 1915. Following the inflationary spiraling of the Finnmark, his pension was raised to 100,000 marks (approximately $5,400), and a citizens' committee collected a "National Gift" from the general public amounting to 150,000 marks. Somewhat earlier, Sibelius had received a special "prize" of 100,000 marks from the Kordelin Foundation and another from his Danish publisher, Wilhelm Hansen. Such recognition of a composer's achievements has rarely been equaled.

As soon as the ceremonies were over, Sibelius once again left for a prolonged stay in Italy, where he worked on two commissioned compositions. The first was *The Hymn of Väinö* (*Väinön virsi*), opus 110, for mixed chorus and orchestra, which Kajanus conducted at a music festival in Sortavala on June 28, 1926. The text is taken from canto XLIII of the *Kalevala,* which deals with Väinämöinen's attempt to steal the magic Sampo. The old man is fortunate enough to obtain some of its fragments, which he sows throughout the land in order to assure abundant crops. In gratitude for divine aid, the chorus sings:

"Grant, O Jumala, Creator,
That we now may live in comfort,

---

[3] *Around his seventieth birthday, Sibelius told Ekman that February 19, 1923—when he presented his Sixth Symphony—marked his last appearance as a conductor in Finland.*

And be joyous in our lifetime,
And thereafter die in honour,
In our pleasant land of Suomi,
And in beautiful Carelia."   (XLIII, 401–6)

Musically, *The Hymn of Väinö* seems to be of a lower order than Sibelius's other *Kalevala* compositions such as *The Origin of Fire* and *Luonnotar*. It was not published until 1945.

The second commission was a tone poem for Walter Damrosch and the New York Symphony Society. The result of these labors was *Tapiola*,[4] opus 112, dedicated to Damrosch. The world *première* took place in New York on December 26, 1926, and the following April it was heard in Finland for the first time with the Seventh Symphony.

For his new tone poem, Sibelius wrote a quatrain that appears in the published score in German, English, and French translations:

Wide-spread they stand, the Northland's
     dusky forests,
Ancient, mysterious, brooding savage dreams;
And within them dwells the Forest's mighty God,
And wood-sprites in the gloom weave magic
     secrets.

"Music is like the wife who must be made pregnant by the husband, and music's husband is poetry," Sibelius had written his friend Erkko in 1893. Although thirty-three years had elapsed since he had penned this youthful confession, Sibelius, the architect of seven "absolute" symphonies, had

---

[4] *The title refers to the realm of Tapio, the forest god in Finnish mythology.*

not completely abandoned this credo. The quatrain for *Tapiola* is similar to the nymph-like vignettes Sibelius wrote for *Florestan* in 1889 and also recalls other early compositions dealing with the same subject, such as *Skogsrået* and *Snöfrid*.

Beyond this, however, the similarities cease. Although Sibelius calls for the special tone colors of the English horn, bass clarinet, and contra basoon, he reverts to the technique employed in his Fourth Symphony and treats the several sections of the orchestra as separate blocks of tone. But the most unusual feature of *Tapiola* is the short and by itself uninteresting little theme upon which it is almost entirely based.

During the eighteen minutes required to perform *Tapiola,* this theme, first stated by the strings in the opening three measures, undergoes a constant evolution in which the listener is never distracted from the central idea by unnecessary episodes. Consequently Sibelius's last great composition must be regarded as a *tour de force* in which with Racinian simplicity he succeeds in duplicating the classical French feat of creating something out of nothing. There may be more than idle daydreaming behind Ernest Newman's assertion that the monothematic structure of *Tapiola* is a deliberate attempt to represent the infinite varieties of life in the forest, all of which spring from a common source. As the English writer Wilfrid Mellers has observed, it is surely one of the most terrifying (spine-chilling) pieces of music ever written.

Tapiola is a fitting climax to Sibelius's long, varied career. The two main streams in his total production—the programmatic tone poems and the seven symphonies—meet here in harmonious combination. Here he stands at the height of his powers, secure in his orchestration, sovereign master of his material. "Even if Sibelius had written nothing else," wrote Cecil Gray, "this one work would be sufficient to entitle him to a place among the greatest masters of all time."

Chapter XVII   The "Silence from Järvenpää"

"Say what you like, but such things do happen
—not often, but they do happen."
                    Gogol

●

After *Tapiola* came what we
have frequently called the "silence from Järvenpää." Techni-
cally this silence was never complete. During the late 1920's
Sibelius wrote some *Masonic Ritual Music* (listed by Ekman
as *Musique religieuse*), opus 113, as well as a few short pieces
for piano, violin, and organ. In 1930, he composed a march
for male chorus entitled *Karelia's Fate (Karjalan osa)* for a
rightest political organization associated with the Lapua movement, which, according to the historian J. Hampden Jackson,
was a conspiracy to establish a form of Fascist dictatorship in
Finland. Gallén-Kallela's death in 1931 inspired him to compose a companion piece to the *Intrada* for organ: *Mournful
Music (Surusoitto)*, opus 111b. Even as late as 1957, he dictated a new accompaniment for one of his songs from *Twelfth
Night*. But for over thirty years no compositions of any stature
appeared.

As time passed, Sibelius found himself living in a
Sibelian world. In the comfort of his home, he enjoyed concerts of his own music, thanks to the radio and phonograph.
He eagerly read all the new books and articles discussing
his life and work, and undoubtedly was both amazed and

pleased to discover so many hidden facets in his art. When
he was depressed, he reread the less flattering criticisms of
earlier years, and, as he later confessed to one Finnish conductor, immediately felt better. He granted interviews to
journalists, musicians, and distinguished figures from all
walks of life, and in time he learned to present the "correct
profile."

When reports of these meetings appeared in print,
Sibelius was invariably described as a genial and gracious
host, a man of refined taste, and a true aristocrat. Some were
amazed to discover that he was a fluent conversationalist
willing to discuss everything from jazz to Homer. He was
silent on only one subject—new compositions in progress,
and especially his Eighth Symphony. In the beginning, it was
an amusing game in which he smilingly parried inquiries
by comparing his music with the delicate wings of a butterfly.
Now and then he would drop a few hints and even promise
to release his new symphony in the indefinite future. But it
failed to materialize. As time passed, his most devoted admirers nervously defended the "silence" while his critics
accused him of being "written out" or of shirking his duties
while enjoying a government pension. It was a most distressing state of affairs, and in time his smiles gave way to frowns.
"You are keeping me from finishing it," he would declare
bluntly, and then either change the topic of conversation or
indicate that the interview was at an end.

Titles being extremely important in Finland, it was
considered proper to address him as Professor Sibelius. But
there were so many professors who had earned their academic
rank, and who consequently looked down upon those with

purely honorary titles, that Sibelius became known as "the Master."

Olin Downes, then recently appointed to succeed Richard Aldrich as music critic for *The New York Times,* journeyed to Finland in 1927 to meet his idol. He had first heard this Finnish music while serving his apprenticeship on the Boston *Post* in 1907, when Karl Muck conducted the First Symphony. The young critic was immediately overwhelmed, and wrote: "Here, oh God, was again grandeur, honor, nobility. . . . A hero was in the world and had spoken. I felt that somewhere in the world was a home." Downes told the Finnish newspapers that Sibelius needed a good press agent in the United States, and upon returning home, he voluntarily assumed the duties. For the rest of his life, he alternately begged and demanded more and more performances of Sibelius in his widely read columns. In 1937, the Finnish government acknowledged his valuable services by appointing him a Commander of the Order of the White Rose.

In 1945, Downes's critical writings and articles on Sibelius were translated into Finnish and published in book form. Shortly before his death in 1955, he wrote a little booklet entitled *Sibelius the Symphonist* for the Philharmonic-Symphony Society of New York. In it, he aimed a few pointed "I told you so's" at his fellow critics and the musicians who through the years had ridiculed what they considered to be his unrestrained enthusiasm. For a special New York concert in honor of his ninetieth birthday, Sibelius wrote: "I sincerely appreciate the thought of combining the celebration of my birthday with the memory of my dear friend, Olin Downes. This warm and wise man has given me so much during many years by his deep, understanding attitude towards music and humanity."

In 1930, Cecil Gray visited Sibelius in order to gather material for his book, which was published the following year. Earlier, Gray had written a survey of contemporary music in which he hailed Sibelius as "one of the few great personalities in modern music." The composer was delighted with these and other complimentary remarks, and pronounced the study excellent in every respect.

When Gray's book appeared, it was entitled merely *Sibelius* and was dedicated to the Finnish people "in sympathy and devotion." Properly speaking, it is not a biography. In the first section—Gray calls it "preliminaries"—the author presents a brief history of Finland and the few facts concerning Sibelius's life which he was able to glean from Furuhjelm's book. Most of the study is devoted to analysis and evaluation of the music, and here Gray may be likened unto the man who so thoroughly enjoyed the water that he jumped into the well.

In one fell swoop, Gray makes a *tabula rasa* of all symphonists after Beethoven with the exception of Sibelius, who is "not only the greatest figure of his generation, but one of the major figures in the entire history of music." Schubert he finds only "potentially" a symphonist; Mendelssohn and Schumann are "lyrical miniaturists"; Berlioz wrote "symphonic poems in disguise"; Brahms is "inferior"; and the works of Bruckner, Mahler, Tchaikovsky, and all who followed them "sin in one or more crucial respects against the symphonic spirit."

Sibelius at fifty

Sibelius at the ceremonies
in honor of his seventieth
birthday

Sibelius in retirement at Järvenpää

It is difficult to determine the importance of Gray's study in contributing to the growing interest in Sibelius in England and the United States, but it must have been considerable. The average music-lover found Gray's enthusiasms contagious and had no reason to question his authority. On the other hand, the book created enemies among those who up to that time had regarded the music of Sibelius with relative indifference. Many were unwilling to replace the "three B's" with "two B's and one S."

Contrary to what one might have expected, the first important Sibelius book in the English language never appeared in Finnish translation. Flattered as the Finns may have been by Gray's touching dedication, they probably did not relish his insistence that their national hero was a "Swede." Gray's shorter study devoted to the symphonies (1935), however, was later translated into Finnish by the composer's son-in-law Jussi Jalas.

Few composers have benefited as much from the invention of the phonograph as has Sibelius. In 1930, the quality of recordings had vastly improved, thanks to the development of an electrical process. For the first time, it was possible to capture the complex sonorities of a symphony orchestra with reasonable fidelity. The Finnish government entered into a financial agreement with the English Columbia Graphophone Company to record the First and Second symphonies, and the aging Kajanus was sent to England to conduct a special ensemble. "Very many men have conducted these symphonies," Sibelius wrote on this occasion, "but there is none who has gone deeper or given more feeling and beauty than Professor Robert Kajanus." The Columbia Company, pleased beyond words by the extraordinary amount of free publicity, announced: "This is the first occasion that any government has interested itself in recording native music for world propaganda purposes."

Two years later, an even more ambitious English recording venture began with the creation of the Sibelius Society. Basically it was a promotion scheme to bolster lagging sales by marketing recordings on a subscription basis, as had already been done with the music of Beethoven and Hugo Wolf. Once again Kajanus was sent to London to conduct the opening concert, which also constituted the first of six large albums: *Pohjola's Daughter, Tapiola,* and the Fifth Symphony. In its prospectus the Society assured potential subscribers that the Eighth Symphony would be included in the first volume "if the parts are available." This is as close as the world has ever come to the most publicized, unheard, and unseen symphony in history. In 1934, Finland sent the Helsinki City Orchestra and its new permanent conductor, Georg Schnéevoigt, to England, where they gave public concerts and made new recordings for the Sibelius Society. "Sibelius stock is booming, and booming hard," observed Scott Goddard in the *Morning Post.*

It was booming even harder in the United States, where Koussevitzky in Boston, Stokowski in Philadelphia, Barbirolli in New York, and Ormandy in Minneapolis were all busy performing and recording Sibelius. During the Boston Orchestra's 1932-3 season, Koussevitzky, who had recently been decorated by the Finnish government,[1] presented the first Sibelius "cycle" given anywhere—all seven symphonies and *Tapiola*. Once again the Eighth Symphony was promised; once again it failed to materialize.

Riding high on the crest of this wave and apparently headed for fame and fortune was a young American conductor named Werner Janssen. Early in 1934, he conducted a concert of Sibelius's music in Helsinki, and the American press reported that his reception had been phenomenal—so much so that Sibelius had embraced him in public and said: "You may say that tonight Finland has for the first time discovered my music." Janssen was awarded the Order of the White Rose, and all of the publicity helped toward his appointment as associate conductor of the New York Philharmonic. He remained for one season: as John Tasker Howard has written, no living creature could have lived up to the advance accounts of Janssen's abilities as a conductor.

And then, in 1935, what seemed to be the impossible happened. Sunday listeners to the concerts broadcast by the New York Philharmonic were asked to indicate their favorite "symphonists," and Sibelius was voted in first place. The other composers in descending order were Beethoven (a close second), Ravel, Brahms, Wagner, Tchaikovsky, Richard Strauss, and Stravinsky. Sibelius *above* Beethoven! There were mutterings that this astonishing state of affairs resulted from the machinations of "a handful of English and American critics." An anti-Sibelius attack in the United States was both imminent and inevitable.

December 8, 1935, was a day of national rejoicing in

---

[1] *Stokowski, Toscanini, and Ormandy received similar decorations in 1955.*

Finland. "If it does not tire you I should like to tell you about the great celebration which our country offered to my husband on his seventieth birthday," Aino Sibelius wrote to Mrs. Newmarch. "The government organized a concert in his honour at which 7000 people were present. My brother, Armas Järnefelt, conducted. It was splendid; nothing like it has ever been known here. The President of the Finnish Republic [P. E. Svinhufvud] presented my husband with a huge crown of laurels on behalf of the Finnish nation. The programme contained his First Symphony—the one you used to like best. It was well played and well accepted. All the outside world sent thousands of letters, telegrams, congratulations and medals, etc. It was a great joy to us. You can imagine how happy I felt!"

Among the seven thousand present were Marshal Mannerheim and former presidents Ståhlberg and Relander; among the many foreign decorations was the Goethe Medal for Science and Art, which Adolf Hitler awarded in recognition of Sibelius's "love of fatherland that permeates his symbolic compositions." No doubt extra-musical considerations were behind Hitler's award, for by 1935, Sibelius's popularity in Germany was at rock bottom. A few years earlier, Herbert Peyser had reported to *The New York Times:* "Today nobody [in Germany] performs his music —neither Furtwängler, Walter, Busch, nor anyone else— and nobody asks to have it performed."

Timed for the seventieth-birthday ceremonies was the appearance of a new Sibelius biography published in the original Swedish and in Finnish translation. It soon appeared in English under the title *Jean Sibelius: His Life and Per-*

sonality. Its author was Karl Ekman, Jr., the son of the well-known Finnish Soprano Ida Ekman, for whom Sibelius had composed many of his art songs. If there is any "authorized" biography, it is Ekman's, and it would not be inaccurate to regard Sibelius as its co-author. A good part of the text consists of direct quotations from the composer which Ekman obtained during a dozen meetings lasting all day. In addition, Sibelius made available carefully selected excerpts from his diary and his letters to Axel Carpelan, which had been returned to him after the latter's death in 1919. The composer's interest in the project was so absorbing that he insisted on reading the publisher's proof.

Ekman's book possesses all the advantages and disadvantages inherent in an authorized biography. It permits us to see how the composer viewed his life and work at the age of seventy. As we have already seen, the picture he paints is a highly idealized one. Modesty is not one of its dominant qualities. Nowhere do we find acknowledgments of genuine indebtedness to his teachers Wegelius and Kajanus, or to such devoted supporters as Faltin, Flodin, and Carpelan. They are either brushed over with a few hurried words or ignored altogether. There is not one word of gratitude to Finland and the Finnish people for the government pension he had been receiving since 1897. Nor does Sibelius mention all of the other public and private financial assistance that he accepted in the hours of his need. The book's central theme is the struggles of a solitary genius against the forces of darkness and misunderstanding.[2]

[2] *In 1956, a revised edition of Ekman's book appeared under the Swedish title* Jean Sibelius och hans verk. *It is basically the same study of*

Sibelius stock continued to boom. In 1936, the English composer-conductor Constant Lambert wrote a book entitled *Music Ho!* in which he asserted: "Not only is Sibelius the most important writer since Beethoven, but he may even be described as the only writer since Beethoven who has definitely advanced what, after all, is the most complete formal expression of the human spirit." Almost everywhere we look, the facts at that time seem to support Lambert's contention. By 1936, it was possible to purchase recordings of the seven Sibelius symphonies—many available in a choice of interpretations—as well as the Violin Concerto, *Voces intimae,* numerous tone poems, and excerpts from his theater music. Bruckner and Mahler were then represented by one recorded symphony each.

In 1937, new Sibelius "cycles" were given by Erno Rapee and the Radio City Music Hall Symphony Orchestra of New York and by Sir Henry Wood at the London Promenade Concerts. The following year, Sir Thomas Beecham presented still another cycle in England; later, he was decorated by the Finnish government. Correspondence with the outside world became so voluminous that Sibelius was compelled to hire a secretary.

For Finland's salute to the New York World's Fair (January 1, 1939), Sibelius temporarily emerged from his retirement in order to conduct the Helsinki City Orchestra in a special performance of his *Andante festivo* which was sent to America via short wave. Finland, the Helsinki announcer said, wished to contribute her share to the promotion of peace and

---

1935. The author has added some new historical material, analyses of the symphonies by Nils-Eric Fougstedt, new photographs, etc.

understanding among nations. Eleven months later, the Soviet Union provoked a border incident, and once again the Finns faced their age-old enemy in what has been called the Winter War.

Following the Russian attack against Finland in 1939, Sibelius refused several invitations to seek safety abroad. Instead, he made a radio appeal for American sympathy and support for the Finnish cause. A special stamp bearing his portrait and the legend "I need your help" was distributed in the United States. In a statement to the Associated Press (July 12, 1941), Sibelius said: "In 1939 my fatherland was attacked by the Bolsheviks. Enlightened American people then realized that we were fighting not only for freedom but for all Western civilization and they gave us valuable assistance. Now that the barbaric hordes of the East are again attacking us in their attempt to Bolshevize Europe, I am convinced that the freedom-loving, intelligent American people will rightly understand and appreciate the present situation, realizing that the Bolshevization of Europe would annihilate freedom and civilization in this continent."

After the outbreak of the so-called Continuation War, when Finland found herself a co-belligerent with Germany, Sibelius was prevailed upon to make public statements concerning the new *Waffenbruderschaft* and his confidence in ultimate victory for the joint cause.[3] One of the amusing sidelights during these troubled times was the creation in Germany of a *Sibelius Gesellschaft*. The Germans, who had

---

[3] *The* Münchner Neuste Nachrichten *(August 21, 1942) reported that Sibelius greeted visiting German soldiers with: "I wish with all my heart that you may enjoy a speedy victory."*

shown no interest in the Finnish composer's music during peacetime, were ordered to mend their ways in time of war!

Finland emerged from the great world conflict bled to exhaustion, but free. Almost miraculously the Finns rebuilt their shattered cities and villages and paid off the staggering war debt imposed by the Russians. Within a relatively short time, life began to resume its normal aspects.

Each birthday brought Sibelius added honors. On the occasion of his eightieth, Finland issued a postage stamp bearing his image. Surely no composer has lived to witness as many national honors as Sibelius. Among these we may list an ensemble known as the Sibelius Quartet, a Sibelius Museum, at least two Sibelius parks, numerous Sibelius streets, and, beginning in 1951, a yearly Sibelius Festival sponsored jointly by the Republic of Finland and the City of Helsinki. Since 1939, the composer's alma mater, Martin Wegelius's old Music Institute, has been known as the Sibelius Academy.

Distinguished foreign visitors found it increasingly difficult to obtain invitations to Ainola. The few who were permitted to pay their respects to "the Master" were warned that the *jeu* about the Eighth Symphony had become the "forbidden question." It was hinted that Sibelius feared to release it because he believed that its performance would be a prelude to his death. The less fortunate joined the tourists who had to be content with distant glimpses of his home and the purchase of souvenir busts, plaques, and albums of photographs depicting a typical day at Ainola. There was no end of fantastic rumors. In 1952, for example, Belgian and Swiss newspapers reported that Sibelius had written an opera entitled *La Vierge au vin,* which he had deposited with a lawyer for release after his death.

Sibelius had all he could do merely to keep abreast of everything that was happening to him. Because he eagerly scanned the daily papers for new information concerning himself, a sort of unofficial censorship existed. When a French journalist who was a guest of the Sibelius Festival sent home glowing criticism, it caused mild Gallic storms in the Paris press. Instead of exposing these amusing outbursts for what they really were, the Finnish papers maintained a discreet silence. When one enterprising Helsinki journalist discovered that the facts did not support Sibelius's lifelong belief that Toscanini had been one of his most active supporters, he was requested not to print his findings, but to spare the old man's feelings.

On September 20, 1957, Sir Malcolm Sargent conducted the Fifth Symphony with the Helsinki City Orchestra. It was a special concert held in conjunction with the British Trade Fair in Helsinki. On such occasions, Sibelius could be expected to remain near his radio and send the guest conductor a polite message indicating his satisfaction with the performance. He would be officially represented at the concert by some or all of his daughters. But that evening the daughters were conspicuously absent. At 9:15 p.m., Jean Sibelius died of a cerebral hemorrhage, only a few months before he would have reached the age of ninety-two.

Within a short time, the newspapers reported that Sibelius had predicted his death only forty-eight hours before it came. "I think," he told his wife, "that the cranes have taken leave of me. It was on my usual walk. The cranes were flying low over Ainola—I have never seen them fly that low before. Straight above Ainola one of them parted with a sad cry and banked in a steep curve around the hill. Almost as if it meant to say good-by." Many Finns knew their Sibelius literature well enough to make an immediate association with his *Scene with Cranes* from the incidental music to *Death (Kuolema)*.

Even more impressive than the elaborate state funeral was the preceding evening, when thousands of Finns waited for hours in front of Helsinki's Great Church in order to pay their respects to the composer's remains. Most of them had never seen Sibelius; to them he was a symbol—a legend. When I visited one journalist who was telephoning composers and conductors throughout the world for eulogies to be included in his paper's special memorial edition, I remarked that the cost of the calls would be tremendous. "Sibelius is the last of Finland's great men," the journalist replied. "It will be a long time before we have another."

Uppermost in many people's minds was the Eighth Symphony. There had even been hints that there might be a Ninth Symphony. "Ask any orchestra conductor what composition, by whom, he would prefer to have the privilege of first presenting to the public," Olin Downes wrote shortly before his own death in 1955. "His answer, almost certainly, would be Sibelius's Eighth Symphony, which the world has awaited for the last thirty years! There is every reason to believe, not only from rumor and report, but from fragmentary references made to friends and to the writer, among others, that it was completed years ago; and there are believed to be a number of other scores which may not be heard until after Sibelius's death, if his enigmatical secrecy about them is indication of their destiny."

The "Silence from Järvenpää"

At last the moment had arrived—the end of the long "silence from Järvenpää." Shortly after Sibelius's death, his eldest daughter issued the terse announcement that there was neither an Eighth Symphony nor, for that matter, any new unpublished composition. To all appearances, Sibelius had been silent for thirty years because of creative sterility.

It is difficult to believe that such was the case. Surely there are no signs of creative sterility in *Tapiola*. As we have seen, the Eighth Symphony was ready, or almost ready, for the opening concert of the English Sibelius Society in 1932. Shortly afterward, Koussevitzky entertained high hopes that he would have the privilege of conducting its world *première* in Boston. As the years passed, Sibelius became less and less definite concerning its date of release, and ultimately he destroyed it. It would be more proper to say that his excessively ardent champions destroyed it.

In 1931, Cecil Gray, who had proclaimed the Seventh Symphony one of the miracles of modern music, wrote: "I should not be surprised in the slightest if in his Eighth Symphony, which I understand has been completed and will probably be produced before this book sees the light, he turns his back on his previous achievements in symphonic form and does something entirely different. . . ." Reading these words, Sibelius must have been concerned with the problem of maintaining the proper musical "profile" before his many admirers. "My Eighth Symphony has been 'finished' many times," he wrote Basil Cameron in 1945, "but I am not content with it yet. When the time comes it will be a pleasure to deliver it into your hands."

"What is the Eighth Symphony really like?" Ralph Wood asked in 1947. "What are the other works lying shelved until the composer's death? Are his survivors to be the happy discoverers of successors to the Sixth Symphony and *Tapiola* or to the Seventh Symphony or to *The Tempest?* The speculation is after all, one realises, not wholly a yearning one. Anxiety and even dread are difficult to exclude."

The proud, sensitive composer was on the horns of a dilemma, and such remarks as these must have caused him many hours of mental anguish. The release of his Eighth Symphony would have involved a calculated risk that he was not willing to take. Would it show the world that he too enjoyed the glowing creative sunset of a Verdi? Would it, on the other hand, be compared with the last feeble efforts of his contemporary Richard Strauss?

A few years before Sibelius's death, Professor Otto Andersson, Director of the Sibelius Museum, visited Ainola in order to describe a recent visit to the United States. Sensing that this was a golden opportunity to raise the "forbidden question," Andersson reported that many Americans had asked him about the Eighth Symphony. "If I return to America, what shall I tell them?" he asked. "Yes," Sibelius repeated nervously, "what shall you tell them? What shall you tell them?" After a moment or two of uncomfortable silence, Aino Sibelius looked up from her knitting and smiled. "Janne," she said, "tell Professor Andersson the truth. There is no Eighth Symphony." "That's right," came the answer, "there is no Eighth Symphony." His face brightened as though a heavy weight had been removed from his shoulders.

"There is no lack of biographies, studies, and analytical notes, but they are all as uncritical as were the pioneer books on Wagner. A scholarly counterblast is badly needed in the case of Sibelius."   *Robert Lorenz*

●

Sibelius's international reputation as a symphonist rests almost exclusively upon his popularity among the English-speaking people—in the United States and England in particular. Various theories have been advanced to explain this phenomenon. Cecil Gray, for example, points out that in Italy, France, and Germany, national art has invariably enjoyed preferential treatment, and that consequently Sibelius has been excluded by a spiritual tariff wall. This theory is undoubtedly correct in part.

We may eliminate Italy from the picture with a few words. Having fed almost exclusively in their operatic pastures for centuries, the Italians could hardly be expected to exhibit more than a mild curiosity about Sibelius. For them, the symphonies were quite naturally foreign, even unattractively so.

The French with their traditional passion for the *lointain* might have been expected to show some interest in music proceeding from so remote a region as Finland, but such was not the case. The concept of a spiritual tariff wall may help to explain the French antipathy toward the symphonies of Brahms and Sibelius, but it completely vanishes when we consider their adoration of Wagner. Sibelius once said that his symphonies would have made great headway in France if given a "proper chance" to become known. As early as 1900, the French had their chance and they declined it. In an article bearing the amusing title "Sibelius, the World's Worst Composer," René Leibowitz examined the Fifth Symphony and concluded that the composer's "originality" resulted from his "ignorance, incompetence, and impotence." In another article, "Sibelius, the Eternal Old Man," Leibowitz characterized his over-all production as a "very heavy dead weight" in the music of the twentieth century. "A craftsman, well and good," wrote "Clarendon" in *Figaro*. "A genius? Really, no." Once when Nadia Boulanger was asked for her opinion, she replied: "Ah, Sibelius! Poor, poor Sibelius! A tragic case!" Whatever that may mean, no one will deny that it is very, very French.

Early in his career, Sibelius pinned his greatest hopes on Germany. In the beginning, the Germans evinced a genuine interest in what they considered to be his Finnish-sounding tone poems, and on at least one occasion so formidable a rival as Richard Strauss conducted his Violin Concerto. When we add to this the fact that Sibelius enjoyed the active support of Breitkopf & Härtel, his conquest of Germany must have appeared a certainty. "I have, indeed, had to suffer a good deal for having persevered in composing symphonies at a time when practically all composers turned to other forms of expression," Sibelius recalled at the age of seventy. "My stubbornness was a thorn in the side to many critics and conduc-

tors, and it is really only in recent years that opinion has be-
gun to change."

These remarks were made with the bitter German defeat in mind. It should be understood, however, that the symphonies were coldly received not because they were so similar
to what the Germans already had in abundance, but because
they were so foreign to what they thought should constitute a
symphony. To them, the symphonies of Sibelius sounded like
the awkward fumblings of a rank amateur trying to write in
a form far beyond his powers of comprehension. Even today
most German musicians and musical scholars regard the music
of Sibelius as completely inconsequential. His popularity in
the United States and England they attribute to one of the
many Anglo-Saxon idiosyncrasies that they cannot understand.

Lacking any deeply rooted musical traditions of their
own, the Americans and the English traded freely in the
world music market and opened their concert halls to all foreign importations. Anything and everything was accepted
with equanimity—Verdi and Wagner, Brahms and Tchaikovsky, Debussy and Richard Strauss. Their catholicity in matters
of musical taste made them ideal guinea pigs for all of the
new -isms of the twentieth century.

"Here abroad you are manufacturing cocktails of all
colors," Sibelius is said to have told Breitkopf & Härtel on one
of his visits to Germany, "and now I come with pure cold water." Sibelius never coined a happier metaphor. After a sur-
feit of -isms, this Finnish water found receptive and even
grateful ears among the Anglo-Saxons. Many found it different, unpretentious, and, above all, sincere. Although it frequently sounded a trifle unfinished—some called it "primi-

tive"—this quality actually served to enhance Sibelius's reputation as an honest composer. Whereas much of the new music tended to wear thin after repeated hearings, the symphonies of Sibelius seemed to improve. Thanks to the phonograph records sponsored by the Finnish government and the Sibelius Society, much of his music could be heard in the home.

Within a short time, there was a great thirst for information concerning Finland and her culture. Such exotic words as Väinämöinen, Lemminkäinen, Luonnotar, Tuonela, Pohjola, and Tapiola prompted the curious to read Kirby's translation of the *Kalevala*. Very little was known about Finland and her people. The Finns were regarded as an honest, industrious race, especially in the United States, where they enjoyed the reputation of being the only Europeans to pay their war debts. In time, the music of Sibelius was associated with Finnish topography and described as bleak, gray, austere, cold, primitive, etc. Photographs of Väinö Aaltonen's bust of the composer seemed to enhance this impression of sternness and vision.

Such authorities as Downes, Gray, Lambert, and Ernest Newman were on hand to remind their readers that this Finnish Music, far from being primitive and unfinished, was in reality complex in structure, even *avant-garde*. Sibelius, they claimed, had been the first composer since Beethoven to blaze a new and musically significant trail.

In 1939, the English writer Robert Lorenz felt that the time had come for a "scholarly counterblast" in order to clear the air and separate the Sibelian chaff from the wheat. In the United States, at least, the "counterblast" was not long in coming. How scholarly much of it was is a debatable matter.

Contemporary American composers who had been trained abroad quite understandably resented this slighting of their own music and that of their teachers. The European composers and scholars residing in the United States had, of course, arrived with preconceived notions concerning Sibelius —they did not like him. In the beginning, the hostile and the wary were willing to bide their time, for they believed that Sibelius was merely a fad that would soon pass. Ironically enough, this was the fate of Frederick Delius, who shared their views. But the "fad" demonstrated extraordinary staying-powers, and the public's capacity for Sibelius appeared to be unlimited. In time, the confidence of the anti-Sibelius group yielded to skepticism, which in turn yielded to anger.

Nadia Boulanger's students—frequently known as products of the *boulangerie*—could not have been expected to display any interest in the "tragic case." Aaron Copland, battling desperately to strike the significant contemporary note in his own compositions, presented his opinions in a book entitled *Our New Music*. All of this "nonsense" about Sibelius, he felt, was owing to the exaggerated commentaries of a handful of English and American critics. They obscured the true picture of a late-nineteenth-century composer who, in Copland's opinion, had nothing significant to say for twentieth-century ears. "The attempt to set Sibelius up as a great modern composer is certain to fail," he predicted.

The versatile composer and critic Virgil Thomson revealed himself as a *summa cum laude* graduate of the *bou-*

langerie when he labeled Sibelius "a provincial beyond description." The composer's whole technique and outlook, he felt, were derived from Tchaikovsky—this in reference to the Seventh Symphony!—and his "dirty-brown orchestral coloring" was proof that he was ignorant in this department. "I realize that there are many sincere Sibelius lovers in the world," Thomson conceded, "though I have never met one among professional educated musicians." Thomson, we should add, has spent a good part of his life in France.

Russian-born Nicholas Nabokov, erstwhile composer-teacher-impresario, received his musical training in St. Petersburg, Berlin, and Stuttgart. Consequently, it is no surprise that he characterized Sibelius as one of the many "demi-vierges of Western musical culture," his symphonies as "antediluvian monstrosities." The Hungarian-born critic and musicologist Paul Henry Láng wrote that he was astounded by the deification accorded to Sibelius by America. The good points in the composer's favor, Láng observed, were offset by the "obesity . . . turgidity, and redundance" in his music, in which the melodies were too long and drawn-out. Paul Rosenfeld, also a critic, complained that Sibelius's melodies were too short and rather uncharitably called the composer "that overstuffed Finnish bard."

In a guidebook for those interested in phonograph records, B. H. Haggin described the Fourth Symphony as "those pretentious snorts of the brass, those ominous drum-rolls, those wild cries of the woodwinds, a bogus mortar of stylistic mannerisms with which Sibelius pads out a few thematic fragments into a symphony movement." Near the end of Haggin's volume, the prospective record-buyer can find

Sibelius's principal compositions listed according to their standards of excellence. *The Swan of Tuonela* is included among the "good," the Second Symphony among the "lesser," the Fourth Symphony among the "poor," and *En Saga* among the "worst" compositions.

Other writers decided to handle the Sibelius problem by ignoring him altogether. In schoolboy fashion, they simply sent him to Coventry. In Lazare Saminsky's *Music of Our Day,* which appeared in 1932, the name of Sibelius is absent. Seven years later, much water had flowed over the dam, and in a revised edition of his book, Saminsky was compelled to reckon with the problem. In a new chapter entitled "Sibelius, a Mind Two-dimensional," he paid tribute to the creator of the early tone poems as a racial and regional genius. But the symphonies he found episodic and poverty-stricken examples of insipid improvisation. Lacking "syntactic originality," Sibelius wrote what amounted to song-symphonies.

A third group of critics neatly avoided both direct attacks and the Coventry treatment. They resorted to an interesting variation of the guilt-by-association type of accusation. They painted Grieg, Borodin, Tchaikovsky, Dvořák, and Smetana, for example, as fine fellows for their times. But when they said that the music of Sibelius was derived from some or all of these composers, they implied that such innocent labels as "romanticism" and "nationalism" were derogatory when applied to a man who had composed most of his music after 1900.

Thus, in many music histories and appreciation manuals, we find the Finnish composer's name relegated to a few lines in chapters entitled "The Late Romantics," "The Post-

Romantics," "The Neo-Romantics," "The Twilight of Romanticism," etc., or with the same prefixes applied to nationalism. Although some of these writers were undoubtedly sincere in their attempts to find the proper niche for a composer who simply did not fit into any textbook classification scheme, many subscribed to the doctrinaire attitude that regards romanticism and nationalism as sins.

Lorenz's call for a counterblast was slightly delayed in England, but when it came, it was somewhat more scholarly than most of the American attacks. This, at least, holds true for Ralph Wood's chapter on the miscellaneous orchestral and theater music in *Sibelius, a Symposium,* which was published in 1947. Many will disagree with Wood's opinions on the merits of individual compositions, but few, if any, will challenge his commendable attempt to separate compositions of genuine worth from the *Valse lyrique* and its many brothers and sisters.

On the occasion of Sibelius's ninetieth birthday, there were a few London echoes of the counterblast. "Such music has to be cultivated sparingly," Eric Blom observed, "and I daresay that we have been dangerously generous in our wholesale acceptance of a number of works—a small number admittedly—by Sibelius." Martin Cooper wrote: "During the Symphony [the Third] and the Violin Concerto it was difficult not to wonder whether England has overrated Sibelius's music and swallowed greedily the whole orchestral output of a composer who is in reality more uneven than most and more the slave of his own clichés. . . . It is not too soon to start a drastic process of weeding in the luxuriant garden of Sibelius enthusiasms." Neville Cardus illustrated his point with an old joke: when a lady was asked if she would like to have a recording of a Sibelius symphony for Christmas, she replied: "But I've got one already."

Since 1950, there has been a continuation of the weeding process. Some Finnish scholars, however, are confident that just the reverse will take place abroad, that such rarely performed compositions as the Third and Sixth symphonies and *Voces intimae* will be hailed as masterpieces. One suspects that they are making the wish father to the thought. It is unlikely that any of the early unpublished manuscripts such as *Kullervo* will enhance the composer's reputation. During his life, Sibelius published his finest works and much that is not fine.

Sibelius's unique position in Finland's cultural life is the greatest guarantee of his continuing popularity in that small country. Generations of school children have been raised on his songs and choral pieces, which are relatively unknown abroad. It is virtually impossible to find any collection of Finnish songs in which Sibelius is not represented by a half-dozen or more. At concerts, his symphonies constitute the "classical" nucleus about which other works are grouped.

Time has converted certain popular compositions into ceremonial numbers. *Spring Song (Vårsång)* always figures in concerts heard around May 1. *Finlandia* is wisely reserved for special occasions as an exaltation of Finnish nationalism. Oddly enough, the once famous *Valse triste* has fallen by the wayside. During a two-year stay in Finland, I heard it only once, in a radio concert emanating from Estonia.

During his thirty years of musical silence, the living Sibelius had a profound—some might say negative—influence on contemporary Finnish music. Openly the younger composers spoke reverently of "the Master" as a shining example; privately many considered him an oppressive cowl. Sibelius's concern for his reputation both at home and abroad precluded any active interest in the work of younger men. On many occasions, to be sure, he permitted his great name to be included on honorary prize committees, but he never used his influence to secure pensions and travel grants for the deserving, as others had done for him.

When one young composer dared to voice such opinions in public, he was severely reprimanded by his elders and informed that the Master was displeased. Indeed, the lot of the younger men has not been a happy one. They could not write in what has come to be known as the Sibelius idiom without the risk of being called caricaturists. In an effort to find distinctive modes of expression, they looked abroad. Consequently much of the post-Sibelius Finnish music betrays the strong influence of Debussy, Ravel, Stravinsky, Schönberg, and—rather surprisingly—Shostakovich and Kabalevsky.

Shortly after the composer's death, a new Sibelius Society was formed in Finland. Constituted along broad regional lines, it has among its members distinguished scholars and musicians and one member of Sibelius's immediate family. Among its many declared objectives are the promotion of the composer's music both at home and abroad, the encouragement of Sibelius scholarship, the restoration of the house in which he was born, and the erection of new monuments. One member of the Society informed me that among the more important long-range objectives will be an attempt to inspire among the Germans and the French a greater understanding and appreciation of Sibelius's music than they have displayed in the past. It will be interesting to see how this formidable task is approached and with what results.

Although such propaganda efforts at this late date are thoroughly understandable, they may strike some as pointing backward instead of forward. The Society's very existence would seem to contradict the assertions that Sibelius's art has long since become universal. In the final analysis, the most powerful agents for such propaganda are the published scores, many of which have been available for more than half a century.

Chapter XIX   The Sibelius Problem

"Sibelius is an aggravatingly difficult person to catalogue."   Lawrence Abbott

•

Historians and other writers have been unable to agree concerning the label needed to indicate Sibelius's position in music. Was he a "classic," "neo-classic," "romantic," "late-romantic," "impressionist," "realist," or "modern"? From a chronological point of view, he appeared to merit inclusion in what has been called the "late-romantic" period. But this tells us nothing if Richard Strauss and Elgar both belong to the same period. Convenient as such labels may be, in the final analysis we must admit that we are playing with words that have no precise meaning. Some writers simply gave up in despair and called Sibelius a "composer in isolation."

Even within himself, Sibelius presented problems for those who divided his music into periods or phases. The most popular was the tripartite division that appeared to work so nicely in the case of Beethoven: (1) *Kalevala—Romantic* (1892–1903), (2) *European—Classical* (1903–19), and (3) *Universal* (1919–26). Some writers insisted that the Second Symphony marked the beginning of the middle period rather than the culmination of the first one; others felt that the Fifth Symphony was more "universal" than "classical."

One writer, David Cherniavsky, established another period to take care of the enigmatic Fourth Symphony, which stands in a class by itself.

Everything collapsed when one was forced to reckon with the many "exceptions." The *Kalevala*-inspired tone poems, *The Swan of Tuonela* (1893), *Pohjola's Daughter* (1906), and *Tapiola* (1926), each belonged to a different period. Which was more or less romantic, classical, or universal than the others, and why? Although many claimed that the third period was characterized by lofty contemplation and a general summing up of experience, it was difficult to detect these qualities in *Valse lyrique, Valse chevaleresque, Suite mignonne, Suite champêtre,* and *Suite caractéristique.* Among the minor instrumental compositions, the little *Epilogue* for violin published in 1888 seemed to be the twin of the *Humoresque* dating from 1929. And then there were all those pieces for the piano—more than 130 of them!

Cecil Gray, in his own tripartite division—(1) *Romantic and National,* (2) *Eclectic and Cosmopolitan,* and (3) *Classic and Universal*—solved this problem by claiming that these periods developed side by side instead of seriatim. He added, however, that throughout the composer's career each of these periods was in the ascendant at different stages. These stages were (1) when the composer lived in Helsinki, (2) when he traveled abroad, and (3) when he sought seclusion in Järvenpää. Apparently Gray did not take into account that Sibelius traveled abroad throughout his active life and that he had nothing to give to the world once the real seclusion at Järvenpää commenced.

The fundamental error in this approach springs from

a desire to prove that there was a definite intellectual and spiritual growth in the music of Sibelius. After his retirement, the composer made frequent references to his "way," and his biographers quite understandably felt compelled to chart it.

In the final analysis, Sibelius's reputation as a great composer rests upon his seven "absolute" symphonies and, to a slightly smaller extent, upon some of his programmatic tone poems. We may with justification exclude both the Violin Concerto and *Voces intimae* as solitary excursions in different directions. One is a highly successful concession to popular taste, the other an attempt to produce a quasi-symphonic string quartet. Although neither of these works could have been written by anyone else, we do not think of Sibelius as the creator of concertos and chamber music.

In the shorter forms, Sibelius is frequently revealed as a conscientious craftsman possessing rare abilities. This especially holds true for his theater music. Here almost everything may be found: the elegant miniatures for *King Kristian II,* the darkly colored interludes for *Pelléas et Mélisande,* the pseudo-Oriental moods in *Belshazzar's Feast,* the delicate background music for two scenes in *The Lizard,* and the gigantic score for *The Tempest.* Sir Thomas Beecham may have had Sibelius's theater music in mind when he wrote: "It is a fact that it is exceedingly difficult to compose good light music, and the study of this branch of his work has suggested to one person at least that Sibelius has done it better than anyone who has yet lived."

We do not think of Sibelius as essentially a composer of choral music and art songs, though his contributions in

these departments have been considerable. Many of the unaccompanied choral pieces based on the *Kalevala* and the
Kanteletar are strikingly original, but they are so closely
wedded to their texts that the linguistic barrier prevents their
being appreciated by non-Finns. Only a few of the more than
one hundred art songs are known outside Finland, though
most of them have been published by Breitkopf & Härtel with
German and English texts. Perhaps their failure to achieve international popularity may be attributed to the fact that they
lack the original qualities associated with the symphonies and
tone poems.

In the first chapter of this study, I posed the following questions: Are the symphonies of Sibelius different from
those of his contemporaries and predecessors primarily because he was unwilling or unable—as some have intimated—
to present his musical ideas in forms that would give them
logic and continuity? Are the forms so highly personalized and
intellectualized as to constitute a veritable revolution in music?

It does seem significant that the great preoccupation
with Sibelius as a radical innovator in matters of form began
after his retirement. Apparently no one was more astonished
by these revelations of highly complex tonal relationships and
the evolution of "germ" motifs than the composer himself.
Musical vivisection was so completely foreign to his way of
thinking that he frequently protested that his admirers were
attempting to turn him into a cerebral composer, whereas in
reality he regarded his symphonies as "poems." Now, poems
may embody intricate rhyming schemes within themselves,
but Sibelius did not have this in mind when making such a

comparison. "Music can reach its true power only when it is guided by poetic meaning," he had written early in his career.

If Sibelius was astonished to discover all these things which he had accomplished, he was also pleased. Conflicting opinions regarding the significance of such and such a thematic fragment—whether it should be properly designated as an introduction, the first theme, the second theme, or the logical evolution of a "germ" announced in an earlier movement —helped to enhance his reputation as a musical enigma. Consequently, he carefully refrained from taking sides in such controversies even when pressed by intimates for a direct answer. In the academic folderol concerning the three- vs. four-movement structure of the Fifth Symphony, Sibelius refused to give Ringbom a direct answer, stating that he was unwilling to take part in a controversy in which both sides were justified in maintaining their respective views. The matter might have been settled to everybody's satisfaction had the scholars been permitted to examine the manuscript of the first version, but Sibelius cannily refused to make it available.

"As usual I am a slave to my themes and submit to their demands," the composer once confessed. This has been used by his admirers and detractors to support their respective positions. The germinal evolution of themes, some argue, so completely dominates Sibelius's approach to music that the consequences seem to be inevitable. On the other hand, there are those who point out that his symphonies are deficient in terms of form precisely because Sibelius is the slave rather than the master of his themes. The symphony, they continue, is one of the most complex forms of musical expression and requires that a composer exercise a high degree of control at all times in order to provide balance and contrast while at the same time imposing a sovereign unity throughout.

Whether one chooses to regard the symphonies as being either highly episodic or highly complex in form, different words are being used to describe the same phenomenon. The Sibelian way of saying things in music is the natural consequence of the composer's personality—indeed, it could not be otherwise. Konow found Janne a most imaginative child capable of inventing plays in which sudden and last-minute changes in the action created "the most preposterous scenes." Karl Flodin was bewildered by Sibelius the music student as a conversationalist, and characterized his train of thought as "confused" and "lacking a firm foundation." "Sibelius sober was like the rest of us when we were drunk," Kajanus recalled. In his early thirties, Sibelius delivered a lecture on folk music which impressed the professors of the Imperial Alexander University as being "mosaic."

As early as 1892, Finnish critics took pains to point out the "mosaic" structure of *Kullervo*. They attributed the many striking musical ideas to the composer's genius, but added that they followed one another in too rapid succession, and consequently were imperfectly developed. The symphonies evoked the same comments from critics who heard them for the first time—"ends that do not seem to meet" or words to that effect.

The more obvious attempts to join these loose ends frequently appear crude and unconvincing: the sustained four-part chords for horns and trombones over a timpani roll, the eternal pedals in the string bass, and the never-ending string tremolos, which nearly drive musicians out of their minds. This may help to explain why many conductors refuse to perform the Sibelius symphonies. They resent what they feel to be the added and unfair duty of having to impose a unity not apparent in the printed scores. When Karl Muck said: "I'm blest if I know what he wants," after rehearsing the Fourth Symphony eight times, he was not admitting his own deficiencies, but pointing out those of the composer in a very tactful manner.

And yet for those who enjoy the symphonies of Sibelius, there is a unity both adequate and satisfying. The abrupt changes of thought and the long periods of uncertainty out of which new ideas slowly and painfully emerge strike them as being the peculiar speech mannerisms of a man who has something significant to say. For them, the greatness of Sibelius resides in the triumph of ideas over form.

Although Sibelius has frequently been hailed as a "folk" composer, no one has been able to prove that he actually employed Finnish folk melodies in his symphonies and tone poems. As early as 1936, however, Professor A. O. Väisänen drew attention to certain marked similarities between Sibelius's melodies and those found in Finnish folk tunes. More recently, the conductor Simon Parmet attempted to show that Sibelius's melodies are based on the rhythms and inflections peculiar to the Finnish language.

When we recall that Sibelius, early in his career, served as a folklorist, additional weight is given to the suspicion that many of his melodies were inspired by folk tunes. For the average Finnish concert-goer, this has been self-evident ever since hearing the music of Sibelius. Whether the melody in question is from one of the seven symphonies or a tone poem, a Finn will invariably tell his foreign guest: "This music is Finnish—I can't explain why, but it belongs to our soil, our culture."

Although the tone poems are every bit as "mosaic" as the symphonies, they are less vulnerable to charges of formal deficiencies for the obvious reason that no one has ever established textbook rules by which to measure tone poems. On the surface, however, it would appear that the programmatic tone poems represent another aspect of Sibelius's art, as opposed to the seven "absolute" symphonies. Oddly enough, Sibelius began and ended his career with programmatic tone poems—*Kullervo* in 1892, *Tapiola* in 1926—and the symphonies all fall between these two extremities.

Kullervo and the *Lemminkäinen Suite* embody highly detailed programs, for they are musical narratives. *Tapiola* is an evocation of the legendary Finnish forest god and his realm inhabited by supernatural creatures; so that there would be no confusion on this point, Sibelius inserted a quatrain of his own writing in the published score. Other tone poems such as *En Saga, Pohjola's Daughter,* and *Night Ride and Sunrise* appear to have no programs other than their titles. Whether some can be said to be more or less programmatic than others is a minor matter, for they are all one in that they were conceived as "literary" music.

As Sibelius's fame as a composer of "absolute" symphonies increased, he made frequent attempts to minimize the programmatic significance of his tone poems, claiming that he was not a "literary" musician and that he believed that music began where words left off. During the spring of 1957, only a few months before Sibelius's death, I published an article on the *Lemminkäinen Suite* in a leading Finnish newspaper. It established beyond any doubt that the composer had printed detailed and lengthy programs for three of the tone poems, and that these differed greatly from those advanced by his biographers. Furthermore, it proved that the first of them, *Lemminkäinen and the Maidens of the Island,* had been published by Breitkopf & Härtel in 1954 under the incorrect title *Lemminkäinen and the Maidens of Saari.*

It would be an exaggeration to say that this article fell like a bombshell in Finnish musical circles, but for a brief spell there was considerable doubt that it could be correct, for Sibelius himself had prepared his manuscripts for publication. However, *Lemminkäinen and the Maidens of the Island* was listed with its correct title during the Sibelius Festival of 1957 for the first time in sixty years, and I was gratified to learn that Mrs. Sibelius pronounced the article correct. But when the composer was consulted on this matter by his secretary, he said that he did not have any specific programs in mind and that one would do just as well as the other.

We have seen that Sibelius's confession to Erkko in 1893 that "absolute music" could not by itself satisfy indicates how literary a composer he was at that time. When, one may properly ask, did he change his views? At the time of the First Symphony? The Second? The Fifth? The Seventh? Did he ever change them? *Tapiola* would indicate that the answer to this last question may be in the negative.

As a logical consequence, we must then ask: how "absolute" are the seven symphonies, and is the First more "absolute" than the Seventh? There are, of course, no ready and satisfactory answers, but once these questions have been posed, they may not be dismissed lightly. They are important if we are to understand how Sibelius thought musically. Ilmari Krohn has been ridiculed for his attempts to attribute programmatic significance to these symphonies in his *Der Stimmungsgehalt der Symphonien von Jean Sibelius,* and few people would accept his theories as having any basis in fact. The importance of Krohn's position is that it is symptomatic of the general suspicion that the symphonies are more deeply rooted in reality than Sibelius would have us believe. A case in point is the Second Symphony, which the Finnish intelligentsia invariably refer to as the "patriotic" symphony, and which, for that reason, is usually played on state occasions.

If the composer decided to conceal the literary background of his symphonies, he slipped up on one occasion after the *première* of his Fourth Symphony. It is difficult to believe that Wasenius could have imagined so distinctive a Sibelian program as impressions of the Koli Mountain. Nor does Sibelius's explanation that he made this up as an April Fool's Day joke ring with sincerity. One could not imagine a less amusing joke than this. Perhaps the composer's letters to Axel Carpelan—if they are ever revealed in their entirety—will help to shed greater light on such matters.

Sibelius is a composer who both merits and can stand a great deal of light. His emotional insecurity and the fear that the world might laugh at him compelled him to seek protection in shadows where he could pose as a musical enigma, a man of mystery. He was eminently successful in maintaining this profile during his lifetime, and his overzealous admirers dutifully held up their mirrors to it. But the time for such blind hero-worship is now over. It would have been over in 1926 if Sibelius the legend had not outlived Sibelius the composer.

Externally, Sibelius's "way" was singularly free from the struggles and anguish associated with other great musical geniuses. His greatest anguish was that of an artist striving to become articulate in his art, and his greatest struggles were within himself. "Musical inspiration is like the children's game of *Word-taking and Word-making*," Sibelius told Mrs. Newmarch. "A spiritual force (call it God) throws down to one a handful of letters—a message—and a voice says: 'Make what you can of this.' Alas, we cannot always make the best of it."

Complete List of Compositions and Arrangements by Jean Sibelius *

Abbreviations of publishers' and printers' names:

A.	Affärstryckeriet, Turku
A.H.	Abraham Hirsch, Stockholm
A.L.	Axel Lindgren, Helsinki
B. & H.	Breitkopf & Härtel, Wiesbaden
C.	Chappell & Co., London
D.	Delanchy-Dupré, Asnières (Seine)
F.	Fazerin Musiikkikaupa Oy, Helsinki
F. & W.	Fazer & Westerlund, Helsinki
H.	Wilhelm Hansen, Copenhagen
J.W.	J. Wikstedtin Kivipaino, Helsinki
K.W.	K. F. Wasenius, Helsinki
L.	Robert Lienau, Berlin—Lichterfelde
L.M.	Laulu-Miehet, Helsinki
M.	Grand Lodge of Free and Accepted Masons of the State of New York
M.A.	Musices Amantes, Turku
M.M.	Muntra Musikanter, Helsinki
M.K.	Musiikkikeskus, Helsinki
N.M.F.	Nordiska Musikförlaget, Stockholm
O.	Kustannusosakeyhtiö Otava, Helsinki
S.	Werner Söderström, Helsinki
Säv. 2	Sävelisto, Vol. 2
S.B.	Silver Burdett, Boston
S.F.V.	Svenska Folkskolans Vänner, Helsinki
S.L.	Suomen Laulajain ja Soittajain Liitto, Helsinki
S.M.	Suomen Musiikkilehti, Helsinki
T.	F. Tilgmann, Helsinki
U.E.	Universal-Edition, Vienna
W.	R. E. Westerlund Oy, Helsinki
Y.L.	Ylioppilaskunnan Laulajat, Helsinki

* A fairly complete list of arrangements by other musicians may be found in Lauri Solanterä's The Works of Jean Sibelius (Helsinki: R. E. Westerlund Oy; 1955).

List of Compositions and Arrangements

The date following the publisher indicates the year in which the work was composed or arranged. The instrumentation is to be read as follows:

2222/4331/11/1/str.

2 flutes	2 oboes	2 clarinets	2 bassoons
4 horns	3 trumpets	3 trombones	1 tuba
timpani	1 percussion		
1 harp			
string orchestra			

A. WITH OPUS NUMBERS

Opus	Title	Publisher	Date
1.	Five Christmas Songs, with piano	W.	1895–1913

    1. *Nu står jul vid snöig port* (Topelius)
        [*Now Christmas Stands at the Snowy Gate*]
    2. *Nu så kommer julen* (Topelius)
        [*Now Christmas Comes*]
    3. *Det mörknar ute* (Topelius)
        [*Outside It Grows Dark*]
    4. *Giv mig ej glans* (Topelius)
        [*Give Me No Splendor*]
    5. *On hanget korkeat* (Joukahainen)
        [*High Are the Snowdrifts*]

Opus	Title	Publisher	Date
2.	Two Pieces for Violin	U.E.	1888 rev. 1912

    1. *Romance* in B minor
        [First version in *Nornan*, 1890]
    2. *Epilogue*
        [First version in *Nuori Suomi*, 1891,
        under title *Perpetuum mobile*]

Opus	Title	Publisher	Date
3.	*Arioso* (Runeberg), song with piano	W.	1893
	With string orchestra	W.	rev. 1913

    Also known as *Flickans årstider*
    [*The Maiden's Seasons*]

Opus	Title	Publisher	Date
4.	String Quartet in B flat major	Ms.	1889
	Presto arranged for string orchestra	Ms.	?
5.	Six Impromptus, for piano	B. & H.	1893
	Nos. 5 & 6 arranged for string orchestra under title *Impromptu* [Probably the composition known as *Andante lirico*]	Ms.	1894
6.	*Cassazione*, for orchestra		1904
	Orchestra 1: 2222/4231/10/0/ str.	Ms.	
	2: 2020/2110/10/0/ str.	Ms.	
7.	*Kullervo*, symphonic poem for soprano, baritone, male chorus, and orchestra	Ms.	1892
	1. *Introduction*		
	2. *The Youth of Kullervo*		
	3. *Kullervo and His Sister*		
	With piano	Ms.	
	Choral parts	J.W.	
	Kullervon valitus [*Kullervo's Lament*], in *Uusi Säveletär*, December 1918		
	4. *Kullervo Leaves for the War*		
	5. *Kullervo's Death*		
	Orchestra: 2222/4331/11/0/str.		
8.	Incidental Music to *Ödlan* [*The Lizard*], by M. Lybeck (Act II, scenes 1 & 3), for solo violin and string quintet	Ms.	1909
9.	*En Saga*, tone poem for orchestra	B. & H.	1892
	Orchestra: 2222/4331/01/0/ str.		rev. 1901
	Original version	Ms.	
10.	*Karelia Overture*	B. & H.	1893
	Orchestra: 3222/4331/11/0/str.		

List of Compositions and Arrangements

Opus	Title	Publisher	Date
11.	*Karelia Suite*	B. & H.	1893

    1. *Intermezzo*
    2. *Ballade*
    3. *Alla marcia*
    Orchestra: 3222/4331/11/0/str.

	Nos. 1 & 2 arranged for piano	A.L.	1897

    See: *Karelia* Music (no opus no.)

12.	Sonata in F major, for piano	B. & H.	1893

    1. *Allegro molto*
    2. *Andantino*
    3. *Vivacissimo*

13.	Seven Songs of Runeberg, with piano	B. & H.	

    1. *Under strandens granar* — 1892
      ['*Neath the Fir Trees*]
    2. *Kyssens hopp* — 1892
      [*The Kiss's Hope*]
    3. *Hjärtats morgon* — 1891
      [*The Heart's Morning*]
    4. *Våren flyktar hastigt* — 1891
      [*Spring is Flying*]
      ·With orchestra: 2000/4000/ 01/0/str. — Ms. — 1914
    5. *Drömmen* — 1891
      [*The Dream*]
    6. *Till Frigga* — 1892
      [*To Frigga*]
    7. *Jägargossen* — 1891
      [*The Young Hunter*]

14.	*Rakastava* [*The Lover*], for male chorus a cappella. Text from Book I of the *Kanteletar*	Y.L.	1893

    1. *Missä armahani?* (canto 173)
      [*Where Is My Beloved?*]
    2. *Armahan kulku* (canto 174)
      [*My Beloved's Path*]
    3. *Hyvää iltaa, lintuseni* (canto 122)
      [*Good Evening, My Little Bird*]

Opus	Title	Publisher	Date
	With string orchestra	Ms.	1894
	For mixed chorus a cappella	Säv. 3	1898
	For string orchestra, triangle, and timpani [rewritten]	B. & H.	1911
	1. *The Lover*		
	2. *The Path of the Beloved*		
	3. *Good Night—Farewell!*		
15.	*Skogsrået* [*The Wood Nymph*], for piano, two horns, and strings to accompany the recitation of verses by Rydberg	Ms.	1894
	Revised as a tone poem for orchestra	Ms.	1894
	Orchestra: 2222/4330/11/0/str.		
	From "Skogsrået," for piano (N.B. The *Impromptu* & *Romance*, opus 24, are not from *Skogsrået*, as Abraham claims)	B. & H.	1895
16.	*Vårsång* [*Spring Song*], tone poem	B. & H.	1894
	Orchestra: 2222/4331/11/0/str.		
17.	Seven Songs, with piano	B. & H.	
	1. *Sen har jag ej frågat mera* (Runeberg)		1894
	[*And I Questioned Them No Further*]		
	With Orchestra: 2222/ 4000/11/0/str.	Ms.	1903
	2. *Sov in!* (Tavaststjerna)		1894
	[*Slumber*]		
	With Orchestra: 2022/ 1000/10/0/str.	Ms.	
	3. *Fågellek* (Tavaststjerna)		1891
	[*Enticement*]		
	With Orchestra: 1100/ 1000/01/1/str.	Ms.	
	4. *Vilse* (Tavaststjerna)		1894
	[*Astray*]		

List of Compositions and Arrangements

Opus	Title	Publisher	Date
	5. *En slända* (Levertin)		1894[?]
	[*The Dragonfly*]		
	With Orchestra: 2122/		
	3000/01/1/str.	Ms.	
	6. *Illalle* (Forsman—Koskim-		
	ies)		1898
	[*To Evening*]		
	7. *Lastu lainehilla* (Calamnius)		1898
	[*Driftwood*]		
18.	Nine Part-Songs, for male chorus a cappella		
	1. *Isänmaalle* (Cajander)	O.	1900
	[*To the Fatherland*]		
	For mixed chorus a cappella	O.	
	Also known as *Yks' voima* [*One Power*]		
	2. *Veljeni vierailla mailla* (Aho)	L.M.	1904
	[*My Brothers Abroad*]		
	3. *Saarella palaa* (*Kanteletar*, I,		
	186)	B. & H.	1895
	[*Fire on the Island*]		
	For mixed chorus a cappella	Säv. 4	1898
	Also known as *Työnsä kumpasellaki*		
	[*Each Has His Job*]		
	4. *Min rastas raataa* (*Kanteletar*,		
	I, 219)	?	1898
	[*Busy as a Thrush*]		
	For mixed chorus a cappella	Säv. 4	1898
	5. *Metsämiehen laulu* (Kivi)	B. & H.	1898
	[*The Woodman's Song*]		
	6. *Sydämeni laulu* (Kivi)	B. & H.	1898
	[*The Song of My Heart*]		
	For mixed chorus a cappella	Säv. 8	1907
	7. *Sortunut ääni* (*Kanteletar*, I,		
	57)	B. & H.	1898
	[*The Broken Voice*]		
	For mixed chorus a cappella	Säv. 3	1898
	8. *Terve kuu* (*Kalevala*, XLIX,		
	403–23)	B. & H.	1901
	[*Hail, Moon!*]		

Opus	Title	Publisher	Date
	9. *Venematka* (*Kalevala*, XL, 1–16) [*The Boat Journey*] For mixed chorus a cappella	B. & H. O.	1893
19.	Impromptu, for women's chorus and orchestra (Rydberg)	B. & H.	1902, rev. 1910
	Orchestra: 2222/4000/11/1/str. With piano Choral parts (first version) in facsimile Also known as *Lifslust* and *Gossar och flickor*	B. & H.	
20.	*Malinconia*, for cello with piano	B. & H.	1901
21.	*Natus in curas*, for male chorus a cappella (Gustafsson)	B. & H.	1896
22.	*Lemminkäinen Suite*, for orchestra	B. & H.	
	1. *Lemminkäinen and the Maidens of the Island* Orchestra: 2222/4330/12/0/str. Through an error, published as *Lemminkäinen and the Maidens of Saari*		1895, rev. 1897, 1939
	2. *Lemminkäinen in Tuonela* Orchestra: 2222/4330/03/0/str.		1895, rev. 1897, 1939
	3. *The Swan of Tuonela* Orchestra: 0112/4030/11/1/str.		1893, rev. 1897, 1900
	4. *Lemminkäinen's Homeward Journey* Orchestra: 2222/4331/13/0/str. (N.B. In 1947, Sibelius indicated that when performed as a suite the order of nos. 2 & 3 should be reversed.)		1895, rev. 1897, 1900
23.	Cantata for the University Ceremonies of 1897, for soloists, mixed chorus, and orchestra (Koskimies)	Ms.	1897
	Choral parts in facsimile Excerpts in *Lauluja sekaköörille* [*Songs for Mixed Chorus*]:	F. & W.	1899
	1. *Me nuoriso Suomen* [*We the Youth of Finland*]		

Opus	*Title*	*Publisher*	*Date*
	2. *Tuuli tuudittele* [*The Wind Rocks*]		
	3. *Oi toivo, toivo, sä lietomieli* [*Oh Hope, Hope, You Dreamer*]		
	4. *Montapa elon merellä* [*Many on the Sea of Life*]		
	5. *Sammuva sainio maan* [*The Fading Thoughts of the Earth*]		
	6a. *Soi kiitokseksi Luojan* [*Let Thanks Ring unto the Lord*] For women's chorus	F.	
	6b. *Tuule, tuule leppeämmin* [*Blow, Blow Gentler*]		
	7. *Lempi, sun valtas ääretön on* [*Love, Your Realm Is Limitless*]		
	8. *Kuin virta vuolas* [*As the Swift Current*]		
	9. *Oi kallis Suomi, äiti verraton* [*Oh Precious Finland, Incomparable Mother*]		
24.	Ten Pieces for Piano	B. & H.	
	1. *Impromptu*		1894
	2. *Romance* in A major		1894
	3. *Caprice*		1895
	4. *Romance* in D minor		1895
	5. *Waltz* in E major		1895
	6. *Idyll*		1898
	7. *Andantino*		1898
	8. *Nocturne*		1900
	9. *Romance* in D flat major		1903
	10. *Barcarola*		1903
25.	(From the music for the "Press Celebrations")		
	Scènes historiques I, for orchestra	B. & H.	1899
	1. *All' Overtura* (Tableau 1) Orchestra: 2222/4330/10/0/str.		rev. 1911
	2. *Scena* (Tableau 4) Orchestra: 2222/4330/13/0/str.		
	3. *Festivo* (Tableau 3) Orchestra: 2222/4330/13/0/str.		

Opus	*Title*	*Publisher*	*Date*
	See: "Press Celebrations" Music (no opus no.)		
26.	(From the music for the "Press Celebrations")		
	Finlandia (Tableau 6)	B. & H.	1899
	Orchestra: 2222/4331/12/o/str.		rev. 1900
	For piano	B. & H.	1900
27.	Incidental music to *King Kristian II*, by A. Paul	B. & H.	1898
	1. *Elegie*		
	2. *Musette*		
	3. *Menuetto*		
	4. *Fool's Song of the Spider*		
	5. *Nocturne*		
	6. *Serenade*		
	7. *Ballade*		
	Orchestra: 2222/4230/11/1/str., and voice		
	Suite for orchestra (less no. 4)	B. & H.	
	Nos. 1–4, for piano	B. & H.	
28.	*Sandels*, improvisation for male chorus and orchestra (Runeberg)	Ms.	1898
	Orchestra: 2222/4230/11/o/ str.	Ms.	rev. 1915
	With piano	Ms.	
	Choral parts	M.M.	
29.	*Snöfrid*, improvisation for mixed chorus, recitation, and orchestra (Rydberg)	Ms.	1900[?]
	Orchestra: 2121/2310/11/o/str.		
	With piano	H.	
	Choral parts	T.	
30.	*Islossningen i Uleå älv*, improvisation for male chorus, recitation, and orchestra (Topelius)	Ms.	1898
	[*The Breaking of the Ice on the Uleå River*]		
	Orchestra: 2222/4331/11/o/str.		
	Choral parts in facsimile		

List of Compositions and Arrangements

Opus	Title	Publisher	Date
31.	1. *Laulu Lemminkäiselle*, for male chorus and orchestra (Veijola)	Ms.	1894[?]
	[*A Song for Lemminkäinen*] Orchestra: 2222/4231/10/0/str. Choral parts in hectograph		
	2. *Har du mod?* for male chorus and orchestra (Wecksell)	Ms.	1904
	Orchestra: 2222/4231/12/0/str.		
	With piano	A.L.	
	Choral parts	W.	
	3. *Atenarnes sång*, for boys' and men's voices with saxhorn septet and percussion (Rydberg)	B. & H.	1899
	[*Song of the Athenians*] Arranged: 2222/4331/11/0/ str. bass	Ms.	
	With piano	B. & H.	
32.	*Tulen synty*, for baritone, male chorus, and orchestra (*Kalevala*, XLVII, 41–110)	Ms.	1902
	[*The Origin of Fire*]		rev. 1910
	Orchestra: 2222/4231/13/0/str.		
	With piano	B. & H.	
	Choral parts	n.p., n.d.	
	Also known as *Ukko the Firemaker*		
33.	*Koskenlaskijan morsiamet*, for baritone or mezzo-soprano and orchestra (Oksanen)	B. & H.	1897
	[*The Rapids-Shooter's Brides*]		
	Orchestra: 2222/4230/13/0/str.		
	With piano	B. & H.	
	Voice part for male chorus	n.p., n.d.	
	Also known as *The Ferryman's Brides*		
34.	Ten Pieces for Piano		1914–16
	1. *Waltz*	B. & H.	
	2. *Dance Air*	B. & H.	

List of Compositions and Arrangements

Opus	Title	Publisher	Date
	3. *Mazurka*	B. & H.	
	4. *Humorous*	B. & H.	
	5. *Drollery*	B. & H.	
	6. *Rêverie*	B. & H.	
	7. *Pastoral Dance*	W.	
	8. *The Harper*	W.	
	9. *Reconnaissance*	W.	
	10. *Souvenir*	W.	
35.	Two Songs, with piano	B. & H.	1907–8

1. *Jubal* (Josephson)
   With orchestra: 2122/2000/
   01/1/str.   **Ms.**

2. *Teodora* (Gripenberg)

36.	Six Songs, with piano	B. & H.	1899

1. *Svarta rosor* (Josephson)
   [*Black Roses*]

2. *Men min fågel märks dock icke* (Runeberg)
   [*But My Bird Is Long in Homing*]

3. *Bollspelet vid Trianon* (Fröding)
   [*Tennis at Trianon*]
   With orchestra: 2011/0000/
   01/1/str.   **Ms.**

4. *Säv, säv, susa* (Fröding)
   [*Sigh, Sedges, Sigh*]

5. *Marssnön* (Wecksell)
   [*March Snow*]

6. *Demanten på marssnön* (Wecksell)
   [*The Diamond on the March Snow*]
   With orchestra: 2020/0000/
   00/1/str.   **Ms.**

37.	Five Songs, with piano	B. & H.	

1. *Den första kyssen* (Runeberg)   1898
   [*The First Kiss*]

2. *Lasse liten* (Topelius)   1898
   [*Little Lasse*]

3. *Soluppgång* (Hedberg)   1898
   [*Sunrise*]

Opus	Title	Publisher	Date
	With orchestra: 2022/4000/ 10/0/str.	Ms.	
	4. *Var det en dröm?* (Wecksell) [*Was It a Dream?*]		1902
	5. *Flickan kom ifrån sin älsklings möte* (Runeberg) [*The Maiden Came from Her Lover's Tryst*] With orchestra: 1122/2030/ 11/1/str.	Ms.	1901
38.	Five Songs, with piano	B. & H.	
	1. *Höstkväll* (Rydberg) [*Autumn Evening*] With orchestra: 0233/4030/ 10/1/str.	B. & H.	1903
	2. *På verandan vid havet* (Rydberg) [*On a Balcony by the Sea*] With orchestra: 0222/4000/ 01/1/str.	Ms.	1902
	3. *I natten* (Rydberg) [*In the Night*] With orchestra: 0012/4000/ 11/0/str.	Ms.	1903
	4. *Harpolekaren och hans son* (Rydberg) [*The Harper and His Son*]		1904
	5. *Jag ville jag vore i Indialand* (Fröding) [*I Wish I Dwelt in India Land*]		1904
39.	Symphony No. 1 in E minor	B. & H.	1899
	1. *Andante ma non troppo—Allegro energico*		
	2. *Andante (ma non troppo lento)*		
	3. *Scherzo (Allegro)*		
	4. *Finale (Quasi una fantasia)* Orchestra: 2222/4331/12/1/str.		
40.	*Pensées lyriques*, for piano		1912–14
	1. *Valsette*	B. & H.	
	2. *Chant sans paroles*	B. & H.	
	3. *Humoresque*	B. & H.	

Opus	*Title*	*Publisher*	*Date*
	4. *Menuetto*	B. & H.	
	5. *Berceuse*	B. & H.	
	6. *Pensée mélodique*	B. & H.	
	7. *Rondoletto*	B. & H.	
	8. *Scherzando*	B. & H.	
	9. *Petite Sérénade*	W.	
	10. *Polonaise*	W.	
41.	*Kyllikki*, three lyric pieces for piano	B. & H.	1904
	1. *Largamente—Allegro*		
	2. *Andantino*		
	3. *Commodo*		
42.	Romance in C major, for string orchestra	B. & H.	1903
	Also known as *Andante for Strings*		
43.	Symphony No. 2 in D major	B. & H.	1901–2
	1. *Allegretto—Poco allegro*		
	2. *Tempo andante ma rubato—Allegro—Andante sostenuto*		
	3. *Vivacissimo*		
	4. *Allegro moderato*		
	Orchestra: 2222/4331/10/0/str.		
44.	Incidental Music to *Kuolema* [*Death*], by A. Järnefelt. Six "scenes" for string orchestra, bass drum, and church bell	Ms.	1903
	No. 1 revised as *Valse triste*	B. & H.	1904
	Orchestra: 1010/2000/10/0/str.		
	For piano	B. & H.	1904
	Nos. 3 & 4 revised as *Scene with Cranes*	Ms.	1906
	See: Opus 62		
45.	1. *The Dryad*, tone poem for orchestra	B. & H.	1910
	Orchestra: 3232/4331/02/0/str.		
	For piano	B. & H.	1910
	2. *Dance Intermezzo*, for orchestra	B. & H.	1907
	Orchestra 1: 2121/4200/11/ 1/str.		

Opus	Title	Publisher	Date
	2: 1020/2100/11/ o/str.	?	
	For piano	B. & H.	1904
46.	Incidental Music to *Pelléas et Mélisande*, by M. Maeterlinck		
	Concert Suite:	L.	1905

1. *At the Castle Gate* (Prelude, Act I, Scene 1)
2. *Mélisande* (Prelude, Act I, Scene 2)
3. *At the Seashore* ("Melodrama," Act I, Scene 4)
4. *A Spring in the Park* (Prelude, Act II, Scene 1)
5. *The Three Blind Sisters* (Mélisande's Song, Act III, Scene 2)
6. *Pastorale* ("Melodrama," Act III, Scene 4)
7. *Mélisande at the Spinning Wheel* (Prelude, Act III, Scene 1)
8. *Entr'acte* (Prelude, Act IV, Scene 1)
9. *Mélisande's Death* (Prelude, Act V, Scene 2)

Orchestra: 1122/2000/11/o/str.

Unpublished:
1. Prelude, Act IV, Scene 2
2. Mélisande's Song (No. 5, original version)

Opus	Title	Publisher	Date
47.	Concerto in D minor, for violin and orchestra	L.	1903 rev. 1905

1. *Allegro moderato*
2. *Adagio di molto*
3. *Allegro ma non tanto*

Orchestra: 2222/4230/10/o/str.

	With piano	L.	
48.	*Vapautettu kuningatar*, cantata for mixed chorus and orchestra (Cajander)	L.	1906

[*The Liberated Queen*]

Orchestra: 2222/4230/13/o/str.

	With piano	L	
	Parts for male chorus	n.p., n.d.	

(Composed to a German translation of the original text and published as *Die gefangene Königin*

Opus	Title	Publisher	Date
	[*The Captive Queen*]. Also known as *Siell' laulavi kuningatar* [*There Sings the Queen*] and *Snellman's Fest Cantata*.)		
49.	*Pohjola's Daughter*, symphonic fantasia for orchestra	L.	1906
	Orchestra: 3333/4431/10/1/str.		
50.	Six Songs, with piano	L.	1906

1. *Lenzgesang* (Fitger)
   [*Spring Song*]
2. *Sehnsucht* (Weiss)
   [*Longing*]
3. *Im Feld ein Mädchen singt* (Susman)
   [*In the Field a Maiden Sings*]
4. *Aus banger Brust* (Dehmel)
   [*Oh, Wert Thou Here*]
   With orchestra: 1012/2000/
   00/1/str.   **Ms.**
5. *Die stille Stadt* (Dehmel)
   [*The Silent City*]
6. *Rosenlied* (Ritter)
   [*Song of the Roses*]

| 51. | Incidental Music to *Belshazzar's Feast*, by Hj. Procopé | | 1906 |
| | Original score: | **Ms.** | |

1. *Alla marcia* (Act I)
2. *Nocturne* (Prelude, Act II)
3. *The Jewish Girl's Song* (Act II)
4. *Allegretto* (Act III)
5. *Dance of Life* (Act III)
6. *Dance of Death* (Act III)
7. *Tempo sostenuto* (Act IV)
8. *Allegro* (Act IV)

Orchestra: 1020/2000/03/0/str.
Concert Suite: **L.**

1. *Oriental Procession* (No. 1)
2. *Solitude* (Accompaniment for No. 3)
3. *Night Music* (No. 2)

Opus	Title	Publisher	Date
	4. *Khadra's Dance* (Nos. 5 & 6) Orchestra: 2120/2000/03/0/str.		
52.	Symphony No. 3 in C major 1. *Allegro moderato* 2. *Andantino con moto, quasi allegretto* 3. *Moderato* Orchestra: 2222/4230/10/0/str.	L.	1907
53.	*Pan and Echo*, dance intermezzo Orchestra: 3333/4431/10/1/str.	L.	1906
54.	Incidental Music to *Swanwhite*, by A. Strindberg Original score: 14 "scenes" Orchestra: 1010/2000/11/0/str. Concert Suite: 1. *The Peacock* 2. *The Harp* 3. *The Maiden with the Roses* 4. *Listen, the Robin Sings* 5. *The Prince Alone* 6. *Swanwhite and the Prince* 7. *Song of Praise* Orchestra: 2222/4000/11/1/str.	Ms. L.	1908
55.	*Night Ride and Sunrise*, tone poem for orchestra Orchestra: 3233/4231/13/0/str.	L.	1907
56.	String Quartet in D minor (*Voces intimae*) 1. *Andante—Allegro molto* 2. *Vivace* 3. *Adagio di molto* 4. *Allegretto (ma pesante)* 5. *Allegro*	L.	1909
57.	Eight Songs, with piano (Josephson) 1. *Älvan och snigeln* [*The Fairy and the Snail*] 2. *En blomma stod vid vägen* [*A Flower Stood by the Path*]	L.	1909

Opus	Title	Publisher	Date
	3. *Kvarnhjulet* [*The Millwheel*]		
	4. *Maj* [*May*]		
	5. *Jag är ett träd* [*I Am a Tree*]		
	6. *Hertig Magnus* [*Duke Magnus*]		
	7. *Vänskapens blomma* [*The Flower of Friendship*]		
	8. *Näcken* [*The Watersprite*]		
58.	Ten Pieces for Piano	B. & H.	1909
	1. *Rêverie*		
	2. *Scherzino*		
	3. *Air varié*		
	4. *The Shepherd*		
	5. *The Evening*		
	6. *Dialogue*		
	7. *Tempo di menuetto*		
	8. *Fisher Song*		
	9. *Sérénade*		
	10. *Summer Song*		
59.	*In Memoriam*, funeral march for orchestra Orchestra: 2333/4331/13/0/str.	B. & H.	1909
60.	Two Songs for Shakespeare's *Twelfth Night*, with guitar or piano	B. & H.	1909
	1. *Kom nu hit, död* (Act II, Scene 4) [*Come away, Death*] With harp and string orchestra	Ms.	1957
	2. *Och när som jag var en liten smådräng* (Act V, Scene 1) [*When That I Was and a Little Tiny Boy*]		
61.	Eight Songs, with piano	B. & H.	1910
	1. *Långsamt som kvällskyn* (*Tavaststjerna*) [*Slowly as the Evening Sun*]		

List of Compositions and Arrangements

Opus	Title	Publisher	Date
	2. *Vattenplask* (Rydberg) [*Lapping Waters*]		
	3. *När jag drömmer* (Tavaststjerna) [*When I Dream*]		
	4. *Romeo* (Tavaststjerna)		
	5. *Romance* (Tavaststjerna)		
	6. *Dolce far niente* (Tavaststjerna)		
	7. *Fåfäng önskan* (Runeberg) [*Idle Wish*]		
	8. *Vårtagen* (Gripenberg) [*Spell of Springtide*]		
62.	(Incidental Music to *Kuolema* [*Death*], by A. Järnefelt)	B. & H.	1911
	1. *Canzonetta*, for string orchestra		
	2. *Valse romantique* Orchestra: 2020/2000/10/0/str. See: Opus 44		
63.	Symphony No. 4 in A minor	B. & H.	1911
	1. *Tempo molto moderato, quasi adagio*		
	2. *Allegro molto vivace*		
	3. *Il tempo largo*		
	4. *Allegro* Orchestra: 2222/4230/11/0/str.		
64.	*The Bard*, tone poem for orchestra	B. & H.	1913 rev. 1914
	Orchestra: 2232/4230/11/1/str.		
65.	Two Part-Songs for mixed chorus a cappella		
	1. *Män från slätten och havet* (Knape) [*People from Land and Sea*]	B. & H.	1911
	2. *Klockmelodin i Berghälls kyrka* (Engström) [*Bell Melody of Berghäll Church*]	B. & H.	1912
66.	*Scènes historiques II*, for orchestra	B. & H.	1912
	1. *The Chase* (Overture) Orchestra: 2222/4000/10/0/str.		

Opus	*Title*	*Publisher*	*Date*
	2. *Love Song*		
	Orchestra: 2222/4000/10/1/str.		
	3. *At the Drawbridge*		
	Orchestra: 3222/4000/11/1/str.		
67.	Three Sonatinas, for piano	B. & H.	1912
	No. 1 in F sharp minor		
	a. *Allegro*		
	b. *Largo*		
	c. *Allegro*		
	No. 2 in E major		
	a. *Allegro*		
	b. *Andantino*		
	c. *Allegro*		
	No. 3 in B flat minor		
	a. *Allegro moderato*		
	b. *Andante*		
	c. *Allegretto*		
68.	Two Rondinos, for piano	U.E.	1912
	No. 1 in G sharp minor		
	No. 2 in C sharp minor		
69.	Two Serenades, for violin and		
	orchestra	B. & H.	
	No. 1 in D major		1912
	Orchestra: 2222/4000/10/0/str.		
	No. 2 in G minor		1913
	Orchestra: 2222/4000/11/0/str.		
70.	*Luonnotar* [*Spirit of Nature*],		
	tone poem for soprano and or-		
	chestra (*Kalevala*, 1, 110–242 *passim*)		1910[?]
	Orchestra: 2232/4230/20/2/		
	str.	Ms.	
	With piano	B. & H.	
71.	*Scaramouche*, music for the tragic		
	pantomime [*sic*] by P. Knudsen		
	and M. T. Bloch	H.	1913
	Orchestra: 2222/4100/12/1/str.		
72.	Six Songs, with piano		

List of Compositions and Arrangements

Opus	Title	Publisher	Date
	1. *Vi ses igen* (Rydberg) [*Farewell*]	Ms. lost	1914
	2. *Orions bälte* (Topelius) [*Orion's Girdle*]	Ms. lost	1914
	3. *Kyssen* (Rydberg) [*The Kiss*]	B. & H.	1915
	4. *Kaiutar* (Larin Kyösti) [*The Echo Nymph*]	B. & H.	1915
	5. *Der Wanderer und der Bach* (Greif) [*The Wanderer and the Brook*]	B. & H.	1915
	6. *Hundra vägar* (Runeberg) [*A Hundred Ways*]	B. & H.	1907
73.	*The Oceanides*, tone poem for orchestra Orchestra: 3333/4330/12/2/ str. First version entitled *Aallottaret* [*Nymphs of the Ocean*]	B. & H. Ms.	1914 rev. 1914
74.	Four Lyric Pieces, for piano 1. *Eclogue* 2. *Soft West Wind* 3. *At the Dance* 4. *In the Old Home*	B. & H.	1914
75.	Five Pieces for Piano 1. *When the Mountain-ash Is in Flower* 2. *The Lonely Fir* 3. *The Aspen* 4. *The Birch* 5. *The Fir*	H.	1914
76.	Thirteen Pieces for Piano 1. *Esquisse* 2. *Étude* 3. *Carillon* 4. *Humoresque* 5. *Consolation* 6. *Romanzetta* 7. *Affettuoso*	H.	1914–?

Opus	Title	Publisher	Date
	8. *Pièce enfantine*		
	9. *Arabesque*		
	10. *Elegiaco*		
	11. *Linnea*		
	12. *Capricietto*		
	13. *Harlequinade*		
77.	Two Pieces for Violin (or Cello) and Orchestra	H.	1914
	1. *Cantique* (*Laetare anima mea*) Orchestra: 2020/2000/10/1/str.		
	2. *Devotion* (*Ab imo pectore*) Orchestra: 2012/4030/00/0/str.		
78.	Four Pieces for Violin (or Cello), with piano	H.	
	1. *Impromptu*		1915
	2. *Romance*		1915
	3. *Religioso*		1919
	4. *Rigaudon*		1915
79.	Six Pieces for Violin, with piano	H.	1915
	1. *Souvenir*		
	2. *Tempo di menuetto*		
	3. *Danse caractéristique*		
	4. *Sérénade*		
	5. *Dance idyll*		
	6. *Berceuse*		
80.	Sonatina in E major, for violin and piano		
	1. *Lento—Allegro*	H.	1915
	2. *Andantino*		
	3. *Lento—Allegretto—Vivace*		
81.	Five Pieces for Violin, with piano	W.	1915–?
	1. *Mazurka*		
	2. *Rondino*		
	3. *Waltz*		
	4. *Aubade*		
	5. *Menuetto*		

261

List of Compositions and Arrangements

Opus	Title	Publisher	Date
82.	Symphony No. 5 in E flat major	H.	1915
	Molto moderato—Allegro moderato		rev. 1916
	Andante mosso quasi allegretto		rev. 1919
	Allegro molto		
	Orchestra: 2222/4330/10/0/str.		
	First version	Ms.[?]	
	Second version	Ms.[?]	
83.	Incidental Music to *Jedermann* [*Everyman*], by H. von Hoffmannsthal, for mixed chorus, piano, organ, and orchestra	Ms.	1916
	Orchestra: 2121/2200/11/0/str.		
84.	Five Part-Songs, for male chorus a cappella		
	1. *Herr Lager* (Fröding)	M.M.	1914
	2. *På berget* (Gripenberg) [*On the Mountain*]	M.M.	1915
	3. *Ett drömackord* (Fröding) [*A Dream Chord*]	M.M.	1915
	4. *Evige Eros* (Gripenberg) [*Eternal Eros*]	M.M.	1915
	5. *Till havs* (Reuter) [*At Sea*]	W.	1915
85.	Five Pieces for Piano	H.	1916
	1. *Bellis*		
	2. *Oeillet*		
	3. *Iris*		
	4. *Aquileja*		
	5. *Campanula*		
86.	Six Songs, with piano	H.	1916
	1. *Vårförnimmelser* (Tavaststjerna) [*The Coming of Spring*]		
	2. *Längtan heter min arvedel* (Karlfeldt) [*Longing Is My Heritage*]		
	3. *Dold förening* (Snoilsky) [*Hidden Union*]		
	4. *Och finns det en tanke?* (Tavaststjerna) [*And Is There a Thought?*]		

Opus	Title	Publisher	Date
	5. *Sångarlön* (Snoilsky) [*The Singer's Reward*]		
	6. *I systrar, I bröder* (Lybeck) [*Ye Sisters, Ye Brothers*]		
87.	Humoresques I–II, for violin and orchestra	H.	1917
	No. 1 in D minor		
	Orchestra: 2222/2000/10/0/str.		
	No. 2 in D major		
	Orchestra: 0000/2000/10/0/str.		
88.	Six Songs, with piano	H.	1917
	1. *Blåsippan* (Franzén) [*The Anemone*]		
	2. *De bägge rosorna* (Franzén) [*The Two Roses*]		
	3. *Vitsippan* (Franzén) [*The Star-flower*]		
	4. *Sippan* (Runeberg) [*The Primrose*]		
	5. *Törnet* (Runeberg) [*The Thorn*]		
	6. *Blommans öde* (Runeberg) [*The Flower's Destiny*]		
89.	Humoresques III–VI, for violin and orchestra	H.	1917
	No. 3 in G minor, with string orchestra		
	No. 4 in G minor, with string orchestra		
	No. 5 in E flat major		
	Orchestra: 2022/0000/00/0/str.		
	No. 6 in G minor		
	Orchestra: 2002/0000/00/0/str.		
90.	Six Songs, with piano (Runeberg)	B. & H.	1917
	1. *Norden* [*The North*]		
	2. *Hennes budskap* [*Her Message*]		
	3. *Morgonen* [*The Morning*]		

Opus	Title	Publisher	Date
	4. *Fågelfängaren* [*The Bird-catcher*]		
	5. *Sommarnatten* [*Summer Night*]		
	6. *Vem styrde hit din väg?* [*Who Has Brought You Here?*]		
91.	1. *March of the Finnish* [27th Royal Prussian] *Jaeger Battalion* (Nurmio)		1917
	For male chorus a cappella, in hectograph		
	For male chorus with orchestra	B. & H.	
	Orchestra: 2232/4330/12/0/str.		
	Song with piano	B. & H.	
	2. *Scout March*, for mixed chorus a cappella (Finne-Procopé)	H.	1917
	With orchestra: 2222/4331/10/0/str.	H.	
	Song with piano	H.	
	Also known as *Det danske Spejderes March* [*The Danish Scout March*] and *The World Song of the World Association of Girl Guides and Girl Scouts*		
92.	*Oma maa* [*Our Native Land*], cantata for mixed chorus and orchestra (Kallio)		
	Orchestra: 2222/4230/11/0/str.	Ms.	1918
	Choral parts	W.	
93.	*Jordens sång* [*Song of the Earth*], cantata for mixed chorus and orchestra (Hemmer)		1919
	Orchestra: 2222/3220/10/0/str.	Ms.	
	Choral parts	W.	
94.	Six Pieces for Piano	W.	1919
	1. *Dance*		
	2. *Novelette*		

Opus	Title	Publisher	Date
	3. *Sonnet*		
	4. *Berger et bergerette*		
	5. *Mélodie*		
	6. *Gavotte*		
95.	*Maan virsi* [*Hymn of the Earth*], cantata for mixed chorus and orchestra (E. Leino)		1920
	Orchestra: 2222/4230/10/0/ str.	W.	
	Choral parts	W.	
96.	1. *Valse lyrique*, for orchestra	H.	1920
	Orchestra: 2222/4230/11/0/str.		
	For piano	H.	
	2. *Autrefois, scène pastorale*, for two voices *ad. lib.* and orchestra	H.	1919
	Orchestra: 2022/2000/10/0/str.		
	For piano	H.	
	3. *Valse chevaleresque*, for orchestra	H.	1920
	Orchestra: 2222/4230/11/0/str.		
	For piano	H.	
97.	Six Bagatelles for Piano	B. & H.	1920
	1. *Humoresque I*		
	2. *Song*		
	3. *Little Waltz*		
	4. *Humorous March*		
	5. *Impromptu*		
	6. *Humoresque II*		
98.	1. *Suite mignonne*, for 2 flutes and strings		
	a. *Petite scène*	C	1921
	b. *Polka*		
	c. *Epilogue*		
	For piano	C	
	2. *Suite champêtre*, for string orchestra		
	a. *Pièce caractéristique*	H.	1921
	b. *Mélodie élégiaque*		

List of Compositions and Arrangements

Opus	Title	Publisher	Date
	c. *Danse*		
	For piano	H.	
99.	Eight Pieces for Piano	F.	1922
	1. *Pièce humoristique*		
	2. *Esquisse*		
	3. *Souvenir*		
	4. *Impromptu*		
	5. *Couplet*		
	6. *Animoso*		
	7. *Moment de valse*		
	8. *Petite Marche*		
100.	*Suite caractéristique*, for harp and string orchestra	Ms.	1922
	1. *Vivo*		
	2. *Lento*		
	3. *Commodo*		
	For piano	H.	
101.	Five Pieces for Piano	H.	1923
	1. *Romance*		
	2. *Chant du soir*		
	3. *Scène lyrique*		
	4. *Humoresque*		
	5. *Scène romantique*		
102.	*Novelette*, for violin and piano	H.	1923
103.	Five Pieces for Piano	H.	1924
	1. *The Village Church*		
	2. *The Fiddler*		
	3. *The Oarsman*		
	4. *The Storm*		
	5. *In Mournful Mood*		
104.	Symphony No. 6 in D minor	A.H.	1923
	1. *Allegro molto moderato*		
	2. *Allegretto quasi andante*		
	3. *Poco vivace*		
	4. *Allegro molto*		
	Orchestra: 2232/4330/10/1/str.		
105.	Symphony No. 7 in C major	H.	1924
	In one movement		

Opus	Title	Publisher	Date
	Orchestra: 2222/4330/10/0/str. Also known as *Fantasia sinfonica*		
106.	Five *Danses champêtres*, for violin and piano	H.	1925
107.	Hymn, for chorus with organ (Probably *Herran siunaus* [*God's Blessing*])	Ms.[?]	1925
108.	Two Part-Songs to texts by Larin Kyösti, for male chorus a cappella	L.M.	1925
	1. *Humoreski*		
	2. *Ne pitkän matkan kulkijat* [*Wanderers on the Long Way*]		
109.	Incidental Music to *The Tempest*, by W. Shakespeare		1925
	Original score: in 34 parts for soloists, mixed chorus, harmonium, and orchestra	Ms.	
	Arranged for concert performance:		
	1. Prelude	H.	
	Orchestra: 3232/4331/13/0/str.		
	2. Suite No. I:	H.	
	a. *The Oak Tree*		
	b. *Humoresque*		
	c. *Caliban's Song*		
	d. *The Harvesters*		
	e. *Canon*		
	f. *Scena*		
	g. *Intrada—Berceuse*		
	h. *Entr'acte—Ariel's Song*		
	i. *The Storm*		
	Orchestra: 3232/4331/13/1/str.		
	3. Suite No. II:	H.	
	a. *Chorus of the Winds*		
	b. *Intermezzo*		
	c. *Dance of the Nymphs*		
	d. *Prospero*		
	e. *Song I*		
	f. *Song II*		

Opus	Title	Publisher	Date
	g. *Miranda*		
	h. *The Naiads*		
	i. *Dance Episode*		
	Orchestra: 2222/4000/10/1/str.		
110.	*Väinön virsi* [*Väinö's Song*], for mixed chorus and orchestra (*Kalevala*, XLIII, 385–422)	W.	1926
	Orchestra: 2222/4330/11/0/str.		
	Choral parts	W.	
111.	Two Pieces for Organ	W.	
	1. *Intrada*		1925
	2. *Surusoitto* [*Mournful Music*]		1931
112.	*Tapiola*, tone poem for orchestra	B. & H.	1926
	Orchestra: 3333/4330/10/0/str.		
113.	Masonic Ritual Music, for male voices, piano, and organ	M.	
	1. *Introduction*		1927
	2. *Thoughts Be Our Comfort* (Schiller)		
	3. *Introduction and Hymn* (Confucius)		
	4. *Marcia* (Goethe)		
	5. *Light* (Simelius)		
	6. *Salem* (Rydberg) (Also known as *Onward Ye Peoples*)		
	7. *Whosoever Hath a Love* (Rydberg)		
	8. *Ode to Fraternity* (Sario)		1946
	9. *Hymn* (Sario)		
	10. *Marche funèbre*		1927
	11. *Ode* (Korpela)		
	12. *Finlandia Hymn* (Sola)		1938
	(First edition copyright 1935; second and enlarged edition copyright 1950)		
114.	Five Esquisses for Piano	Ms.	1929
	1. *Landscape*		
	2. *Winter Scene*		
	3. *Forest Lake*		
	4. *Song in the Forest*		
	5. *Spring Vision*		

Opus	Title	Publisher	Date
115.	Four Pieces for Violin, with piano	B. & H.	1929
	1. *On the Heath*		
	2. *Ballade*		
	3. *Humoresque*		
	4. *The Bells*		
116.	Three Pieces for Violin, with piano	B. & H.	1929
	1. *Scène de danse*		
	2. *Danse caractéristique*		
	3. *Rondeau romantique*		

B. WITHOUT OPUS NUMBERS

Title	Publisher	Date
Aamusumussa [*Morning Mist*], for three children's voices a cappella (Erkko)	O.	1896
For male chorus	O.	
For mixed chorus	Säv. 4	
Also known as *Päiv' ei pääse*		
Academic March		
See: *Promotiomarssi*		
Allegretto, for piano	Ms.	1889
Andante cantabile, for violin with piano	Ms.	1887
Andante festivo, for string quartet		1922
In *Kertomus Säynätsalon tehtaitten 25-vuotisjuhlasta*, 28, XII, 1922		
For string orchestra with timpani *ad. lib.*	W.	
Andante for Strings		
See: Opus 42		
Andante lirico, for string orchestra		
See: *Impromptu*, for string orchestra		
Andantino, for clarinet, 2 cornets, 2 horns, baritone, and tuba	Ms.	1890–1
Andantino, for piano	Ms.	1888
Andantino, for cello with piano	Ms.	1884[?]
Au crépuscule, for piano	Ms.	1887

Title	Publisher	Date
Ballet Scene, for orchestra	Ms.	1891
Orchestra: 2222/4221/02/0/str.		
Ballet Scene, for orchestra	Ms.	1909
Orchestra: 2222/4230/11/0/str.		
Björneborgarnes March, arr. for orchestra	Ms.	1900
Orchestra: 2222/4330/02/0/str.		
Brusande rusar en våg [*The Roaring of a Wave*], for male chorus a cappella (Schybergson)	W.	1918
Cantata for the Coronation of Nicolas II, for soloists, mixed chorus, and orchestra (Cajander)	Ms.[?]	1896
Choral parts in facsimile		
Cantata to Words by W. von Konow, for women's chorus a cappella	A.	1911
Cantata for the University Ceremonies of 1894, for mixed chorus and orchestra (K. Leino)	Ms.	1894
Orchestra: 2222/2221/12/0/str.		
Choral parts in hectograph		
Juhlamarssi [*Festival March*], for mixed chorus a cappella	O.	
Carminalia, Latin songs for students arranged for soprano, alto, and bass a cappella or soprano and alto with piano and harmonium, from melodies and texts collected by Elise Stenbäck	K.W.	1899
1. *Ecce novum guadium*		
2. *Angelus emittitur*		
3. *In stadio laboris*		
Cortège, for orchestra	?	?
(Listed by Gray as composed in 1901 and unpublished)		
Drömmarna [*Dreams*], for mixed chorus a cappella (Reuter)	S.F.V.	1912
Ej med klagan [*Not with Lamentations*], for mixed chorus a cappella (Runeberg)	Säv. 8	1905

List of Compositions and Arrangements

Title	Publisher	Date
Also known as *Till minnet av Albert Edelfelt* [*To the Memory of Albert Edelfelt*] *Ett ensamt skidspår* [*The Lonely Ski Trail*], for piano to accompany the recitation of verses by B. Gripenberg	N.M.F.	1925
For harp and string orchestra	Ms.	1948
Erloschen [*Extinct*], song with piano (Busse-Palmo)	S.M.	1906
Fantasia, for cello with piano	Ms.[?]	1900
Finnish Folk Songs, arranged for piano	B. & H.	1903

1. *Minun kultani* [*My Beloved*]
2. *Sydämestäni rakastan* [*I Love You with All My Heart*]
3. *Ilta tulee* [*Evening Comes*]
4. *Tuopa tyttö, kaunis tyttö* [*That Beautiful Girl*]
5. *Velisurmaaja* [*The Brother's Murderer*]
6. *Häämuistelma* [*Wedding Memory*]

Title	Publisher	Date
Finnish Runos (17 fragments transcribed by Jean Sibelius), in *Kalevala*, Vol. II, *Selityksiä* [*Comments*], Helsinki: Suomalaisen Kirjallisuuden Seura; 1895		1895
Florestan, suite for piano with descriptive text by the composer	Ms.	1889

1. *Moderato*
2. *Molto moderato*
3. *Andante*
4. *Tempo primo*

Title	Publisher	Date
Fridolins dårskap [*Fridolin's Folly*], for male chorus a cappella (Karlfeldt)	A.H.	1917
Gossar och flickor See: Opus 19		
Grefvinnans konterfej [*The Countess's Portrait*], for string orchestra to accompany the recitation of verses by Z. Topelius	Ms.	1906
Also known as *Porträtterna* [*Portraits*]		
Herran siunaus [*God's Blessing*], hymn with organ	S.	1925

271

List of Compositions and Arrangements

Title	Publisher	Date
(Probably the Hymn for chorus with organ, opus 107)		
Hymn to Thais, song with piano (Borgström)	Ms.	1900
Impromptu, for string orchestra	Ms.	1894
(Probably the composition known as *Andante lirico*. See: Opus 5)		
Isänmaalle		
See: Opus 18, no. 1		
Johdantovuorolauluja [*Introductory Antiphons*], for mixed chorus	S.	1925
1. *Palmusunnuntaina* [*Palm Sunday*]		
2. *Pyhäinpäivänä* [*All Saints Day*]		
3. *Rukouspäivänä* [*General Prayers*]		
Jone havsfärd [*Jonah's Voyage*], for male chorus a cappella (Karlfeldt)	S.	1918
Published as *Joonaan meriretki*		
(Finnish translation by Nortamo), in Hj.		
Nortamo (ed.): *Laulajapoika*, I–II, 1945		
Juhlamarssi		
See: Cantata for the University Ceremonies of 1894		
Jungfrun i tornet [*The Maid in the Tower*], opera in one act (Hertzberg)	Ms.	1896
Orchestra: 1121/2110/01/0/str.		
With piano	Ms.	
Kansakoululaisten marssi [*Folk School Children's March*], for children's voices a cappella (Onnen Pekka)		1910
In *Kansakoulun lauluja*, Helsinki, 1910		
Also known as *Uno Cygnaeuksen muistolle* [*To the Memory of Uno Cygnaeus*]		
Karelia Music (original score)	Ms.	1893
1. *Overture* (Opus 10)		
2. *Più lento*		
3. *Moderato assai*		
4. *March in the Old Style* (Opus 11, no. 1)		
5. *Tempo di menuetto* (Opus 11, no. 2)		

List of Compositions and Arrangements

Title	Publisher	Date
6. *Moderato, ma non tanto*		
7. *Alla marcia*—"*Based on an old motif*" (Opus 11, no. 3)		
8. *Vivace*		
9. *Moderato—Allegro molto—Vivace molto—*		
Maestoso e largamente (The		
Finnish national anthem, *Vårt Land,* by Pacius)		
Orchestra: 2222/4331/11/o/str.		
Karjalan osa [*Karelia's Fate*], march for		
male chorus with piano (Nurminen)	M.K.	1930
Choral parts	M.K.	
Also known as *Patriotic March*		
Kavaljeren [*The Cavalier*], for piano		1900
In *Fyren,* December 1900		
Kehtolaulu [*Lullaby*], for violin and kantele		1899
In *Musiikkitieto,* December 1935		
Kotikaipaus [*Nostalgia*], for three women's		
voices a cappella (Von Konow)	S.M.	1902
In *Suomen Musiikkilehti,* December 1935		
Koulutie [*The Way to School*], for children's		
voices a cappella (Koskenniemi)	S.	1925
Kuutamolla [*In the Moonlight*], for male		
chorus a cappella (Suonio)	Y.L.	1916
Lauloit piennä		
See: *Till Thérèse Hahl*		
Lifslust		
See: Opus 19		
Likhet [*Resemblance*], for male chorus a		
cappella (Runeberg)	M.A.	1922
Mandolinato, for piano	H.	1917
Menuetto, for clarinet, 2 cornets, 2		
horns, baritone, and tuba	Ms.	1890–1
Menuetto, for orchestra	Ms.	1894
Orchestra: 1122/4331/01/o/str.		
Also known as *Menuet—Impromptu*		
and *Tempo di menuetto*		
Min rastas raataa		
See: Opus 18, no. 4		

273

List of Compositions and Arrangements

Title	Publisher	Date
Morceau romantique sur un motif de M. Jacob		
de Julin, for piano	D.	1925
For orchestra	Ms.	
Also known as *Pièce romantique*		
Narciss, song with piano (Gripenberg)	W.	1918[?]
Näcken [*The Watersprite*], two songs for the		
fairy-tale drama by G. Wennerberg	Ms.	1888
Onward Ye Peoples		
See: Opus 113		
Overture in E major	Ms.	1890–1
Orchestra: 2222/4221/11/0/str.		
Overture in A minor	Ms.	1902
Orchestra: 2222/4421/10/0/str.		
Päiv' ei pääse		
See: *Aamusumussa*		
Patriotic March		
See: *Karjalan osa*		
Perpetuum mobile		
See: Opus 2, no. 2		
Pièce romantique		
See: *Morceau romantique*		
Porträtterna		
See: *Grefvinnans konterfej*		
Presto, for string orchestra		
See: Opus 4		
"Press Celebrations" Music	Ms.	1899
Preludium, for clarinet, 2 cornets,		
2 horns, baritone, and tuba		
Tableau 2: *Andante, ma non troppo lento*		
Orchestra: 2222/4230/02/0/str.		
Tableau 5: *Grave*		
Orchestra: 2222/4330/11/0/str.		
See: Opus 25		
Promotiomarssi [*Academic March*], for orchestra		
Orchestra: 2222/4200/11/1/str.	Ms.	1919
Quartet for Strings in E flat major	Ms.	1885
Quartet for Strings in A minor	Ms.	1889
Quartet for Piano and Strings in E minor	Ms.	1881–2

List of Compositions and Arrangements

Title	Publisher	Date
Quartet for Piano, Two Violins, and Cello in C major	Ms.	1891
Quartet for Piano, Harmonium, Violin, and Cello in G minor	Ms.	1887
Quintet for Piano and Strings in G minor	Ms.	1889
Rondo, for viola with piano	Ms.	1893
Scène de ballet		
See: Ballet Scene		
Scherzo, for piano	Ms.	1888[?]
Scherzo, for string orchestra	Ms.	1894

(Probably an arrangement of the *Presto* movement from the String Quartet in B flat major, opus 4)

Segelfahrt [*Sailing*], song with piano (Öhqvist) — 1899
In *Brohige blad*, 1899

Serenade, song with piano (Runeberg) — 1888
In *Det sjungande Finland*, No. 45, 1888

Serenade, for baritone with orchestra (Stagnelius)
Orchestra: 0222/4000/00/0/str. — Ms. — 1895

Siltavahti [*The Guard of the Bridge*], for male chorus a cappella (Sola)
In *Helsingin työväen mieskuoro*, 1938 — J.W.

Skogsrået
See: Opus 15

Små flickorna [*Small Girls*], song with piano (Procopé) — 1920
In *Lucifer*, 1920

Snellman's Fest Cantata
See: Opus 48

| Sonata for Violin and Piano in D minor | Ms. | 1881–3 |
| Sonata for Violin and Piano in F major | Ms. | 1886[?] |

Souda, souda sinisorsa [*Row, Row, Duck*], song with piano (Koskimies) — F. — 1899

Spagnuolo, for piano — 1913
Printed in facsimile by Karisto, Hämeenlinna

Die Sprache der Vögel [*The Language of the Birds*], drama by A. Paul

Title	Publisher	Date
Wedding March for Act III	Ms.	1911
Orchestra: 2130/0220/13/0/str.		
Suite in A major, for string trio	Ms.	1889
Suur' olet, Herra [*You Are Mighty, Oh Lord*], hymn for mixed chorus a cappella (Korpela)	S.L.	1927
For male chorus	L.M.	
Svartsjukans nätter [*Nights of Jealousy*], for violin, cello, and piano to accompany the recitation of verses by Runeberg	Ms.	1888
Tanken [*The Thought*], duet for two sopranos with piano (Runeberg)	Ms.	1915
Tempo di menuetto		
See: *Menuetto*, for orchestra		
Theme and Variations in C sharp minor, for string quartet	Ms.	1888
Three Songs for American Schools	S.B.	1913
1. *Autumn Song* (Dixon)		
2. *The Sun upon the Lake Is Low* (Scott)		
3. *A Cavalry Catch* (Macleod)		
In *Progressive Music Series*, Vols. III and IV [1915]		
Tiera, tone poem for brass ensemble and percussion	O.	1898
Ensemble: 3 cornets, alto, tenor, baritone, tuba, cymbals, and bass drum		
Till minnet av Albert Edelfelt		
See: *Ej med klagan*		
Till Thérèse Hahl [*To Thérèse Hahl*], for mixed chorus a cappella (Wasastjerna)	Säv. 7	1902
also known as *Lauloit piennä*		
Till trånaden [*To Longing*], for piano		1913
In *Lucifer*, 1913		
Trånaden [*Longing*], for piano to accompany the recitation of verses by Stagnelius	Ms.	1887
Trio in A minor [fragments], for violin, cello, and piano	Ms.	1881–2

Title	Publisher	Date
Trio in G minor, for violin, viola, and cello	Ms	1885[?]
Trio for Violin, Cello, and Piano (the so-called "Korpo Trio")	?	1887
Trio in C major, for violin, cello, and piano (the so-called "Loviisa Trio")	Ms.	1888
Two Italian Songs, arranged for mixed chorus	Ms.	?

   1. *Ohi, Caroli*
   2. *Trippole Trappole*

Työkansan marssi [*Workers' March*], for
   mixed chorus a cappella (Erkko)   1893–6
   In *Työväen kalenteri*, Vol. IV, Viipuri, 1896

Työnsä kumpasellaki
   See: Opus 18, no. 3

Uno Cygnaeuksen muistolle
   See: *Kansakoululaisten marssi*

Ute hörs stormen [*One Hears the Storm Outside*], for male chorus a cappella
   (Schybergson)   W.   1918

Uusmaalaisten laulu [*Song for the People of Uusimaa*], for mixed chorus a cappella (Terhi)   O.   1912
   For male chorus a cappella   O.

Veljeni vierailla mailla
   See: Opus 18, no. 2

Viipurin Laulu-Veikkojen kunniamarssi [*Honor March of the Singing Brothers of Viipuri*],
   for male chorus a cappella (Eerola)   1920
   First version: in *Viipurin Laulu-Veikot* (*W.S.B.*), *1897–1922*
   Second version   J.W.

Water Drops, for violin and cello pizzicato   Ms.   1876

Wedding March
   See: *Sprache der Vögel*

Yks' voima
   See: Opus 18, no. 1

Bibliography

Abraham, Gerald (ed.) :
  Sibelius: A Symposium
  London: Lindsay Drummond; 1947

Andersson, Otto:
  Finlandssvenska musikfester under 50 år
  Åbo: Förlaget Bro; 1947

———:

  Jean Sibelius i Amerika
  Åbo: Förlaget Bro; 1955

———:

  Jean Sibelius och Svenska Teatern
  Åbo: Förlaget Bro; 1956

———:

  "När Jean Sibelius erhöll statsstipendium"
  Hufvudstadsbladet, January 3, 1957

———:

  "Sibelius-Nummer I–II"
  Tidning för Musik, Nos. 14–16 (December 1915)

———:

  "Sibelius och Kajanus som konkurrenter"
  Hufvudstadsbladet, December 8, 1956

Bantock, Granville:
  "Jean Sibelius"
  Monthly Musical Record, December 1935, pp. 217–19

Bax, Arnold:
  Farewell, My Youth
  London: Longmans, Green; 1943

Beecham, Thomas:
  "Sibelius the Craftsman"
  Living Age, February 1939, pp. 576–7

Bibliography

Born, Elsa von:
"Den underbara resan"
Finlands Röda Kors, Julhälsning 1935, pp. 5–7

Copland, Aaron:
Our New Music
New York: Whittlesey House; 1941

Demuth, Norman:
Musical Trends in the Twentieth Century
London: Rockliffe; 1952

Diktonius, Elmer:
"Opus 12," Musik
Helsingfors: Holger Schildts Förlag; 1933

Downes, Irene (ed.):
Olin Downes on Music
New York: Simon and Schuster; 1957

Downes, Olin:
Sibelius the Symphonist
New York: The Philharmonic-Symphony Society of New York; 1956

Dyson, George:
"Sibelius"
The Musical Times, November 1936, pp. 987–9

Ekman, Karl:
Jean Sibelius: His Life and Personality
New York: Alfred A. Knopf; 1938

———:
Jean Sibelius och hans verk
Helsingfors: Holger Schildts Förlag; 1956

Fenby, Eric:
Delius as I Knew Him
London: Quality Press; 1936

Bibliography

Flodin, Karl:
Finska musiker
Helsingfors: Söderström & Co.; 1900

——:

Musikliv och reseminnen
Helsingfors: Söderström & Co.; 1931

Furuhjelm, Erik:
Jean Sibelius: hans tondiktning och drag ur hans liv
Borgå: Holger Schildts Förlag; 1916

Gelatt, Roland:
The Fabulous Phonograph
Philadelphia: J. B. Lippincott Company; 1955

Goossens, Eugene:
Overture and Beginners
London: Methuen & Co.; 1951

Gray, Cecil:
Peter Warlock
London: Jonathan Cape; 1934

——:

Predicaments, or Music and the Future
London: Oxford University Press; 1926

——:

Sibelius
London: Oxford University Press; 1931

——:

"Sibelius, or Music and the Future"
The Nation and Athenaeum, December 24, 1927, pp. 483-4

——:

Sibelius: The Symphonies
London: Oxford University Press; 1935

Bibliography

Häkli, Pekka:
Arvid Järnefelt
Helsinki: Werner Söderström; 1955

Halonen, Antti:
Taiteen juhlaa ja arkea
Helsinki: Tammi; 1951

Hannikainen, Ilmari:
Sibelius and the Development of Finnish
Music
London: Hinrichsen Edition; [1948]

Helasvuo, Veikko:
Sibelius and the Music of Finland
Helsinki: Otava; 1957

Jackson, J. Hampden:
Finland
New York: The Macmillan Co.; 1940

Jalas, Jussi:
"Valse triste och musiken till 'Kuolema' "
Musik-Världen, May 1948, pp. 138–40

Johnson, H. Earle:
Symphony Hall, Boston
Boston: Little, Brown & Co.; 1950

Johnson, Harold E.:
"Finlandia ja 'Sanomalehdistön päivän' mu-
siikki"
Helsingin Sanomat, October 5, 1958

———:
"Jean Sibeliuksen alkusoitto"
Helsingin Sanomat, February 28, 1958

———:
"Jean Sibeliuksen 'Andante lirico' "
Helsingin Sanomat, June 15, 1958

281

Bibliography

Johnson, Harold E.:
"Jean Sibeliuksen 'Lemminkäis-sarja' "
Helsingin Sanomat, May 19, 1957

———:
Jean Sibelius: The Recorded Music
Helsinki: R. E. Westerlund Oy; 1957

———:
"Jean Sibeliuksen 'Työkansan marssi' "
Helsingin Sanomat, July 5, 1958

———:
"Sibeliuksen seitsemäs sinfonia ja 'Fantasia
sinfonica' "
Helsingin Sanomat, September 22, 1957

———:
"Sibelius fjärde symfoni—en stråkkvartett?"
Nya Pressen, June 7, 1958

———:
"Sibelius ja ohjelmamusiikki"
Helsingin Sanomat, June 8, 1958
Jukola, Martti:
Juhana Heikki Erkko
Helsinki: Kustannusosakeyhtiö Otava; 1939

Konow, Walter von:
"Janne"
Veckans Krönika, December 4, 1915, pp. 429–30

———:
"Muistoja Jean Sibeliuksen poikavuosilta"
Aulos, 1925
Krohn, Ilmari:
*Der Formenbau in den Symphonien von Jean
Sibelius*

Helsinki: Annales Academiae Scientiarum Fennicae
BXLIX; 1942

Krohn, Ilmari:
Der Stimmungsgehalt der Symphonien von
Jean Sibelius, I–II
Helsinki: Annales Academiae Scientiarum Fennicae
BLVII–BLVIII; 1945–6

Lambert, Constant:
Music Ho!
London: Charles Scribner's Sons; 1934

Láng, Paul Henry:
"Melody: Is It Dated?"
The Saturday Review of Literature, January 11, 1947,
pp. 28–9

——:
Music in Western Civilization
New York: W. W. Norton & Co.; 1941

Leibowitz, René:
Sibelius, le plus mauvais compositeur du
monde
Liège: Aux Editions Dynamo; 1955

Levas, Santeri:
Nuori Sibelius
Helsinki: Werner Söderström; 1957

Lönnrot, Elias:
Kalevala: The Land of Heroes, I–II, trans.
W. F. Kirby
New York: E. P. Dutton; 1951

Lorenz, Robert:
"Afterthoughts on the Sibelius Festival"
The Musical Times, January 1939, pp. 13–14

Bibliography

MacLean, Charles:
"Sibelius in England"
Zeitschrift der I.M.G., Vol. IX (1908), pp. 271–3

Madetoja, Leevi:
"Jean Sibelius oppetajana"
Aulos, 1925

Marvia, Einari:
AB Fazers Musikhandel, 1897–1947
Helsingfors: Fazer; 1948

——:
"Jean Sibeliuksen musikaalinen sukuperintö"
Uusi Musiikilehti, No. 9 (1955), pp. 49–81

Mazour, Anatole G.:
Finland Between East and West
New York: D. Van Nostrand & Co.; 1956

Mellers, Wilfrid:
"Sibelius at Ninety: A Revaluation"
The Listener, December 1, 1955, p. 969

Mueller, John H.:
The American Symphony Orchestra
Bloomington: Indiana University Press; 1951

Newmarch, Rosa:
Jean Sibelius: A Finnish Composer
Leipzig: Breitkopf & Härtel; 1906

——:
Jean Sibelius: A Short History of a Long Friendship
Boston: C. C. Birchard & Co.; 1939

Nieman, Walter:
Jean Sibelius
Leipzig: Breitkopf & Härtel; 1917

Bibliography

Pajanne, Martti:
"Muusikkojen muistelmia mestarista orkester-injohtajana"
Uusi Musiikkilehti, No. 9 (1955), pp. 15–16
Parmet, Simon:
Sibelius Symfonier
Helsingfors: Söderström & Co.; 1955
Paul, Adolf:
En bok om en människa
Stockholm: Albert Bonniers Förlag; 1891
——:
Profiler
Stockholm: Fahlcrantz & Co.; 1937
Ranta, Sulho (ed.) :
Suomen säveltäjiä
Porvoo: Werner Söderström; 1945
Ringbom, Nils-Eric:
Helsingfors orkesterföretag, 1882–1932
Helsingfors: Frenckellska Tryckeri; 1932
——:
Jean Sibelius: A Master and His Work
Norman: University of Oklahoma Press; 1954
——:
De Två versionerna av Sibelius' tondikt "En Saga"
Åbo: Åbo Akademi; 1956
Robinson, Edward:
"Jean Sibelius"
The American Mercury, February 1932, pp. 245–9
Roiha, Eino:
Die Symphonien von Jean Sibelius
Jyväskylä: K. J. Gummerus; 1941

Saminsky, Lazare:
Music of Our Day
New York: Thomas Y. Crowell Co.; 1939

Scholes, Percy A.:
The Mirror of Music (1844–1944)
London: Novello & Co.; 1947

Shore, Bernard:
The Orchestra Speaks
London: Longmans, Green & Co.; 1938

——:

Sixteen Symphonies
London: Longmans, Green & Co.; 1938

Slonimsky, Nicolas (ed.):
Lexicon of Musical Invective
Boston: Coleman-Ross; 1953

——:

Music Since 1900
Boston: Coleman-Ross; 1949

Solanterä, Lauri (ed.):
Jean Sibelius—Manuscripts
Helsinki: R. E. Westerlund Oy; 1945

——:

The Works of Jean Sibelius
Helsinki: R. E. Westerlund Oy; 1955

Stoeckel, Carl:
Some Recollections of the Visit of Jean Sibelius to America in 1914
Manuscript in Yale University Library

Suomalainen, Yrjö:
Robert Kajanus
Helsinki: Kustannusosakeyhtiö Otava; 1952

Bibliography

Tawaststjerna, Erik:
  The Pianoforte Compositions of Sibelius
  Helsinki: Kustannusosakeyhtiö Otava; 1957

Thomson, Virgil:
  The Musical Scene
  New York: Alfred A. Knopf; 1945

Törne, Bengt von:
  Sibelius: A Close-up
  London: Faber & Faber; 1937

Väisänen, A. O.:
  Sibelius ja kansanmusiiki
  Helsinki: Kalevalan vuosikirja No. 16; 1936

———:
  "Sibelius om sina Kalevala-kompositioner"
  Musikern, December 1, 1925, pp. 663–4

Voipio, Anni:
  "Sibelius as His Wife Sees Him"
  The New York Times, January 28, 1940, IX, 8:3

Wood, Henry J.:
  My Life of Music
  London: Victor Gollancz; 1938

Index

Index

Index

Flodin, Karl Teodor, 56, 211, 235; *quoted* 130; background, 19; first meeting with Sibelius, *quoted* 20; re Sibelius's growing reputation in Europe, 102; describes Sibelius's conducting, 129; on Sibelius's student compositions, *quoted* 20–1; on Sibelius's early songs, *quoted* 40–1; re *Impromptu*, 102–3; on *Karelia Music*, *quoted* 58; on *Kullervo*, *quoted* 45–8; on *Lemminkäinen Suite*, 66, 69, 72, *quoted* 71; on Overture in A minor, *quoted* 103; on *Pelléas et Mélisande*, *quoted* 119; re *Pohjola's Daughter*, 128; on *Rakastava*, *quoted* 60; on *Sandals*, *quoted* 83; re *Serenade* for baritone and orchestra, 63; re First Symphony, 85; on Third Symphony, *quoted* 130; re Violin Concerto, 115–16

Fougstedt, Nils-Eric, 212 *n*

France: Sibelius concerts, 78, 94–7; Sibelius's visit, 124; Sibelius's reputation in, 215, 219–20

Friedrich Karl, Prince of Hesse, 181

Fuchs, Robert, 32

Furtwängler, Wilhelm, 210

Furuhjelm, Erik: re *Water Drops*, 13; quotes Sibelius on early musical training, 14; *Jean Sibelius: hans tondiktning och drag ur hans liv*, 21, 170–1, 206; on *Kullervo*, 41–2, *quoted* 47; re *The Maid in the Tower*, 73; re Fourth Symphony, 144

Gallén-Kallela, Akseli, 28, 117, 203; *Symposium*, 64–5

Gattermann, Ludwig, *Über die Heide*, 113

Genetz, Emil, *Hakkapelitta*, 59–60; *Arise, Finland!* 93–4

Gericke, Max, 157

Germany: Sibelius as student in Berlin, 28–31; later sojourns, 82, 100–2, 118, 124; medical treatment in Berlin, 132; response to Paris tour,

Germany (*continued*)
97–8; Heidelberg Festival (1901), 100–2; popularity of Sibelius in, 136, 145, 210, 219–21; *King Kristian II* performed in Leipzig, 81; reception of Fourth Symphony, 146; Strauss conducts Violin Concerto, 116

Gluck, Alma, 162

Goddard, Scott, *quoted* 208

Gogol, Nikolai, *quoted* 203

Goldmark, Carl: as Sibelius's teacher, 32–3, 103; *Rustic Wedding Symphony*, 195

Goltz, Rüdiger von der, 181

Goossens, Eugene, Jr., on Sibelius, *quoted* 137–8

Gray, Cecil: on Sibelius's genealogy, *quoted* 2; re Sibelius's admiration for Johann Strauss, 190; re Sibelius's international reputation, 219, 222; classifies Sibelius's music, 231–2; on *In Memoriam*, *quoted* 139–40; re *Kullervo*, 46; on *Luonnotar*, *quoted* 157; re *The Maid in the Tower*, 73; re *Oceanides*, 162; re *Pelléas et Mélisande*, 119; re *Pohjola's Daughter*, 128; re *Spring Song*, 62; re First Symphony, 85; re Second Symphony, 105–6; analyzes Fifth Symphony, 171; analyzes Sixth Symphony, 191–2; re Seventh Symphony, 196; re "Eighth Symphony," 217; on *Tapiola*, *quoted* 202; first visit to Finland, 206; *Sibelius*, 206–7

Grieg, Edvard, 44, 81, 97, 225; *Peer Gynt*, 50

Gripenberg, Bertel, 120

Gustafsson, Fridolf Vladimir, 72

Gustavus Adolphus II, 90

Hadley, Henry, 163

Haggin, B. H., 224–5

Halir, Karl, 116

Halonen, Pekka, 117

Halvorsen, Johan, 182, 187

Handel, George Frideric, 194

Index

Hansen, Wilhelm: commissions music for *Scaramouche*, 152–3; publishes Fifth Symphony, 171; signs contract for Seventh Symphony, 193; re manuscript of *The Tempest*, 197; awards Sibelius "prize," 199

Hanslick, Eduard, 24, 71

Haydn, Franz Joseph, 49, 194

Helasvuo, Veikko, 23–4

Helsinki City Orchestra, 22 *n*, 74, 77, 108, 173, 179, 198, 208, 212, 215; Paris tour 95–8; Mahler conducts, 129–30

Henry, Bishop of Uppsala, 90

Hitler, Adolf, 25, 210

Hjelt, Edvard, 169

Høeberg, Georg, 182

Hoffmann, E. T. A., 25

Hofmannsthal, Hugo von, *Everyman*, 176

Howard, John Tasker, 209

Hufvudstadsbladet, review of *Breaking the Ice on the Uleå River*, 88

Humiston, William Henry, on Fourth Symphony, *quoted* 136

Imperial Alexander University, 15, 17, 66, 235; competition for teaching post, 73–8

Imperial Music Academy (Vienna), offers Sibelius position, 150

Indy, Vincent d', 137

Italy: Sibelius visits Rapallo, 100–1; popularity of Sibelius in, 219; Sibelius conducts Second Symphony in Rome, 105; Sibelius works on *Tapiola*, 199

Jackson, J. Hampden, 4, 203

Jadassohn, Salomon, 18

Jagellonica, Catharina, 90

Jalas, Jussi, 207

Janssen, Werner, 209

Järnefelt, Aino, *see* Sibelius, Aino

Järnefelt, Armas, 24, 71, 108, 129, 165; friendship with Sibelius, 26–7; conducts *Pohjola's Daughter*, 128–9; conducts First Symphony, 210; *Andante* for strings, 96; *The Birth of*

Järnefelt *(continued)*
Finland, 82; *Korsholm*, 62; *Prelude* for orchestra, 96

Järnefelt, Arvid, 27, 140; *Death*, 111–12, 114, 142

Järnefelt, August Alexander, 27, 47

Järnefelt, Eero, 24, 27, 148

Järnefelt [Palmgren], Maikki, 71, 96

Johann, Grand Duke of Finland, 90

Josephson, Ernst Abraham, 139

Julin, Jacob von, 198

Jürgensburg, Elisabeth Clodt von, 27

Kabalevsky, Dimitri, 228

Kajanus, Robert, 33, 41, 60, 62, 71, 73, 82, 92, 101, 106, 128–9, 165, 169, 176, 179, 180, 181, 199, 211; *quoted* 89, 144, 235; background, 22–4; presents tribute to Sibelius, 44; influence on Sibelius, 47, 49–50, 52–3, 65, 166; in University competition, 74–8; on Paris tour, 95–6, 98; records Sibelius, 207–8; *Aino Symphony*, 23, 30–1, 96; *Finnish Rhapsodies*, 23, 96; *Kullervo's Death*, 23; *Summer Memories*, 96

Kalevala, 90, 91, 128, 160, 162, 230, 233; re influence on Sibelius, 7, 9, 23, 31, 65; as source material for *The Boat Journey*, 54; *The Building of the Boat*, 127; *The Hymn of Väinö*, *quoted* 199–200, 222; *Lemminkäinen Suite*, 65, *quoted* 66–8, 71–2; *Luonnotar*, *quoted* 155–6; *The Origin of Fire*, *quoted* 108–9; *Pohjola's Daughter*, 56; *The Swan of Tuonela*, 56–7; *Tapiola*, 231; *Tiera*, 84; *see also* Lönnrot, Elias

Kalevala Society, 71–2

Kalisch, Alfred, 137, 184; on Fourth Symphony, *quoted* 146; on Fifth Symphony, *quoted* 183

Kanteletar, 60, 233

Kirby, W. F., 222

Kivi, Aleksis, *The Seven Brothers*, *quoted* 111

Klemetti, Heikki, 144, 168

Klingenberg, Alf, 185–7

Knudsen, Poul, 152

iv

Index

Index

Index

Index

Index

Index